# GROUP INTERVENTIONS IN SCHOOLS

# The Guilford Practical Intervention in the Schools Series

Kenneth W. Merrell, Founding Editor
T. Chris Riley-Tillman, Series Editor

*www.guilford.com/practical*

This series presents the most reader-friendly resources available in key areas of evidence-based practice in school settings. Practitioners will find trustworthy guides on effective behavioral, mental health, and academic interventions, and assessment and measurement approaches. Covering all aspects of planning, implementing, and evaluating high-quality services for students, books in the series are carefully crafted for everyday utility. Features include ready-to-use reproducibles, lay-flat binding to facilitate photocopying, appealing visual elements, and an oversized format. Recent titles have Web pages where purchasers can download and print the reproducible materials.

### Recent Volumes

Promoting Academic Success with English Language Learners:
Best Practices for RTI
*Craig A. Albers and Rebecca S. Martinez*

Integrated Multi-Tiered Systems of Support: Blending RTI and PBIS
*Kent McIntosh and Steve Goodman*

The ABCs of CBM, Second Edition:
A Practical Guide to Curriculum-Based Measurement
*Michelle K. Hosp, John L. Hosp, and Kenneth W. Howell*

DBT Skills in Schools:
Skills Training for Emotional Problem Solving for Adolescents (DBT STEPS-A)
*James J. Mazza, Elizabeth T. Dexter-Mazza, Alec L. Miller, Jill H. Rathus,
and Heather E. Murphy*

Interventions for Disruptive Behaviors:
Reducing Problems and Building Skills
*Gregory A. Fabiano*

Promoting Student Happiness:
Positive Psychology Interventions in Schools
*Shannon M. Suldo*

Effective Math Interventions:
A Guide to Improving Whole-Number Knowledge
*Robin S. Codding, Robert J. Volpe, and Brian C. Poncy*

Emotional and Behavioral Problems of Young Children, Second Edition:
Effective Interventions in the Preschool and Kindergarten Years
*Melissa L. Holland, Jessica Malmberg, and Gretchen Gimpel Peacock*

Group Interventions in Schools: A Guide for Practitioners
*Jennifer P. Keperling, Wendy M. Reinke, Dana Marchese, and Nicholas Ialongo*

Transforming Schools: A Problem-Solving Approach to School Change
*Rachel Cohen Losoff and Kelly Broxterman*

Evidence-Based Strategies for Effective Classroom Management
*David M. Hulac and Amy M. Briesch*

# Group Interventions in Schools

A Guide for Practitioners

JENNIFER P. KEPERLING
WENDY M. REINKE
DANA MARCHESE
NICHOLAS IALONGO

THE GUILFORD PRESS
New York    London

Copyright © 2017 The Guilford Press
A Division of Guilford Publications, Inc.
370 Seventh Avenue, Suite 1200, New York, NY 10001
www.guilford.com

Printed in Canada

This book is printed on acid-free paper.

Last digit is print number:   9   8   7   6   5   4   3   2   1

**Library of Congress Cataloging-in-Publication Data**

Names: Keperling, Jennifer P., author.
Title: Group interventions in schools : a guide for practitioners / Jennifer
    P. Keperling, Wendy M. Reinke, Dana Marchese, Nicholas Ialongo.
Description: New York : The Guilford Press, [2017] | Series: The Guilford
    practical intervention in the schools series | Includes bibliographical
    references and index.
Identifiers: LCCN 2016047424 | ISBN 9781462529452 (paperback)
Subjects: LCSH: School mental health services. | Group psychotherapy for
    children. | Crisis intervention (Mental health services) | BISAC:
    PSYCHOLOGY / Psychotherapy / Child & Adolescent. | SOCIAL SCIENCE / Social
    Work. | EDUCATION / Counseling / General. | PSYCHOLOGY / Psychotherapy /
    Group.
Classification: LCC LB3430 .K47 2017 | DDC 371.7/13—dc23
LC record available at *https://lccn.loc.gov/2016047424*

*To Ryan and my family:*
*Thank you for always encouraging and supporting me*

*And to my beautiful daughter, Adelyn:*
*May you always be surrounded by our love*
*as you choose your own path in life*
*—J. P. K.*

*To Keith and Kennedy:*
*I am ever inspired by each of you*
*—W. M. R.*

*To Vic and my family:*
*Thank you for all of your love and support*
*—D. M.*

*To Jenn, Dana, and Wendy:*
*Thanks for all your hard work and your perseverance*
*—N. I.*

*To future group leaders:*
*No matter how difficult or demanding the task may seem,*
*we hope that you find answers and assistance in this guide*
*and persevere through challenging times*

# About the Authors

**Jennifer P. Keperling, MA, LCPC,** is a Faculty Member and Research Associate in the Department of Mental Health at the Johns Hopkins Bloomberg School of Public Health. She has extensive experience implementing evidence-based group interventions in school settings with students and families and coaching teachers in implementing evidence-based techniques in classrooms. She also coordinates schoolwide initiatives aimed at reducing risks for mental health disorders in Baltimore City Public Schools.

**Wendy M. Reinke, PhD,** is Associate Professor in School Psychology at the University of Missouri and Co-Director of the Missouri Prevention Center. She developed the Classroom Check-Up, an assessment-based, classwide teacher consultation model. Her research focuses on preventing disruptive behavior problems in children and increasing school-based implementation of evidence-based practices. She is Associate Editor of *School Psychology Quarterly* and serves on the editorial boards of several other scholarly journals. Dr. Reinke presents nationally, has published numerous peer-reviewed articles, and has coauthored five books on teacher consultation and effective practices in schools.

**Dana Marchese, PhD,** is a Research Associate in the Department of Mental Health at the Johns Hopkins Bloomberg School of Public Health. Dr. Marchese coordinates and implements evidence-based interventions with children and families in Baltimore City Public Schools. She has extensive experience coaching and consulting with teachers to increase implementation of evidence-based practices in the classroom.

**Nicholas Ialongo, PhD,** is Professor in the Department of Mental Health at the Johns Hopkins Bloomberg School of Public Health, where he is also Director of the Center for Prevention and Early Intervention. Dr. Ialongo has a particular interest in adolescent mental health promotion and is the author of numerous publications in this area.

# Acknowledgments

We would like to acknowledge the many teachers, families, and students with whom we have worked through the years. We are grateful to have had the opportunity to learn from each of them. Funding to support the research upon which this book is based has come from the National Institute of Mental Health and the National Institute on Drug Abuse (Grant No. MH086043). We are especially grateful to Jen Cox, Kelly Willis, Michael Green, Charles Hines, and Courtney Vaughan, who implemented school-based groups and provided us with essential feedback and ideas to include within this book, and to Tiffany Stuart, who provided suggestions and edits as we finalized this book for publication. A special thank you to the postdocs, clinicians, and interns from the Johns Hopkins Bloomberg School of Public Health Center for Prevention and Early Intervention and the University of Maryland Center for School Mental Health, who spent numerous hours preparing for and assisting with implementation of school-based groups. We are appreciative of Drs. Keith Herman, John Lochman, Nicole Powell, Caroline Boxmeyer, and Catherine Bradshaw for providing ongoing supervision and support for clinicians and group leaders implementing school-based groups. We would also like to thank Drs. John Lochman and Carolyn Webster-Stratton, who have influenced the field of prevention science with their innovative group-based interventions and have provided support and assistance to enhance implementation of school-based groups. Finally, we would like to acknowledge our own families, who have been supportive of each of us in every way.

# Contents

# CHAPTER 1

# Facilitating Successful Child and Parent Groups

Approximately one in five children and adolescents have a clinically significant mental health diagnosis that negatively impacts their functioning at home and/or school (Costello, Mustillo, Erkanli, Keeler, & Angold, 2003). Sixteen percent of children receive mental health services, and the majority (70–80%) receive these services in schools (Farmer, Burns, Philips, Angold, & Costello, 2003). School-based mental health professionals have the unique advantage of being able to effectively identify such students in need and then address that need. Yet the numbers can be daunting. Delivering an evidence-based intervention to a *group* of students is an efficient and effective use of a practitioner's time and resources. Group interventions mean that a larger number of students can receive services compared with individual therapy of students. Furthermore, a host of group-based interventions have been shown to be effective and are readily available to school-based practitioners (National Academy of Sciences & Institute of Medicine, 2009).

However, our own past experiences have taught us that it's not enough to select the best group intervention, or as simple as following the intervention manual. The purpose of this book is to help school-based mental health practitioners overcome the challenges of running intervention groups in schools. This book offers specific strategies to assist with recruitment, group organization, managing the behavior of group members, effectively dealing with crises within the group, and engaging group members throughout the process of implementing effective group interventions. You can use this book in conjunction with any group-based intervention offered to elementary and middle school students and their parents. While this book is tailored to implementing child groups and parenting groups simultaneously, the essential ideas within each section can be used when implementing either independently.

## BENEFITS OF GROUP INTERVENTIONS

Group interventions are essential components of a practitioner's tool kit. In addition to the skills and strategies in the intervention content, there are benefits through the group process and the relationships developed among group members. Over time, group members begin to behave with other group members as they interact with other people in their everyday lives (Yalom, 1995). This gives the group leader insight into students' problems and where to intervene that may not become evident in individual work.

There is a significant amount of research showing that students with behavior problems have social skills deficits with their peers (Dodge et al., 2003). Aggressive–disruptive behavior can lead to other problems for students, such as peer rejection, poor academic achievement, and school dropout (Darney, Reinke, Herman, Stormont, & Ialongo, 2013). Conducting group interventions is an effective way of helping students practice important social skills, such as how to make friends, emotion regulation skills for frustrating experiences, and problem solving.

Group members receive support and feedback from peers in addition to that from the group leader. Hearing that other students have similar challenges normalizes these feelings and experiences so students feel less alone. Hearing about other group members' successes can provide hope of accomplishing similar goals. Groups give their members the chance to think more critically about their own personal situations and view things in a different light. While group conflict can be uncomfortable, it can be a great learning experience and beneficial in the change process. If set up effectively, the group setting offers a safe place where group members appropriately interact with one another and achieve goals together.

As a group leader, or future group leader, you may be aware of the benefits of group interventions. However, you may ask yourself, "Where do I find group interventions that work, and how do I successfully integrate these interventions into my current practices?" This book will provide key strategies on how to set up and successfully implement a group intervention, as well as how to effectively overcome any challenges that may arise within a group setting. Specifically, in Chapter 2, we look at resources and examples of evidence-based group interventions that can be utilized in your current practices.

## CHALLENGES IN IMPLEMENTING GROUP INTERVENTIONS

Despite growing evidence of the efficacy of particular group interventions, their use in educational settings has met with limited success (Herschell, McNeil, & McNeil, 2004; Stormont, Reinke, & Herman, 2011). A number of barriers impede the transportability of evidence-based interventions from research to applied settings (see Kratochwill, 2007; Kratochwill & Shernoff, 2003).

First, school environments are inherently more complex and often have limited resources compared with the carefully controlled conditions of research trials. Practitioners who work in the schools understand the inherent challenges of reaching those families and children with the greatest needs. Therefore, practitioners who hope to utilize an evidence-based intervention need to employ innovative strategies to reach those families and children who need services. Second, while many interventions are manualized for dissemination purposes, often these manuals lack practical information about how to engage students and families in the intervention and maintain their participation. Attendance and behavior management can be major obstacles. An intervention will not be effective if you are unable to get parents or caregivers to attend parenting groups, or are unable to manage students' challenging behaviors in a child group. To overcome these challenges, group leaders need to know and use effective strategies for recruiting, engaging, and sustaining group participation. This book is designed to teach you effective strategies and offers guidance on using them.

Perhaps you can relate to this scenario: You decide to run a group intervention that targets the parents of students in your school who have the highest needs (e.g., aggressive behaviors, noncompliance, lack of engagement in school). You send an invitation to the parents. Perhaps you call and leave messages for as many parents as possible. You determine the date and time the group will occur. Then, you wait patiently for the parents to arrive. You may have even brought snacks, found a time after school, and plan to provide child care as needed. Time goes by and one parent arrives. You decide to wait a bit for others to arrive. No other parents arrive. Your group has turned into an individual intervention.

Research has documented a number of factors that influence whether parents agree to allow their children to engage in services or to participate themselves, and whether they continue their participation over time (McKay, McKernan, Atkins, Hawkins, & Lynn, 2003; Morrissey-Kane & Prinz, 1999). Socioeconomic disadvantage, ethnic-minority status, severity of child dysfunction, caregiver stress and depression, lack of support (including caring for children and elderly caregivers), family member resistance, lack of parenting knowledge and skills, and lack of confidence all play significant roles in determining whether a family engages in and makes use of services (McKay et al., 2004; Nock & Kazdin, 2005).

For instance, many caregivers from low-income or diverse racial or ethnic backgrounds have children who would benefit from services but the caregivers have often had negative interactions with the educational system. These parents may find additional interactions quite aversive. Further, many of them may have had negative experiences as students in school. Some parents expect social or racial discrimination, blaming, and poor treatment outcomes from involvement with services. Being aware that past negative experiences may influence a parent's decision to participate in group programs is critical. McKay and colleagues' (2004) model confronts this challenge by having practitioners engage in direct conversations with caregivers about their prior experiences and perceptions. For example, during an initial phone call to caregivers, the practitioner asks questions to gauge the caregiver's attitudes about previous experiences with services, and collaboratively identifies solutions to overcoming obstacles that stand in the way of engagement. McKay and colleagues' work demonstrates the importance of integrating evidence-based engagement strategies into service delivery by using supportive phone techniques from the very first contact and clarifying the role of the interventionist. These strategies are typically not outlined in treatment manuals for group interventions.

In addition, the structural and cultural contexts in which an intervention is delivered can contribute to participants not showing up for group-based services. Understanding these contexts is critical to our ability to design and deliver interventions. For example, negative perceptions of school personnel affect engagement in services (Stormshak, Dishion, Light, & Yasui, 2005), and are likely to be amplified when families do not feel supported by the school or educational institution. Each family is unique, and families are less likely to participate and continue involvement in an intervention when they do not believe it is responsive to their needs (Dishion & Patterson, 1992; Sue, Bingham, Porché-Burke, &

Vasquez, 1999). Maximizing positive outcomes requires attention to the potential barriers that can impede parent and child engagement and ongoing participation in interventions.

## OVERCOMING THE CHALLENGES

In our work with students, teachers, and caregivers in the Baltimore city schools, we experienced the challenges of working in school settings and engaging those participants who may benefit most from a group intervention. Yes, we have had that one parent show up for our group interventions. We have encountered difficulties setting up groups, building participation in groups, maintaining participation in groups, and effectively providing the important content of the groups to parents and students. Solutions for such issues were not adequately outlined in the intervention program manuals. As a result, we developed strategies for overcoming these challenges. This book presents several decades of experience in overcoming barriers to leading school-based intervention groups. By sharing these strategies and tips from the field with practitioners, more children and families can benefit from efficacious interventions, helping to bridge the gap between research and practice.

### How This Book Is Organized

This book focuses on important implementation issues associated with any school-based group intervention and can be used by school psychologists or other school-based mental health practitioners. However, many of the practical strategies discussed throughout the book can be utilized in settings outside the school building as well. Our past experiences have taught us that it's not enough to select the best intervention. Instead, we have learned to think of all the strategies outlined in this book as much a part of the intervention as the manual and materials provided. Each chapter describes procedures that have repeatedly been shown to be effective in our work running parent and child groups.

In Chapter 2, we discuss how to locate and select effective group interventions for specific behavior areas. It can be challenging to identify evidence-based groups that fit the needs of the population, area, and setting in which you work. However, it is critical to identify group interventions that have been proven effective in reducing symptoms of behavioral and emotional disorders in children and adolescents. We review a variety of evidence-based group interventions that are proven and promising, along with resources for further in-depth reviews and critiques. While this is by no means a comprehensive list of all group interventions, we hope that we've provided a starting place for you to find proven and promising groups for your setting.

After locating an evidence-based group intervention, the second step is the successful recruitment of individuals who will benefit from the intervention. Chapter 3 describes ways to effectively recruit members for both student groups and parent groups. Group leaders will need to figure out the best plan of action to select appropriate students while following school and program procedures. This often involves a process of nominations, referrals and assistance from teachers, consent from parents, and assent from each student participating in the group. Tips for overcoming initial implementation barriers include frequent check-ins with potential group members.

In Chapter 4, we discuss how to develop a plan of action for implementing all aspects of student and parent groups, involving all the key people (e.g., teachers, administrators, parents). This includes planning out logistics such as location, time, and how to get students to and from the group in a way that ensures sessions will start and end on time. We also discuss some of the benefits of having a co-leader, if that is a possibility in your setting.

Chapter 5 covers how to set rules and manage behaviors within child groups. By setting clear expectations, group rules, and structure, the group leader begins the process of creating a successful group. You will want to act as a "fortune-teller" by anticipating possible group pitfalls and planning accordingly. We also provide tips for establishing confidentiality, seating group members, ignoring inappropriate behavior, and praising positive behavior. Last, we discuss the importance of choosing the best behavior management system and being *consistent* with the system. Chapter 6 covers how to set rules and manage behaviors in parent groups, including tips on how to deal with questions about group leader qualifications and challenges to the leader's ability to understand and help parents.

Chapter 7 presents strategies for engaging group members and building group morale and cohesion. Developing rapport, group cohesion, and morale are critical to keeping group members coming to each session. They need to feel a connection with the group, enjoy coming, and feel it is important to attend, or they may stop attending. This chapter discusses how to build group cohesion to keep members excited about and actively attending group sessions.

Chapter 8 covers how to respond to more difficult group situations, such as reporting child abuse or neglect, suicidal ideation, and members in crisis who may need referrals outside of the group. We provide examples of what to do following a group member's report of suicidal ideation or disclosure of abuse. However, it is important to follow the policies and procedures outlined by your school district, agency, and state.

Chapter 9 describes how to use data to select appropriate group members, and monitor group progress and outcomes. Matching the intervention to the needs of the students is vital. For example, a student with social phobia would be less likely to benefit from a group intervention on anger management skills than a group that specifically targets the student's problem. Additionally, some students will not fully benefit despite participating in an evidence-based group intervention, and they may need additional supports. Using data to determine whether students are improving as intended is a large part of the role of group leader.

At the end of Chapters 3–9, we offer questions to help facilitate reflection and role-play scenarios for applying the key principles in each chapter to parent and child groups. Real-life examples from our work with Baltimore city parents, students, teachers, and clinicians are also provided. Finally, the Appendices contain a wealth of materials—such as group reminder fliers, goal sheets, and recruitment scripts—to help you recruit and run successful groups.

This book can be utilized by the growing population of school-based mental health clinicians, school social workers, psychologists, behavior specialists, and other professionals who serve as group leaders. This book may also be used as a text for graduate courses focused on group-based interventions and therapy most often found in school psychology, counseling, public health, and social work programs. Often it is difficult for practitioners to translate theory into practice, especially for many evidence-based interventions that lack the necessary details to effectively implement these programs in real-world school settings. This unique book provides the necessary link between these two areas of training and practice.

### Learning Objectives

The aim of this book is to provide a practical step-by-step guide for group leaders to locate, plan, implement, and maintain effective parent and child group interventions. In reading this book, we intend for you to learn to do the following:

1. Successfully locate evidence-based group interventions for specific behavior areas in which you serve and practice.
2. Identify ways to recruit group members and overcome initial implementation barriers.
3. Understand how to establish group organization and develop ways to maintain group members within the group process.
4. Develop ways to manage behaviors and set rules within the group.
5. Learn ways to engage group members and build group morale and cohesion.
6. Identify ways to handle more difficult group situations, such as dealing with group crises, group termination, and sensitive topics.
7. Utilize data and group outcomes to select group members, monitor group progress, and successfully plan for termination and future practices.

## SUMMARY

This chapter provided a brief overview of some of the challenges and barriers to successful group interventions. We highlighted that the content of the book includes specific strategies that have been developed in response to the difficulties we ourselves have experienced over decades of implementing group interventions in school settings among children and families with significant risk factors. We now share these strategies, step-by-step guidelines, and resources with you so that you can maximize the outcomes for those participating in your school-based group interventions.

## CHAPTER 2

# Locating Evidence-Based Group Interventions

The American Psychological Association Presidential Task Force on Evidence-Based Practice (2006) defines evidence-based practice as "the integration of the best available research with clinical expertise in the context of patient characteristics, culture, and preferences" (p. 280). Locating effective, evidence-based interventions for a specific psychological or behavioral area can be challenging. Given the number of interventions available, the cost of the interventions, and the availability of training and intervention materials, the task of identifying the best intervention can be daunting. In this section of the chapter, we review a variety of evidence-based group interventions that are proven or promising, along with resources that provide further in-depth reviews and critiques of evidence-based practices, in reducing mental health symptoms in early and middle childhood.

The U.S. Department of Health and Human Services Substance Abuse and Mental Health Services Administration (SAMHSA; 2014) offers a wide variety of interventions on their website (*www.samhsa.gov/ebp-web-guide*), organized by the following behavioral health areas: substance abuse prevention, substance abuse treatment, mental health treatment, and prevention of mental health disorders. Once you select an intervention title on this website, it will link you to the website associated with that title, offering a description of the intervention, the intended audience, reviews of the programs, and intervention implementation.

Group leaders can also search SAMHSA's *National Registry of Evidence-Based Programs and Practices*, which offers a registry of more than 310 substance abuse and mental health interventions (*www.nrepp.samhsa.gov*). This registry is helpful if you have a specific intervention in mind and would like to find out more regarding implementation, outcomes, target populations, settings, adaptations, program costs, and contact information. You can also search for interventions within a certain behavioral area by typing in a keyword or phrase and then browsing through the interventions listed.

The *Promising Practices Network,* operated by the RAND Corporation (a nonprofit research organization), is a group of individuals and organizations committed to providing quality unbiased, evidence-based information about what works to improve the lives of children, families, and communities. On their website (*www.promisingpractices.net/programs.*

*asp*), they offer a wide variety of proven and promising programs listed by intervention title. Clicking on an intervention title will take you to an overview of what the program offers, including program participants, evaluation methods, key evaluation findings, implementation detail, issues to consider, contact information, and other available resources.

Finally, the *Blueprints for Healthy Youth Development* website (*www.blueprintsprograms.com*), in partnership with the Annie E. Casey Foundation, offers over 65 model and promising programs that promote healthy youth development. You can review all programs listed based on program outcome, target population, program specifics, and risk and protective factors, and then select a specific program. You can also type in a keyword or phrase and search the list. Selecting a program allows you to view overall project information, target population statistics, funding strategies, and benefits minus costs data.

All of the above resources provide a wealth of information regarding evidence-based practices that include individual, group, and schoolwide interventions. They also give information on how to access these interventions and learn more about implementation in your own practices. In the rest of this chapter, we provide information and resources on specific evidence-based group interventions by behavioral area: social–emotional interventions (including violence and substance abuse prevention), interventions that focus on externalizing behaviors (problem solving, social skills, and self-control), interventions that focus on internalizing behaviors (depression, anxiety, and mood), and trauma and suicide. Most of the interventions we review can fall under multiple behavior areas. However, we have placed them where they fit best based on search criteria; they are listed alphabetically within each behavior area. The group practices listed are found to be proven or promising based on the "evidence criteria" on the Promising Practices Network site, and they are included as evidence-based interventions on the other sites listed above (see Table 2.1 for evidence criteria; visit the website for more information). Additionally, many of the interventions listed in this chapter have been acknowledged by the World Health Organization (2004) as effective evidence-based prevention programs. Not all evidence-based practices are reviewed here. However, we provide a good variety of programs as examples of group interventions in each behavior category. More detailed information regarding the programs in each area can be found using the resources listed above or by searching for evidence-based mental health group interventions on a reliable internet search engine (e.g., Google).

## SOCIAL–EMOTIONAL INTERVENTIONS

The interventions listed below cover social–emotional curricula and violence and substance abuse prevention. These interventions are often listed as violence and substance abuse prevention resources on many internet search engines.

### The Curriculum-Based Support Group Program

The *Curriculum-Based Support Group Program* (CBSG; Brown, 2004; Hedl, 2009) is designed to increase resiliency and reduce risk factors among children and adolescents identified as being at elevated risk for early substance use, future delinquency, and vio-

**TABLE 2.1. RAND Corporation Promising Practices Network (PPN) Evidence Criteria**

| Type of information | Proven program: Program must meet all of these criteria to be listed as "proven" | Promising program: Program must meet at least all of these criteria to be listed as "promising" | Not listed on site: If a program meets any of these conditions, it will not be listed on the site |
|---|---|---|---|
| Type of outcomes affected | Program must directly impact one of the indicators used on the site. | Program may impact an intermediary outcome for which there is evidence that it is associated with one of the PPN indicators. | Program impacts an outcome that is not related to children or their families, or for which there is little or no evidence that it is related to a PPN indicator (such as the number of applications for teaching positions). |
| Substantial effect size | At least one outcome is changed by 20%, 0.25 standard deviations, or more. | Change in outcome is more than 1%. | No outcome is changed more than 1%. |
| Statistical significance | At least one outcome with a substantial effect size is statistically significant at the 5% level. | Outcome change is significant at the 10% level (marginally significant). | No outcome change is significant at less than the 10% level. |
| Comparison groups | Study design uses a convincing comparison group to identify program impacts, including randomized control trial (experimental design) or some quasi-experimental designs. | Study has a comparison group, but it may exhibit some weaknesses (e.g., the groups lack comparability on preexisting variables or the analysis does not employ appropriate statistical controls). | Study does not use a convincing comparison group (e.g., the use of before and after comparisons for the treatment group only). |
| Sample size | Sample size of evaluation exceeds 30 in both the treatment and comparison groups. | Sample size of evaluation exceeds 10 in both the treatment and comparison groups. | Sample size of evaluation includes less than 10 in the treatment or comparison group. |
| Availability of program evaluation documentation | Publicly available. | Publicly available. | Distribution is restricted (e.g., only to the sponsor of the evaluation). |

*Note.* From Promising Practices Network (2014). Copyright © 2014 Promising Practices Network. Reprinted by permission.

lence. The program targets children and youth ages 4–17 who are living in adverse family situations, lack coping and social skills, and display early indicators of antisocial behaviors. The intervention is based in cognitive-behavioral and competence-enhancement models of prevention. Core elements include a focus on coping with difficult family situations, resisting peer pressure, setting and achieving goals, refusing substances, and reducing antisocial behaviors. The 10–12 CBSG lessons are taught weekly, are 1 hour in length, and address topics such as self-concept, anger and feeling awareness, setting future goals, making healthy choices, peer pressure, making friends, assessing life challenges, and making a public commitment to stay substance free. Lesson content and objectives are tailored for age and developmental status.

## I Can Problem Solve

*I Can Problem Solve* (ICPS; Shure, 1993, 2001a, 2001b) is a universal school-based program for enhancing the interpersonal cognitive processes and problem-solving skills of children ages 4–12. The ICPS curriculum offers an array of engaging activities such as games, stories, puppets, illustrations, and role plays to help children learn problem-solving techniques, identify feelings, discover alternate thinking strategies, and become more aware of consequences linked to behaviors. This program aims to assist children in thinking for themselves, considering consequences, and solving their own problems. It also aims to prevent and reduce early high-risk behaviors and promote prosocial behaviors. ICPS consists of three age-specific programs: preschool, kindergarten and primary school, and intermediate elementary school. ICPS lessons are 20 minutes in duration and are taught three to five times per week for the length of the program. The program course ranges from 59 to 83 lessons based on the age group. Typically, the program has been used classwide but it can also be delivered by a group leader to a small group of children.

## Life Skills Training

*Life Skills Training* (LST; Botvin, 2000; Botvin & Eng, 1980; Botvin & Griffin, 2002) is a school-based substance abuse prevention curriculum that aims to modify drug-related knowledge, attitudes, and norms. It teaches skills for resisting social influences that encourage drug use, while it fosters the development of general personal and social skills. The LST program is used in elementary schools through high schools in classwide or group settings. The program runs across 3 years and consists of 15 lessons in the first year, followed by 10 booster lessons during the second year, and five booster lessons in the third year.

## Promoting Alternative THinking Strategies

*Promoting Alternative THinking Strategies* (PATHS; Greenberg, Kusche, Cook, & Quamma, 1995; Greenberg & Kusché, 2006, 2011) is for children in preschool through elementary school. The intervention enhances social–emotional development through teaching self-control, self-esteem, emotional awareness, social skills, friendship, and interpersonal problem-solving skills, while also reducing aggression and other behavior problems. The

PATHS curriculum introduces skill concepts through direct instruction, discussion, modeling, storytelling, role playing, and video presentations. The PATHS curriculum is offered in three age-specific programs: preschool PATHS (3–5 years old), the PATHS Turtle Unit (kindergarten), and the PATHS Basic Kit (grades 1–6). The PATHS curriculum includes 131 lessons that range from 20 to 30 minutes in length. Although the program is typically used classwide, it can also be delivered by a group leader to a small group of children.

### Strong Kids

*Strong Kids* programs (Merrell, Carrizales, Feuerborn, Gueldner, & Tran, 2007; Merrell, Juskells, Oanh, & Buchanan, 2008) are brief curricula designed to teach social and emotional skills, promote resilience, strengthen assets, and increase coping skills of students. There is a *Strong Start* for PreK and one for grades K–2; Strong Kids is designed for students in grades 3–5. Session topics are designed to be developmentally appropriate and include identifying and understanding emotions, social skills, cognitive reframing, relaxation strategies, and problem-solving strategies. The curriculum can be used by a group leader in a small group or with an entire class.

## INTERVENTIONS FOR EXTERNALIZING BEHAVIORS

The interventions listed within this behavioral area have been found to be proven or promising in the area of externalizing behaviors, which includes problem solving, social skills, and self-control. Programs that focus on reducing other externalized negative behaviors in children and adolescents can be found using the resources listed above.

### Be Proud! Be Responsible!

*Be Proud! Be Responsible!* (BPBR; Jemmott, Jemmott, & McCaffree, 1994; Advocates for Youth, 2012) is a decision-making intervention about sex. It helps adolescents (ages 12–18) gain knowledge and change behaviors that put them at risk of contracting and transmitting human immunodeficiency virus (HIV) and other sexually transmitted diseases. The curriculum is intended to delay the initiation of sexual activity, reduce the frequency of unprotected sex, and support adolescents in their decisions about their own sexual behaviors. BPBR consists of six 50-minute modules that can be delivered over the course of 1 day or at a rate of one module per week. Each module incorporates a theme that encourages group members to be proud of themselves and their community, to behave responsibly, to consider consequences for their actions, and how these consequences can impede their future goals.

### The Coping Power Child Program

The *Coping Power Child Program* (Lochman & Wells, 2002; Lochman, Wells, & Lenhart, 2008), which developed out of the Anger Coping Program, is a preventive intervention for at-risk children in the late elementary school and early middle school years (ages 8–12), typically delivered in school settings. Sessions are also offered to parents of these children and are described in more detail below. The Coping Power Child Program is offered once a week for 34 group sessions that run for 1 hour each. The program is based in cognitive-behavioral theory and the key factors of social competence, self-regulation, problem solving, and positive relationships are addressed. Session content includes how to set goals, organization and study skills, anger management skills, social skills, problem-solving skills, how to resist peer pressure, and how to enter positive peer groups. The program typically lasts 15–18 months (across 2 school years). However, an abbreviated version encompassing 1 school year is also available (24 group sessions) and is currently being field tested.

## The Coping Power Parent Program

The *Coping Power Parent Program* (Lochman & Wells, 2002; Wells, Lochman, & Lenhart, 2008) is a preventive intervention delivered to the parents of at-risk children in the late elementary school and middle school years (ages 8–12), typically in school-based settings. Parents of these at-risk children play a central role in helping them develop effective social and emotional skills. The Coping Power Parent Program is offered once a week for 16 group sessions that run 1 hour each. Session content includes praise and positive attention, set-ting clear rules and expectations, promotion of child study skills, appropriate discipline practices, parental stress management, family communication and problem solving, and reinforcement of problem-solving skills learned in the Coping Power Child Program. The parent group typically runs in conjunction with the child group, but it can be run as a sepa-rate intervention for parents.

## The FRIENDS Programs

The *FRIENDS* (feelings, remember to relax, I can try my best, explore solutions and coping step plans, now reward yourself, do it every day, smile) programs (Barrett, Lowry-Webster, & Turner, 2000; Shortt & Fox, 2001) are cognitive-behavioral interventions that focus on the promotion of emotional resilience to prevent anxiety and depression in childhood through adulthood. The FRIENDS curriculum is offered in four age-specific programs: *Fun FRIENDS* (ages 4–7), *FRIENDS for Life* (ages 8–11), *My FRIENDS Youth* (ages 12–15), and *Adult Resilience* (ages 16 and older). The FRIENDS curriculum includes 10 weekly sessions, as well as two booster sessions held following program completion. Two sessions are also offered to parents at the start and halfway through the program. The FRIENDS curriculum addresses the attachment, physiological, cognitive, and physical symptoms that occur while experiencing anxiety through play-based activities, role play, and other hands-on activities.

## The Incredible Years Child Programs

*The Incredible Years Small Group Dinosaur Curriculum* (Webster-Stratton, 2013b; Webster-Stratton & Reid, 2003; Webster-Stratton, Reid, & Hammond, 2004), also called "Dinosaur School," is for children ages 3–8. It aims to strengthen children's social and emo-tional competencies. The small-group program consists of 18–22 weekly sessions that are 2 hours in length and focuses on topics such as anger management, problem-solving skills, manners, learning friendship and conversational skills, and how to behave appropriately in the classroom. Dinosaur School offers an interactive curriculum, utilizing videotaped vignettes, life-size puppets, role plays, and other engaging hands-on activities. The Incredible Years Small Group Dinosaur Curriculum is part of a series of interlocking, comprehensive, and developmentally based programs targeting parents, teachers, and children. Dinosaur School is just one of the programs within The Incredible Years series. The parent programs are described next.

## The Incredible Years Parenting Programs

*The Incredible Years Parenting Programs* (Webster-Stratton, 2013a; Webster-Stratton & Reid, 2003; Webster-Stratton et al., 2004) focus on strengthening parent–child interactions and relationships, reducing harsh discipline, and fostering parents' ability to promote children's social, emotional, and language development. The basic parenting training is offered across four age-specific programs: *Babies Program* (0–1 years), *Toddler Program* (1–2 years), *Preschool or Early Childhood Program* (3–5 years), and *Early School-Age Program* (6–12 years). The curriculum ranges from 8 to 20 weekly group sessions (depending on the age-specific program). Sessions are 2 hours in length and focus on topics such as respecting and understanding children and their developmental abilities; modeling social skills; child-directed play; descriptive commenting, coaching, ignoring, and praising; setting clear expectations; and self-control. All the parenting curricula offer interactive approaches to parenting through videotaped vignettes, role playing, brainstorming discussions, and other engaging hands-on activities. The Incredible Years Parenting Programs are part of a series of interlocking, comprehensive, and developmentally based programs targeting parents, teachers, and children. The parenting programs are just one aspect within The Incredible Years series. The child programs are described above.

## Making Proud Choices!

*Making Proud Choices!* (Jemmott et al., 1994; Jemmott, Jemmott, & McCaffree, 1998, 2003) is a multimodule, decision-making intervention about sex, designed to be educational and culturally sensitive. It is based on cognitive-behavioral theories and offers adolescents the knowledge, confidence, and skills necessary to reduce their risk of sexually transmitted diseases, HIV, and pregnancy. The program is typically used in the school setting with adolescents ages 12–18. The program is eight sessions long, with each session 1 hour in length. The curriculum is engaging and involves group discussions, videos, games, brainstorming, hands-on exercises, and skill-building activities.

## The Triple P—Positive Parenting Program

*The Triple P—Positive Parenting Program* (Triple P; Sanders, 1992, 1999) is a multilevel system of providing parenting and family support that is designed to prevent social, emotional, behavioral, and developmental problems in children. It offers practical strategies to help parents confidently manage their children's behavior and build healthy relationships. The program is based in social learning theory and has been effective for families with children from birth to age 12. The Triple P program offers five intervention levels of increasing intensity: level 1 (Universal Triple P), level 2 (Selected Triple P), level 3 (Primary Care Triple P), level 4 (Standard Triple P and Group Triple P), and level 5 (Enhanced Triple P). Level 4 is an intensive strategy for parents of children with more severe behavior difficulties, and is designed to teach positive parenting skills in eight group sessions each of which is 1 hour in length. All other levels are community based, individual, or family based. Sessions offer interactive seminars, real-life discussions, and a toolbox of strategies based on the parent's need.

## INTERVENTIONS FOR INTERNALIZING BEHAVIORS

The interventions listed within this behavioral area have been found to be proven or promising in the area of internalizing behaviors, which includes prevention surrounding depression, anxiety, and mood symptoms and disorders.

### The Adolescent Coping with Depression Course

The *Adolescent Coping with Depression Course* (CWD-A; Clarke, Lewinsohn, & Hops, 1990; Clarke, Rohde, Lewinsohn, Hops, & Seeley, 1999) is a skills-based small-group treatment program for actively depressed adolescents ages 9–18. The intervention consists of core components such as increasing social skills and pleasant activities, and decreasing anxiety and depressive symptoms. Other skills include how to be assertive in stressful situations, relaxation skills, cognitive restructuring techniques, monitoring mood, problem solving, conflict-resolution techniques, and planning for the future. The intervention consists of 16 structured sessions delivered over the course of 8 weeks with two sessions per week. Each session lasts 2 hours. Group members have repeated opportunities to practice skills, develop contracts, and participate in group activities. There are also homework assignments. There is a parallel group intervention for the parents of depressed adolescents. It informs parents of the CWD-A core components and encourages their support and reinforcement of the adolescent's use of skills. Parents are also taught communication and problem-solving skills.

### The Cool Kids Child and Adolescent Anxiety Management Program

The *Cool Kids Child and Adolescent Anxiety Management Program* (Cool Kids; Rappee & Lyneham, 2006; Neil & Christensen, 2009) is an individual or group program involving children (ages 6–18) with a separate parent component. The program teaches anxiety management skills, including identifying anxious thoughts, feelings, and behaviors, and challenging these thoughts; approaching avoided situations/events; and using additional coping skills for dealing with teasing and bullying. The Cool Kids curriculum is offered in 10 individual or group sessions with the child during the school day. The parent component helps the parent or primary caregiver to support the child's use of new skills. Parents also learn and practice strategies for parenting an anxious child. Sessions are focused on a topic (e.g., understanding emotions, followed by experiential learning activities such as discussion, modeling, role play, and application to real-life experiences).

## Coping Cat

*Coping Cat* (Albano & Kendell, 2002; Kendall, 2006; Kendall, Robin, Hedtke, & Suveg, 2005) is a cognitive-behavioral group intervention that assists children ages 6–17 in recognizing anxious feelings and physical reactions to anxiety, being cognitively aware in anxiety-provoking situations, and developing a plan to help cope with the situation. The intervention uses techniques such as modeling real-life situations, role playing, relaxation training, and reinforcement. The curriculum is made up of 16 sessions broken into two parts. In sessions 1–8, the curriculum introduces the basic concepts, which are practiced and reinforced. In sessions 8–16, the child practices the new skills in both imaginary and real-life situations varying from low stress, low anxiety to high stress, high anxiety.

## Structured Psychotherapy for Adolescents Responding to Chronic Stress

*Structured Psychotherapy for Adolescents Responding to Chronic Stress* (SPARCS; DeRosa et al., 2006; DeRosa & Pelcovitz, 2008) is a group intervention designed to address the needs of chronically traumatized adolescents who may still be living with ongoing stress and depression. The aim of the program is to help adolescents cope more effectively in the moment, enhance self-efficacy, connect with others and establish supportive relationships, cultivate awareness, and create meaning in their lives. The program consists of 16 weekly sessions that run for 1 hour each. Session topics include mindfulness practice, relationship building, communication skills, distress tolerance, and problem solving.

# INTERVENTIONS FOR TRAUMA AND SUICIDE PREVENTION

The interventions listed below have been found to be proven or promising in the area of trauma and suicide prevention.

## Cognitive Behavioral Intervention for Trauma in Schools

*Cognitive Behavioral Intervention for Trauma in Schools* (CBITS; Jaycox, 2003; Jaycox, Kataoka, Stein, Langley, & Wong, 2012) is a school-based group and individual intervention for students in grades 3–8 (ages 6–12) who have experienced some form of trauma in their lives. It is designed to reduce symptoms of posttraumatic stress disorder (PTSD), depression, and behavioral problems (e.g., school violence, physical abuse, domestic violence, death, and natural disasters). It also strives to improve peer and parent support and enhance coping skills. The CBITS program includes 10 group sessions and one to three individual sessions, and is designed to be delivered within the school setting. The program also offers two parent psychoeducational sessions and a teacher educational session.

### Combined Parent–Child Cognitive Behavioral Therapy

*Combined Parent–Child Cognitive Behavioral Therapy* (CPC-CBT; Runyon & Deblinger, 2013; Runyon, Deblinger, & Steer, 2010) is a structured group or individual treatment program that targets a more severe population than other programs. It often includes families in which child physical abuse by parents has occurred, families that have had multiple referrals to child protection services (CPS) agencies, and parents who have reported significant stress and fear that they may lose control and hurt their child. The intervention aims to reduce children's PTSD symptoms and behavior problems while improving parenting skills and parent–child relationships. It aims to reduce the use of corporal punishments by parents and offer a healthier home life. CPC-CBT is based in cognitive-behavioral theory and is suited for children ages 3–17 and their parents or caregivers. The group therapy program consists of 16 to 20 sessions that are 2 hours each. The sessions are grouped into four phases: engagement, skill building, safety, and clarification. Parents practice implementing communication, positive parenting, and behavior management skills within the group session, and then with their children. Group leaders also conduct child- and parent-only sessions within the treatment protocol.

### The Grief and Trauma Intervention for Children

The *Grief and Trauma Intervention for Children* (GTI; Salloum, 1997; Salloum & Overstreet, 2008) is an individual or group intervention designed for children ages 6–12 with posttraumatic stress due to witnessing or being a direct victim of one or more types of violence or a disaster. The GTI curriculum includes 10 sessions of approximately 1 hour each. There is also one session conducted with parents and an additional individual session with the child if the curriculum is delivered in a group setting. The techniques used in the sessions are grounded in cognitive-behavioral therapy and narrative therapy utilizing methods such as art, drama, and play, while focusing on dreams/nightmares, questioning, anger, and guilt.

## SUMMARY

It can be challenging to identify evidence-based practices that fit the needs of the population, area, and setting in which you work. This chapter provided an overview of some of the resources available to group leaders when searching for and selecting effective interventions for use in schools or other settings. We provided examples of proven and promising interventions available across four main behavior areas: (1) social–emotional interventions, (2) externalizing behaviors, (3) internalizing behaviors, and (4) trauma and suicide prevention. Although this chapter is by no means a comprehensive list, we hope that we've provided a starting place for you to locate effective groups for your setting.

## CHAPTER 3

# Recruiting for Child and Parent Groups

Once a proven or promising evidence-based group intervention is selected, the next steps are planning the group and successfully recruiting individuals who will benefit from it. Recruitment and group planning sometimes happen simultaneously. However, it can be helpful to plan key group logistics prior to recruiting for the groups—for instance, a day, time, and location for your group meetings. If you plan to use fliers or send letters out to potential group members (covered later in this chapter), you can then include relevant information about the location and time of the group. In some circumstances, you will need to know who is in the group before you can determine the dates and times of meetings and so you will need to recruit group members first. This chapter describes how to recruit students and parents for groups, and techniques to overcome barriers that may get in the way of recruiting them. It first describes how to identify students for groups and then discusses linking their parents or caregiver(s) to a parent group. However, implementing a child group in conjunction with a parent group presents its own unique challenges, and so we address the implementation of child and parent groups simultaneously and individually. Chapter 4 discusses planning logistics. Chapter 9 goes into detail on how to use existing data and teacher rankings to determine which students and parents are in need of support offered by group interventions.

It is important to note that biological parents are not always the primary caregivers of the identified students. When we use the term "parent" throughout this book we mean those individuals responsible for providing care for the students. These individuals can vary in their roles (e.g., parents, grandparents, aunts, uncles, legal guardians, older siblings). Explore this issue with the family to ensure that those attending the parent group are the individuals who are most likely to benefit and will maximize positive outcomes for the student.

Recruiting students and parents for a group can be challenging work, especially within the school setting. You will need to figure out the best plan of action to select appropriate students while following school and program procedures.

# CHILD GROUPS

## *Involving School Staff in the Recruitment Process*

### *Meeting with the Principal*

To begin, we suggest meeting with the principal or school administrator. Explain the purpose of the child group and who would be recruited to participate. We have found it helpful to provide principals, teachers, and others with a handout that briefly overviews the group and the key skills students will learn in it. The handout helps them to understand the overarching purpose and logistical needs of running the child group. Discuss plans for recruitment and potential teachers or classes with students who may be involved in the group. The principal may have suggestions of possible student referrals and may want to discuss potential group meeting times. Involve the principal in brainstorming logistical issues, such as when and where groups should occur. Discuss the number of sessions, and the roles of the teachers and principal in supporting the development, organization, and generalizing of skills the students will learn in the group. It is always a good idea to keep the principal well-informed of the important logistics of the group, the dates of teacher meetings (in case he or she wants to be present), when recruitment is starting, when the group is beginning, and how long the group will run. You may also want to talk to the principal about using existing school data to determine those students in need of support. See Chapter 7 to find out more about using existing data in determining students' need of group interventions.

> **Involve the principal and teachers. Discuss the purpose of the child groups, number of sessions, and roles of the teachers and principal in helping support the development, organization, and generalizing of skills the students will learn in the group.**

### *Meeting with Teachers*

Next, arrange to meet with the classroom teachers during a time that is convenient for them. Ask them to bring their student roster to the meeting. Have a folder prepared containing a program summary of topics to be covered in the group (see Appendix 1 for a sample Program Summary), and any documents that you will be reviewing during the meeting (e.g., see Appendices 2 and 4 for a Consent/Permission Form and a Teacher Nomination Form).

At this initial meeting with the teachers, you may want to cover the following topics:

#### GROUP INTERVENTION PURPOSE AND PROCESS

Describe the purpose and process of the groups to the teachers and answer any questions they may have. Also review details including the number of group sessions and the skills students will be learning (e.g., problem-solving techniques, calming-down strategies).

## THE TEACHER'S ROLE

Teachers will be asked to help by sending home parental consent forms (see Appendix 2 for a sample Consent/Permission Form), reminding students to bring back signed consents, and making sure that signed consent forms are returned to you. Teachers are also involved in developing and monitoring goal setting with participating students. Discuss these teacher roles and address any questions or concerns with the roles (e.g., time, relationships with students) and make sure to discuss how you can help the teachers with their roles and responsibilities.

## TEACHER NOMINATION FORM (IF APPLICABLE)

If you are asking teachers to nominate students as the primary group recruitment method, give teachers the nomination form and explain the nomination procedures (see Appendix 4 for a sample Teacher Nomination Form). The sample Teacher Nomination Form included in Appendix 4 lists behaviors for nominating students for a coping and social skills group. The behaviors to be listed on the form will change depending on the group's focus. The classroom teacher is to rank order 10 students according to the guidelines on the nomination form. Ask the teacher to discuss relationships among the students on their ranked list (e.g., "Do students ranked '3' and '5' get along?"; "Would they be a good fit for the group if they were in the group together?"). Discuss parent involvement (e.g., "Has the teacher had contact with the student's parents?"; "Do they have a phone?"; "Is the teacher able to get in touch with the parents if needed?"). Next, discuss with the teacher how students will be selected for the group. Explain that the students ranked at the very top may not be selected because their disruptive behavior may need more intensive intervention (e.g., individual therapy) than can be provided in the group. Address any concerns that the teacher may have with the criteria for selecting group participants.

## TEACHER INCENTIVE(S)

You may want to provide the teachers and any other school staff involved in the recruitment process with an incentive (e.g., gift card, teaching supplies) to show appreciation for their involvement and to encourage them to stay motivated and involved in the program.

## SCREENING TOOLS (IF APPLICABLE)

If a screening or assessment tool is warranted in the recruitment process (e.g., trauma screening for a trauma-focused intervention), you will first need to obtain consent from parents of the identified students or ask the principal about the school procedure for implementing class-level or schoolwide screening tools. You may also need assistance from parents in filling out measures based on their child's behavior. Some screening tools can be filled out directly by a child and some are to be completed by the child's parent. We discuss the identification and selection of screening tools in more detail in Chapter 7.

## Reviewing Your Current Caseload

If you are a counselor, clinician, social worker, or school psychologist at the school, you may want to begin reviewing your current caseload to determine whether any of these students are appropriate for the group. Since you already have parental consent for the students in your caseload, you can use a screening tool to determine which ones would make a good fit for the group you are planning. Otherwise, you will need to obtain parental consent prior to screening any individual student.

## Meeting with Other School Professionals

It may be helpful to involve any other school counselors, social workers, school psychologists, or other school professionals in the nomination and referral process. Their referral may be more appropriate in some cases (e.g., when implementing a trauma-focused group). You may want to ask school staff to make referrals in a confidential manner (e.g., fill out a referral form). Explain the purpose of the group to school staff (see above for teacher example) to ensure their understanding of who is an appropriate referral for the group.

## Selecting Prospective Group Members

After receiving the nomination form, referrals from appropriate sources, and scoring your screening measures (if you already have parental consent), identify a group of students to be contacted for potential participation in the group. In doing this, consider the relationships among the students on the nomination form. Do they get along with one another? Will each student be a good fit for a group intervention? Are the parents involved based on the information that the teacher has provided? It is also a good idea to observe the students on the nomination list in multiple settings (e.g., classroom, cafeteria, gym, hallways) so that a balanced group can be formed. For example, you may want to have a mix of students with shy, disruptive, aggressive, and inattentive behaviors. Striking a good balance between aggressive and nonaggressive (e.g., shy, prosocial) students will be extremely helpful in effectively and efficiently running groups.

## Setting Group Meeting Times

Once the potential group members have been identified, discuss possible times during the day that the students can be taken from the classroom to attend the group. Collaboratively work with the teachers and principal to identify a day and time that would work best to have the child group. At times, teachers or principals may express concern regarding the amount of instruction students will miss while attending the group. In these situations, point out the specific skills students will be learning in the groups and how they will help improve students' ability to engage more effectively with academic material when they are in the classroom (e.g., increase appropriate classroom behavior, increase the ability to organize and complete schoolwork). Consider having the child group meet during lunch, after school, or partially at the end of the school day and partially after school. If you decide to conduct the group after school, you will want to get parents' permission for students to stay after school. You will also need to have the support of the school building administrator to have students remain after school hours.

## Identifying a Meeting Room

Identify an appropriate room in the building to hold group meetings. The room should allow adequate space for all members to participate in required intervention activities. Ideally, the room is comfortable and welcoming to group members. In addition, you will want to ensure the room selected is private enough for the children to discuss confidential issues, but also public enough to ensure safety concerns that may arise (e.g., having easy access to gaining adult support if physical fights or other crisis situations occur). Make sure the room is safe if there is a crisis (e.g., student with aggressive behavior). For example, scissors should be kept in a closed container or in a cup with points down and stored away from the group area. You will want to declutter the room to be sure that there are no distracting items in the room (e.g., toys, games). If you need video equipment or other materials (e.g., TV, DVD player, LCD projector), make sure that the room is equipped with the appropriate capabilities.

## Contacting Parents

Once a decision has been made about potential student participants, the next step is to obtain parents' or caregivers' contact information, including their names, relationship to student, phone numbers, and addresses. Next, contact each student's parent by phone (be sure to keep a log of all contact attempts and outcomes; see Appendix 5 for a sample Caregiver Contact Log).

The following topics may be reviewed with parents during the initial contact:

### Introduction and Greeting

Greet the parent and introduce yourself (e.g., name, role at the school). It is important to be friendly, enthusiastic, and professional, and to engage the parents in this first phone call.

### Purpose of the Group

Explain the purpose of the child and parent groups (see Appendix 6 for a sample Recruitment Script). Include details such as number of sessions and the skills students will be learning (e.g., problem-solving techniques, calming-down strategies). Last, answer any questions the parent(s) may have.

### Interest in and Commitment to the Group

Determine parents' interest in allowing their child to participate and their interest in participating in the parent group. Identify and problem solve any potential barriers such as transportation, child care, scheduling, time constraints, or previous negative experience with the school or mental health services.

## Use of Screening Tools

If a screening tool is to be utilized prior to selecting group members, make sure this is clear and that the parent fully understands what the screening tool is and how it will be used to select group members. It is important to use simple terms and provide a clear explanation of what the group will entail and how students are recommended for the group, but also be careful about using terms such as "mental health," "disorder," and other such words that may trigger a negative or defensive reaction from parents. This may be the first time they are hearing that their child may be showing signs of a mental disorder and that others are reporting this claim (e.g., through nomination by the teacher). If the screening tool is to be used to select parents for a parent group, be empathic and sensitive to the questions within the screening tool and the parent's responses to them. See Chapter 7 for more information on selecting and identifying screening forms.

There may be times when it is easy to reach parents by phone. There may also be times when it is extremely difficult to reach parents (e.g., phone is not working or turned off, parent works shift work, parent may not answer calls from unknown numbers). Here are some suggestions for how to proceed in these situations:

- *If parents are reachable by phone and are able to come in to meet in person,* schedule a time to meet with the parent to discuss both the child and parent group further. At the meeting, review group logistics, sign consent forms, and identify days and times he or she may be available to attend the parent groups (see Appendix 7 for a sample Parent Group Survey).

- *If parents can be reached on the phone but are unable to meet, send home information with the student.* Inform the parents that the child will be bringing home information regarding a new group at school (see Appendix 8 for a sample Letter to Parent/Caregiver), a consent form to be signed and returned, a summary of the program (see Appendix 1 for a sample Program Summary form), and a survey for the parent to fill out regarding group logistics (see Appendix 7 for a sample Parent Group Survey). It may be helpful to review the purpose of the group with the student and explain the paperwork.

- *If parents are not able to be reached by phone,* explain the purpose of the group to the student and send home the Letter to the Parent/Caregiver, the Program Summary, the Consent/Permission Form, and the Parent Group Survey (see sample forms in Appendices 1, 2, 7, and 8).

- *If parents are not able to be reached by phone and it is not appropriate to send information home with the student,* mail home the Program Summary, the Consent/Permission Form, the Parent Group Survey, and the Letter to Parent/Caregiver (see sample forms in Appendices 1, 2, 7, and 8) and enclose a stamped self-addressed envelope for return of the materials to you at the school. If appropriate, you could also attempt to visit the home or try to talk to the parents when they drop off or pick up their child at school. If you decide to visit the home, consider going with another individual for safety and always tell someone the address of the student's home and when to expect your return. One last suggestion—if the teacher or principal has a good relationship with the parent, ask him or her to recommend the group to the parent.

## *Obtaining Parental Consent*

You will need signed consent forms from all students. Check in with each potential group member to determine if the parent signed and returned the consent form. If the student does not have the consent form, give him or her another packet of group information, including the Program Summary, the Consent/Permission Form, the Parent Group Survey, and the Letter to Parent/Caregiver (see sample forms in Appendices 1, 2, 7, and 8). Discuss the importance of giving the papers to the parent and returning the consent form signed.

You may want to set up an incentive system with students to increase the likelihood they will return the consent form. Tell them that they will earn a reward for returning the signed consent form by the end of the week regardless of their parent's decision to let them participate. It is important to set a specific deadline for return of the forms to school. If the student returns the form within the timeline, provide a small reward (e.g., sticker, pencil, prize from prize box). If the student's parent has already come in for a meeting or has an appointment to come in to discuss the group and sign forms, you may want to reward the student when the parent comes for the meeting.

## *Obtaining Student Assent*

Once the student returns the signed parental consent form, meet with the student to discuss the group in more detail. The following topics could be discussed:

### *Purpose of the Group*

Discuss the purpose of the group, goals, number of sessions, and the skills students will be learning in the group (e.g., problem-solving techniques, calming-down strategies). Answer any questions the student may have (e.g., "Why was I chosen for the group?" "Do I have to attend every session?"). It is essential to assess each student's individual feelings about being in the group. There are times when students do not know why they were chosen for a group or they are unsure about the content that will be discussed in the group. They may be concerned about what their peers will think or say about them participating in a group. Let students know the purpose of the group, how they were selected, and ask if they would like to participate in the group. For instance, you may say something like:

> "Your teacher mentioned that you were having some trouble getting along with others in the classroom. I know you were sent to the office last week for getting into a fight with another student. So, we want to help you work on getting along with others. I would like you to join me once a week in a group meeting with other students to help you learn ways to stay calm, get along with others, and learn problem-solving skills. Students who have been in this group in the past have had fun and learned a lot about how to problem solve and cope with difficult school issues. How does this sound to you?"

See Table 3.1 for appropriate group leader responses to frequently asked questions by students.

**TABLE 3.1. Questions Frequently Asked by Students and Appropriate Responses by Group Leaders**

*Question 1:* "Why was I chosen for the group?"

*Appropriate response:* "All fourth-grade teachers at the school were asked to identify several students they think may benefit from participating in the groups. The groups are designed to increase your organizational skills, help you choose positive friends, help you solve problems, and to make good choices for yourself. Your teacher thinks you may benefit from practicing these skills. Do you think this is something you would be interested in?"

*Question 2:* "Do I have to attend the groups?"

*Appropriate response:* "If your mom says that you can be in the group, we would love for you to attend the group. It is helpful if you are at as many sessions as possible so that you don't miss anything. We have many fun activities and cool prizes to give out when you attend the group, participate, and follow the rules. However, you are free to decide not to be in the group if you do not wish to participate."

*Question 3:* "What do we do in the group?"

*Appropriate response:* "We will do all sorts of fun things while learning important skills that everyone could learn more about . . . even me. We will play games, practice skills through role plays and other activities, we will watch some video clips, and have fun. It's a place where you can talk about everyday problems that everyone deals with in school, at home, and in your life. The group is designed to help you develop the skills that you will need to make a successful transition to the next grade level. Some things we may talk about are organization and study skills, getting along with teachers and classmates, and dealing with peer pressure. But there are many other skills we will learn and things we will discuss."

*Question 4:* "When will I attend the group?"

*Appropriate response:* "We will set a time that works with your school schedule. Most likely the group will occur during your resource period so that we don't take you out of your core academic classes."

*Question 5:* "Will people make fun of me for being in the group?"

*Appropriate response:* "It is unlikely that you will be made fun of for being in the group. This has never been a significant problem for children in this type of group in the past. In fact, most students enjoy the group, and many students who are not included want to be in the group. If this ever were to happen, you can let me know and we will figure out a way to stop that from happening."

*Question 6:* "Will you tell my mom what I say in the group?"

*Appropriate response:* "That is a really good question. The answer has two parts. We will not tell anyone (including your mom) what you talk about or what anyone talks about in the group. It is a safe place where you can feel free to share whatever you would like and we want you to feel confident that it will stay within our group. This will be a rule that we make with the other group members and we will make sure that everyone agrees with this before moving on with any of the sessions. There are a couple of cases where I will have to share information that was discussed in group. One case is if you came into the group and told us that someone had hurt you or was going to hurt you. Another case is if you came into the group and told us that you were going to hurt yourself. In both these cases I would need to tell someone and make sure that you were safe from harm. Other than that, everything stays within our group. If your mom asks what we are learning in the group, I may share that information with her, but if she asks what you are saying in the group, I will not share that information. Does this make sense?"

## Expectations

Discuss group rules and expectations, as well as the consequences, if a student does not follow the rules. It is important to discuss expectations with each student individually as well as collaboratively with the group.

## Group Logistics

Let students know about group logistics (e.g., day, time, location) and if they need to bring any materials to the group (e.g., pencil, book bag, paper). Discuss the procedure for missing class, assignments, or activities if the group is held during the school day.

## Assent

Ask students if they would like to participate in the group and have each sign an assent form (if needed; see Appendix 3 for a sample form). Explain any screening tools that you will be using and be sensitive to questions within the screening tool and how the student responds; asking students if they would like to be a part of this group (and/or complete a screening measure) shows respect for their autonomy and their opinion. Many students enjoy the opportunity to be a part of a group. However, there are times when the topic is sensitive (e.g., trauma-focused groups) and students are not willing to participate or fill out screening measures. In these instances, encourage the student to attend a few sessions and take some time to decide about continuing with the group. If a screening tool is used, explain it in detail and remind them of confidentiality and its limits.

This first meeting can also be used to answer any questions the student has about the group. He or she may feel confused about being selected or anxious about being in a group with peers. Identifying possible concerns prior to the group starting or in the early stages of the group may help to make members feel more comfortable. Ask the students to be open regarding their thoughts and feelings about participating in the group. This is also a good time to discuss confidentiality with each group member. It can be easier to fully explain confidentiality and its limits, and ensure individual understanding in a one-on-one setting. However, confidentiality should also be reviewed during the first group session and in subsequent sessions as needed to guarantee understanding.

## Overcoming Child Group Recruitment Barriers

Frequent check-ins with potential group members are essential during recruitment, especially if you have offered an incentive based on a deadline. For students who have not returned their parental consent form within 2 days: (1) remind each to return the form as soon as possible and remind him or her of the incentive for its return, regardless of the parent's decision; (2) contact each parent by phone or e-mail (if applicable) to determine whether the form was received and if he or she plans to provide consent for the child's participation.

If the student does not return the form within the timeline, double check to be sure the student gave the forms to the parent. If the form did not make it home with the student, give him or her another form or mail it along with other information about the group to the parent. You could also phone the parents to let them know another form has been sent home either with their child or by mail.

If parental consent is not granted or a significant amount of time has passed since the consent return deadline, select additional students from the nomination list and begin the recruitment process again (see "Contacting Parents" and "Obtaining Parental Consent").

## Parent Gives Consent, but Student Refuses

There are times when a student may not want to be in the group but the parent has signed the consent form. This could be due to the other students in the group or being unsure of the group. It is important to obtain assent from all students before continuing with the group process (at least verbal assent and in some cases written assent is needed, too). Explain the group in full detail to each student and inform each of the group requirements.

Ultimately, it is a student's choice whether or not to participate in the group. One option is to call the student's parents and explain the situation since the parents may assume that their child is participating in the group after signing the consent form. It may be helpful to let the student know that you are available to discuss this in further detail now or in the future. Invite the student to attend the first couple of groups and make a decision after trying it out. If the student refuses, you may want to recruit other students but keep this student in mind for future groups.

## Parent Does Not Give Consent, but Student Is Interested

Similarly, there may be situations in which a student wants to participate in the group but his or her parent will not give consent. For example, the student may have heard about the group at school and be interested in participating, or the student may want to participate because classmates have returned signed parental consent forms. You must have parental consent for each student in the group. One option is to contact the parent to further explain the group, answer any questions the parent may have, and express the student's interest in being in the group. If the parent still will not sign the consent form, you could consider briefly but compassionately explaining the consent procedure to the student and apologize for not being able to include him or her in the group. At the end of this chapter there is a sample role play on how to process the concerns when a parent is not interested in his or her child participating in the group (see role-play scenario 1 at the end of this chapter).

## The Student Is Interested in the Group, but the Group Is Full

There are times when other students want to be in the group but they were not "nominated," they may not have met criteria for the group, or the group was already full. It is important to briefly but compassionately explain to the student that the group is currently full, but that you will keep the student in mind for future groups.

# PARENT GROUPS

As discussed earlier, involve school staff and parents early in the process of planning a group. To aid recruitment for parent groups, you may want to form a steering committee of school administrators, teachers, family support workers, and parents. The purpose of the committee would be to provide advice for recruitment of more families, locations for the group, and relevant material. Discuss the purpose of the groups with the school administrators, teachers, and parents actively involved in the school to gain support for implementation of the program. Having strong support from individuals in the school who have frequent contact with parents (e.g., parent liaison) can be helpful when recruiting parent participation, as well as maintaining ongoing participation. You will also want to ask the teachers when is a good time to catch the parent at school (e.g., parent–teacher conferences). This is especially helpful for parents who are difficult to contact by phone or e-mail. At the end of this chapter there is a sample role play on how to set up a mock steering committee of school administrators, teachers, parents, and family advocates for the purpose of discussing barriers and solutions to recruitment and implementation of parent groups in the community (see role-play scenario 2 at the end of this chapter).

## Parent Group Recruitment

### Selecting a Time and Day for Meeting

You may begin by surveying the parents of the students in the child group to determine the days and times they would most likely be able to attend a parent group (see Appendix 7 for a sample Parent Group Survey). Is there a possibility of scheduling the group during parents' lunchtime, after work, weekends, or on days they are off from work? Another possibility is to offer the group at two separate times that are convenient for parents. It may also be possible to rotate or alternate the group time so that all parents can attend when it's convenient for them.

Select a time and day that is most convenient for the parents planning to attend and then contact the parents to inform them of the day, time, and length of the group sessions. Be sure to express enthusiasm and tell them that you are looking forward to having them in the group. Invite all caregivers for each student (e.g., stepparents, grandparents, aunts, uncles) to attend. Discuss any barriers to attendance and help brainstorm possible solutions with each parent. If you are able to provide food and drink, emphasize that food and drinks will be provided at each group. If you are able to provide child care or transportation for parents, highlight these resources in your conversation.

You may want to provide each parent with a calendar of group session dates and times. Send home reminder fliers prior to each session (see Appendix 9 for a sample Parent Group Reminder Flier) and make reminder calls to parents a day or two before the parent group or even the morning of the session. Some parents may prefer a text or an e-mail reminder.

### Identifying a Meeting Place

Find a location that allows the most parents to attend. This is likely to be close to where students' parents live and work. Make sure that the location has adequate space and furniture (e.g., chairs, tables) for the number of parents expected to attend the groups and child care (if provided). The school is often an excellent choice for holding parent groups (e.g., library, conference room, extra classroom). However, depending on the circumstances, churches or community centers may be better choices. Some parents may feel uncomfortable attending meetings held at the school due to negative past experiences. Make sure the location is private (e.g., confidentiality), warm, and welcoming to all parents. If you need video equipment for the group, make sure the selected room has the appropriate capabilities.

Be prepared to answer questions about the group content and logistics. Parents often have questions regarding both the child and parent groups (e.g., "Why was my child chosen for the group?" "Does my child have to attend the group?"). See Table 3.2 for appropriate group leader responses to frequently asked questions by parents.

## Involving More Parents in the Group

Occasionally the group leader may want to offer the group to other parents, in addition to the parents who have children in a child group. Here are a few recruitment suggestions:

### Create Fliers

Create a flier that can be sent out to parents who have children in the same grade level as the students in the child group (see Appendices 10 and 11 for a sample Parent Group Invite Letter and a Parent Group Invite Flier).

### Attend Back-to-School Nights and Other Activities

Attend Back-to-School Nights, Parent Nights, or be available at the start and end of each day to talk to parents about the program. Be enthusiastic! Be sure to have all important information (e.g., parent group topics, group logistics) and the Parent Group Invite Letter or Parent Group Invite Flier (see Appendices 10 and 11) on hand to offer as information about the group.

### Involve Teacher(s)

Ask the teachers to help advertise the parent group by handing out fliers, reminding students to take home the fliers, and sharing information about the group during meetings with parents (e.g., parent–teacher conferences).

## Overcoming Parent Group Recruitment Barriers

Potential barriers may be encountered during recruitment and the start of the group. It is best to prepare in advance for these and try to problem solve with each parent to increase the likelihood that he or she will be able to be a part of the parent group. At the end of this chapter there is a sample role play on how to handle a situation where a parent is interested in attending the parent group, but offers a list of reasons why this will be difficult for him or her (see role-play scenario 3 at the end of this chapter).

**TABLE 3.2. Questions Frequently Asked by Parents and Appropriate Responses by Group Leaders**

*Question 1:* "Why was my child referred? How was he or she chosen for the group?"

*Appropriate response:* "All fourth-grade teachers at the group leader's school were asked to identify several students they think may benefit from participating in the groups. The groups are designed to increase your child's organizational skills, help him or her to choose positive friends, help him or her solve problems, and to make good choices. Your child's teacher thinks he or she may benefit from practicing these skills."

*Question 2:* "Do I have to attend the parent groups?"

*Appropriate response:* "It is strongly recommended that parents attend the parent groups. Research about this program shows that, while children benefit from the child component, they get the maximum benefit when parents attend the parent groups as well. However, parents are free to decline any part of the intervention and may agree to allow their child to participate in the child group even if they do not wish to participate in the parent groups."

*Question 3:* "What will my child get out of this program?"

*Appropriate response:* "This group is designed to help children develop the skills that they will need to make a successful transition to the next grade level. These skills include organization and study skills, taking responsibility for assignments, getting along with teachers and classmates, and dealing with peer pressure. The program extends across the school year during which students have ample opportunity to learn, practice, and consolidate the skills they learn before they graduate from their current grade level."

*Question 4:* "Will participating in this program make my child fall behind in his or her studies (i.e., because he or she will be missing class)?"

*Appropriate response:* "We will work with your child's teacher to set the weekly group time so as not to interfere with important academic periods. The skills learned in the group are likely to have a positive impact on students' academic performance. Topics addressed include learning how to set goals and work toward achieving them, as well as interpersonal and behavioral skills (e.g., getting along with others and anger management) that can lead to better classroom performance."

*Question 5:* "Will my child be teased or ridiculed for being a part of this program?"

*Appropriate response:* "It is unlikely that your child will be teased. This has never been a significant problem for children in this type of group. In fact, most students enjoy the group, and many who are not included in the groups express a desire to participate."

*Question 6:* "Will you tell me what my child says during the group?"

*Appropriate response:* "During parent group meetings we will review what your child has been learning in the group. This will allow parents to encourage and reinforce the skills. Should your child share information that leads to concern about his or her safety or that of another person, the counselor will notify you and, if necessary, other relevant individuals. Otherwise, all other information remains confidential, as we want your child to feel comfortable sharing with the group without feeling like we are telling others his or her personal information."

## Difficulty Contacting Parents

There are times when it is difficult to reach parents because you have an incorrect phone number, the parent is not answering calls, or the parent does not have a working phone. When possible, leave a detailed phone message describing who you are and the purpose of the call. You may also want to request that the parent contact you to review the group materials and provide a phone number where he or she can be reached. Talk to the student's classroom teacher to see whether the parent comes to school or if the teacher has any contact with the parent. If the parent visits the classroom to pick up his or her child or has a meeting scheduled with the teacher, try to make arrangements to stop by and talk with the parent during that time at the school. If the parent uses a cell phone but does not answer during the day, try calling after peak hours. The parent may be saving his or her minutes, only using the phone at night. Keep cell phone conversations brief and offer to call at a different number to save minutes. Keep a log of the days and times you call parents and vary the time of day and days of the week you call.

There are also times when the contact information you have for the parent may be incorrect. It may be helpful to send a letter home with the student requesting updated contact information from the parent. Another strategy is to talk to the teacher or school administrative assistant to see if they may have more up-to-date contact information. Or you could look at the student's emergency contact card at school. These cards often contain information on a second contact person that can be used to obtain current contact information for the family. Last, request correct information through Information (411; XXX-555-1212) or on *whitepages.com*.

## Parent Time Constraints and Other Commitments

Some parents work or have other commitments, and groups may not be offered during a time that is convenient for them. Try to brainstorm times they may be available to attend groups. If parent groups cannot be scheduled at a time that is convenient for the parent, encourage him or her to attend the group as often as possible and explain that materials will be sent home after each group. Set up times with the parent to discuss the parenting group materials by phone. You may also want to e-mail the materials to the parent (e.g., handouts, session worksheets), but it is extremely important to review the materials with the parent so that he or she understands them, especially the more advanced parenting skills such as time-out.

## Finding Child Care

Lack of child care can interfere with parent group attendance. If resources are available, provide child care during parent groups. However, this is not always feasible. During the initial conversation with the parent regarding recruitment and attendance, brainstorm with the parent about potential individuals who may be able to care for the children during the group (e.g., aunt, uncle, neighbor). Another option is for the parent to attend the first group and talk to other members about who cares for their children during the group meeting.

Determine if it is possible for them to share child care providers. If there are resources available for child care during the group, review this option and process it with the parent. For example, some group leaders have had interns or externs working with them who provided child care during the parent groups. In these situations it is recommended that you discuss liability issues with parents prior to providing child care.

## Transportation

Transportation also plays a role in maintaining parent group attendance. If possible, it is helpful to provide a bus token or taxi fare for parents to attend the group. During the initial conversation with the parent, brainstorm ways for the parent to obtain a ride to the group with someone they know or connect with other group members who may have access to private transportation. It may also be helpful to prepare a list of taxi companies and phone numbers as well as bus route and schedule information for parents. Another option is to encourage parents to carpool to group if possible.

## Remembering Commitment to the Group

Another barrier to parent group attendance is their forgetting the group meeting day and time. As mentioned earlier, you can provide the parents with a calendar showing dates and times of group meetings, and a magnet for putting the calendar on the refrigerator at home. Make reminder phone calls a day or two before the meeting; you may even need to call the morning of the session to remind parents about the group. Have an individual meeting and teach the parent how to use a planner or add the meeting dates to his or her planner if the parent already has one. Reward parents for remembering to come to the meeting on time (e.g., a raffle ticket, praise).

## Uncertainty about the Group

Some parents may have unrealistic expectations of what it is like to belong to a group. Other parents may have had negative experiences with groups or mental health services. These experiences may cause parents to feel uncomfortable, have misconceptions about the group, or miss the first session. Identifying parents' concerns prior to the group or in the early stages of the group may help to make members feel more comfortable. You may want to meet with each parent individually or have a phone conversation with the parents to explore what they are expecting. Then, discuss in what ways their expectations are aligned with or not aligned with what will happen. Be sure to explain the structure and the purpose of the group. You will want to ask parents to state their honest reactions, feelings, and thoughts about participating in the group. It may be helpful to generate a list of expectations of the group from the group members during the first meeting. Then, have a group discussion about what is realistic and unrealistic.

Assure parents that they are welcome to any or all of the parent group meetings and encourage them to try it out during the first session. Send reminder fliers home prior to each group meeting and send home parent group materials after each session with a letter encouraging parents to call you if they wish to review the materials. Provide parents with your contact information and a phone number where you can easily be reached.

There will be some parents who will seem committed and interested in the group right from the start. You may still want to ask parents to share barriers that may prevent them from coming to the group (see role-play scenario 4 at the end of this chapter). Then, brainstorm solutions to those barriers with all members of the group. Discussing these barriers in the group setting can lead to innovative solutions that allow parents to attend despite not having resources. Parents will find ways to overcome barriers if they find the group to be important and helpful. In fact, parents who understand how the content of the group will benefit them and the lives of their family are the most likely to come and engage in the group process, regardless of barriers to attendance.

## Sending Home Materials

It is important to use your clinical judgment as to whether or not to send home all parent materials without reviewing them first with the parent. For example, you may feel comfortable sending home materials about praise or building a positive relationship with the child, but you may not want to send home materials on more advanced parenting skills such as time-out. It is a best practice to review these materials with the parent so that he or she completely understands them and so that you are not enabling the parent to miss another group session.

Don't give up! Be persistent, consistent, and continue to encourage family participation whenever you have an opportunity to interact with parents in person, by phone, or through written correspondence (e.g., send home a "We missed you at group" note or letter that encourages them to come to the group). You do not want to make parents feel guilty about missing a session but always convey that you hope to see them at the next session. Always empathize with the parent's stress and busy schedules. This is an excellent opportunity to build rapport with parents.

## Multiple Caregivers

There are times when the primary caregiver is not the student's legal guardian and this becomes a barrier. The primary caregiver may be another relative or child care worker, taking care of the student throughout the day while the legal guardian (e.g., mother, father) works. The student may live full-time with another relative (e.g., grandmother, aunt, uncle), although the biological parents are the legal guardians. Some students may be in foster care or state may be the legal guardian. In these situations, it is recommended that informed consent be conducted with the legal guardian but the primary caregiver could still be involved in the group. When possible invite and encourage all of the student's caregivers to attend the parent groups. It is important to consult with the primary caregiver and legal guardian about who should be invited.

# MANAGING YOUR OWN TIME

It can be difficult to find time in your busy schedule to make phone calls and write notes to parents. When possible try to make time in your schedule. This is easier said than done! For instance, plan to stay a few minutes after work to make phone calls or come in a few minutes early and tackle a few phone calls before the day gets hectic. It is often helpful to split the phone calls up and make them throughout the day. It is important to block off the time in your day (e.g., shut the door and tell people you are unavailable for 30 minutes to make calls). Sometimes reframing how we view these administrative tasks is helpful. For example, think about making phone calls to parents as part of your job as a group leader and *not* something extra that needs to be done. In fact, contacting parents to recruit for the child and parent groups is the main priority at the beginning. It is not possible to have a successful group without parents attending the groups.

Challenge yourself to find creative ways to contact and engage families that are difficult to reach. Don't fall into the trap of recruiting only the most easily accessible families for participation. Sometimes the families that are difficult to contact need the most help! Put extra time in your schedule for families that are more difficult to contact (e.g., take home the phone number and call from home in the evening or on the weekends). When calling families from home or from a personal cell phone, you may want to use the "block" function (*67) to ensure that your personal number does not appear on caller ID. However, some individuals may not answer blocked calls and some phones will not allow blocked calls.

Before the first session begins, prepare templates for letters to send home later to parents, (e.g., "Thank you for coming to group"; "We missed you at group"; "Just a reminder about group"). Save them electronically on your computer so that you do not have to re-create them each time they need to be sent home. Also prepare mailing labels ahead of time and have envelopes ready for letters to be sent home. Some changes will need to be made to the letters before you print them out (e.g., group times and logistics) or you may want to write a personal message on the letter to the parent. But preparing most of it in advance can save you much time.

# SUMMARY

Successful recruitment of students and parents requires careful planning and consideration. Begin the recruitment process by thinking about group content and material, logistics, and the dynamics of the group. Involving principals, teachers, and other school staff is essential for the successful recruitment of students and parents, as they can be of great assistance.

There are times where you may want to utilize a screening measure to select members for your group. You will need consent in order to administer a screening measure to a student and you should make sure all parties involved (e.g., parent and student) are aware of not only the group selection process but also the use of the screening tool. See Chapter 7 for more details regarding the selection and use of screening tools.

Sometimes there are barriers that can get in the way of recruiting and continuing to engage students and parent group members. Be aware of these barriers and have a plan for solving problems that may arise. Strike a balance between flexibility and structure.

# MATERIALS

The following is a list of materials discussed in this chapter that can support you in the recruitment process. You will find examples of most of these materials in the Appendices.

- Program Summary (Appendix 1) prompts you to include a brief description of the purpose of the program, number of sessions, what each session entails, and the role of student and parent in the program.
- Consent/Permission Form (Appendix 2) for participation in individual and group counseling.
- Student Assent Form (Appendix 3).
- Teacher Nomination Form (Appendix 4).
- Caregiver Contact Log (Appendix 5) includes contact information, including current phone and address of primary caregiver.
- Recruitment Script (Appendix 6).
- Parent Group Survey (Appendix 7) asks parents for the best days and times for holding parent sessions.
- Letter to Parent/Caregiver (Appendix 8).
- Parent Group Reminder Flier (Appendix 9).
- Parent Group Invite Letter (Appendix 10).
- Parent Group Invite Flier (Appendix 11).
- Calendar of meeting dates.*
- A list of questions to help elicit feedback from the steering committee (e.g., suggestions for recruitment, making the group relevant, finding appropriate location and time, potential barriers and solutions).*
- Incentives for teachers who assist with recruitment.*
- Parent contact list with all group members' contact information.*
- Bus schedules and taxi numbers to assist in finding transportation for parents.*

# REFLECTION AND ROLE PLAYS

Here we provide a series of reflection exercises and role-play activities to help you further hone your group facilitation skills.

## *Reflection*

After reviewing this chapter, ask yourself the following questions:

1. "How will I appropriately involve administrators, teachers, and other staff in the recruitment process?"

---

*These materials are not included in the Appendices, but may be referenced within this chapter and are also helpful when implementing parent and child groups.

2. "Have I reviewed Table 3.2, 'Questions Frequently Asked by Parents and Appropriate Responses by Group Leaders'? Am I prepared to answer questions that may come up regarding student and parent participation in the groups?"

3. Not only are there barriers for group leaders in preparing for and running group interventions, but there are also barriers for parents in committing to attend the group. "How will I assist parents in overcoming barriers so that they and their children can participate in the group intervention?"

## *Role Plays*

After reviewing the reflection questions, apply your understanding of what has been covered in this chapter by responding to the following four scenarios:

### Scenario 1

The parent is not interested in his or her child participating in the group. The parent states that his or her child does not need the group. As the group leader, process the concerns or issues that may be causing the lack of commitment to participating in the group.

EXAMPLE SCRIPTED ANSWER[†]

GROUP LEADER: We are looking forward to having your child in the group and excited to start both the parent and child groups next week! As we discussed, the parent groups will be held on _____ [date and time of group]. Is there anything that you can think of that could possibly get in the way of you attending the first group?

PARENT: I really do not think Kayla needs to be in a group. How was she chosen to be in the group?

GROUP LEADER: Kayla was identified by her teacher as a student who may benefit from learning ways to stay on-task in the classroom and help with study skills. It is completely up to you if you want Kayla to participate, and if you find that it is not helping, she can stop at any time. One of the things I noticed when I am in Kayla's classroom is that she is often distracted by her peers during independent seatwork or looking out the window. Have you also noticed this behavior at home?

PARENT: Actually, this is something I have noticed at home and her teacher often calls home to tell me she is concerned about Kayla passing the fifth grade because she is not completing her assignments.

GROUP LEADER: A lot of kids I work with have benefited from learning some basic organizational and study skills to help them be more successful in the classroom.

PARENT: Well, that sounds OK. I just did not want Kayla "airing all of our family's dirty laundry" in the group. I am really concerned about confidentiality and everyone in the neighborhood knowing our business. We saw a therapist when she was little and she told all of the teachers everything we told her.

GROUP LEADER: I am really sorry to hear that. It's so unfortunate that you had that horrible experience. (*Listens and empathizes with the parent.*)

PARENT: I have not talked to anyone since that happened.

---

[†]For all role-play scenarios, attempt to respond to the scenario first, prior to reading the script.

GROUP LEADER: I completely understand. I can promise you that everything Kayla and I talk about is completely confidential, unless she were to tell me that she wanted to hurt herself or others, or someone was hurting her. I will not be sharing confidential information with Kayla's teachers or other school staff, not even the principal. This is, however, a group and Kayla may share things with the other group members. I unfortunately cannot guarantee the confidentiality of the other group members. However, we make this a rule at the start of the group that everything that is said in group stays in the group [except for the limits to confidentiality—explain further if needed]. The group members have all agreed to this rule and respect it so we are hopeful that all information will remain within the group. If a student were to ever break this rule, there would be serious consequences, such as removal from the group. So I can promise that we make it very clear to the students what can be shared with others and what can absolutely not be shared with others, and we also discuss consequences if someone breaks the rule. Typically, group members don't share personal information until they feel a certain level of trust in the group and its members, and at that point the bond is formed and oftentimes this rule is followed. Does this make sense?

PARENT: That sounds good. I'm a little concerned with other group members talking about what Kayla shares outside of group, but it sounds like you prepare for this and that the students will share only if they feel comfortable with the other group members and leaders.

GROUP LEADER: Yes, we prepare for this as best as possible. So would you be interested in having Kayla in the group?

PARENT: I will think about it.

GROUP LEADER: I think that sounds like a good idea. Why don't you and Kayla talk it over and then I'll give you a call in a couple days and we can discuss it further then. How does that sound?

PARENT: That sounds great.

## Scenario 2

Set up a mock steering committee of school administrators, teachers, parents, and family advocates for the purpose of discussing possible barriers and solutions to recruitment and implementation of parent groups in the community. Use the activity to develop a list of questions that need to be asked before and during the planning of parent groups in the community.

### EXAMPLE SCRIPTED ANSWER

GROUP LEADER: Thank you so much to everyone for taking the time out of their busy days to attend this meeting and help us brainstorm ways for us to have a successful parent group. We really appreciate you being here today. Let's begin by making a list of topics that you think parents would be interested in learning more about.

SCHOOL COUNSELOR: I have had a lot of trouble getting parents to come to the school, so we need to make it a topic that really interests parents.

PRINCIPAL: I have had a lot of parents ask about help with their children being disrespectful and not following their rules.

GROUP LEADER: Wow, these are great ideas, so under "Barriers" I am going to write that we really need to find a way to engage parents since it can sometimes be difficult to get them to come up to the school, and under "Topics" I am going to add disrespect and following parent rules. Does anyone have anything they have done in the past that has been successful with getting parents to come to school?

TEACHER A: I have had a potluck dinner for my families and parents really seem to like all the different types of food. It is also helpful that they do not have to cook dinner.

GROUP LEADER: Wonderful. I am going to add to our list that it would be helpful to provide dinner at the groups. Anything else you have tried?

TEACHER B: My sister works at Walmart and each year they donate a $50 gift certificate. I have a raffle at Back-to-School Night to increase parent attendance.

GROUP LEADER: That's an excellent idea! I am going to add that we can try to get donations from local businesses and have a raffle at our parent group. Now, are there any other barriers parents may have to attending school events?

SCHOOL SOCIAL WORKER: I know a lot of our families have trouble with transportation and some students take several buses just to get here from across town each day. It would be really helpful if we could give families bus tokens or pay for their cab fare.

GROUP LEADER: Great. I am going to add transportation to our list of barriers. Does anyone know of any resources or funds we could use to pay for the food or transportation?

PRINCIPAL: I can check to see if we have any bus tokens left over from another project we had last year and get back to you.

GROUP LEADER: Thanks so much, we really appreciate that. Now, does anyone have any ideas about providing child care to the children while their parents are in the parent group?

TEACHER C: I wonder if we could talk to the after-school program to see if they would be able to watch a few extra children.

TEACHER B: We also have some practicum students from Towson University who may be able to help with child care.

GROUP LEADER: Nice. I am going to add these to our list for possible help with child care. Is there anything else you can think of regarding the parent group?

SECRETARY: If it is helpful, I could print out a list of contact numbers for all of the students/families. I could also pass out fliers when parents come to the office to pick up students.

SOCIAL WORKER: I would love a few fliers to give to the families in my caseload.

GROUP LEADER: This is amazing! Thanks so much to everyone for all of your great ideas and all of your support in making this a successful parent group.

## TIP

Here is a possible list of questions to use in your steering committee discussions:

- "What types of groups (topics) would parents be most interested in attending?"
- "What are the possible barriers to parents attending the group?"
- "Is it possible to offer child care? Are there any volunteers to help with child care?"
- "Do we have any funding to provide dinner and/or raffles?"
- "Do we have any resources to offer transportation?"
- "Is the school the best place to hold the groups or are there other places (e.g., local church, community center)?"
- "How will we recruit parents? Will we call them? Make fliers?"

## Scenario 3

The parent agrees that his or her child will benefit, but has a list of reasons why attending the parent group will be difficult. For instance, the parent has a full-time job and there are no groups offered during a convenient time. Or there could be no child care offered during the parent group. Try to come up with solutions to the barriers offered.

### EXAMPLE SCRIPTED ANSWER

GROUP LEADER: We are looking forward to having your child in the group and excited to start both the parent and child groups next week! As we discussed, the parent groups will be held on [date and time of group]. Is there anything that you can think of that could possibly get in the way of you attending the first group?

PARENT: I am a little concerned about getting everything done on the evenings we have the group. I work long hours and often when I get home there are a million things I need to do before the kids go to bed, such as homework, dinner, baths, get the kids ready for the next day, etcetera.

GROUP LEADER: I completely understand. You have a lot on your plate right now! (*Listens and empathizes with the parent's stress.*)

PARENT: Yes, the group sounds really great but we have so much going on right now, especially with Kayla starting flag football.

GROUP LEADER: I'm wondering if there is anything we could do to help. For example, sometimes we have provided dinner at the groups so that families do not have to worry about cooking on the nights we have group. Is that something you would be interested in?

PARENT: Wow. That would be really helpful.

GROUP LEADER: Another thing we offer is child care during the parent groups. We have an intern who plays games with the children and helps with their homework. You could also bring Kayla's brothers if that would be helpful.

PARENT: That would be nice if I could bring all of the children and we could eat here on the nights we have group.

GROUP LEADER: Great. If you have any other concerns in the upcoming weeks, I hope you will let me know so we can see if there are ways that we can work around them so that you can be at the weekly parent groups. I know you mentioned that you thought the group would really help improve your and Kayla's relationship and possibly help her to be more successful at school. We want to do anything we can to help you attend the group and help Kayla have a great year in the fifth grade!

## TIP

It will be important to remind the parent of the reasons he or she expressed for being interested in attending the group, or ways the student and parent could benefit from participating in the group. Examples include helping improve the parent–child relationship, the parent's positive parenting skills, helping the child's behavior at home or school, or helping the child to be more successful academically.

## Scenario 4

The parent is willing to have his or her child in the group, is interested in being in the parent group, and asks no difficult questions. As the group leader, process with the parent the barriers to attending a parent group.

EXAMPLE SCRIPTED ANSWER

GROUP LEADER: We are looking forward to having your child in the group and excited to start both the parent and child groups next week! As we discussed, the parent groups will be held on [date and time of group]. Is there anything that you can think of that could possibly get in the way of you attending the first group?

PARENT: I can't think of anything.

GROUP LEADER: Since the parent group will be held after school in the evenings, do you have any concerns with child care for your other children?

PARENT: I have arranged for my other two children to stay with my neighbor that evening.

GROUP LEADER: Will you have transportation to the group?

PARENT: I was planning on taking the light rail after work, but then I'll need to figure out the bus lines and schedule to get to the school.

GROUP LEADER: Wonderful. Would you like me to look up the bus lines and schedule and print out a copy for you?

PARENT: Sure. That would be very helpful!

GROUP LEADER: (*Prints out bus information and gives it to the parent.*) Are there any other concerns you have about attending the group?

PARENT: No, not right now.

GROUP LEADER: Great. If you have any other concerns in the coming week, I hope you will let me know so we can see if there are ways that we can work around them so that you can be at the weekly parent groups.

## TIP

You may want to think about one or two specific barriers that could possibly be an issue for the parent based on previous conversations. For example, if the parent has mentioned that he or she works long hours, you may want to ask whether dinner or getting the evening routine completed (e.g., homework, baths) may be a concern. Another example would be to ask whether the parent is comfortable coming to the school if there has been a possibly negative relationship between the parent and the student's teacher or other school staff.

# CHAPTER 4

# Planning, Organizing, and Establishing the Group

Effective group organization is essential in implementing a successful child and parent group. Take the time up front to determine the logistical aspects of running a group and involve all key individuals in the planning (e.g., teachers, administrators). This will allow groups to run smoothly. For instance, planning logistics such as location, time, and how you will get students to and from the group will help ensure that the group starts and ends on time. By planning ahead, everything will be ready to go for a group session. You can also anticipate potential problems and prepare solutions.

Planning and problem solving the logistics of your groups can be challenging. This chapter discusses strategies for establishing and maintaining successful child and parent groups while troubleshooting common issues that may arise at the start of a group.

## CHILD GROUPS

### Establishing the Group

#### Preparing for Group Members' Arrival to Meetings

There are some things to consider when setting up your group arrival plan. First, determine whether you will allow students to use the restroom prior to, after, or during the group. It may be best to have the students use the restroom on the way to the group rather than leaving the group to use the restroom. Again, you will want to teach, model, and practice how you want students to go to and from the restroom or water fountain. If the students will be bringing their belongings to the group, plan for how items will be stored and accessed during the group (e.g., piled neatly under a desk or chair, coats hung in the corner). Find a way to limit the amount of time and distraction caused by having these additional items in the room.

## SEATING ARRANGEMENTS

Determine the seating arrangements for the group meetings. We highly recommended you have a seating arrangement prior to the students entering the room. For instance, there may be group members who do not get along very well. You may want to sit these students apart from one another during group meetings. Similarly, there may be group members who know each other too well and don't need to be seated together. You may want group members who do not know each other well to sit beside each other, allowing them to interact more. If you have group members who are constantly vying for your attention, you may want to sit between them, keeping them in close proximity to give them attention while managing their behavior. You will want to think about who will work well together, rotating seats so everyone meets one another.

Consider in advance whether the group members should sit in desks, at a table, in chairs, or on the carpet in a circle. There are benefits and challenges to each option. Tables are beneficial when the group members need to write, but they can also be a distraction for students. For example, students can play under the table, kick other students, etc., without being "seen" by the group leader. Students may also put their heads down on the table, and this can be distracting when you are trying to engage group members. If the students are seated in a circle in chairs (or on the carpet/floor), it is easier to engage them in activities; be in close proximity to control for behavior management; and offer individual reinforcement using tokens, stickers, points, or other reinforcers for appropriate behavior. However, students could lie down on the carpet, touch other group members, or become more fidgety when sitting on the ground or in a chair. It is important to continually assess the group and decide how the group should be set up for the best chance for success. Some group leaders find it helpful to switch from sitting on the carpet to sitting at the table for certain activities. This allows for movement and change within the group setting, which may help keep students on-task and focused.

It may be helpful to put name tags or folders on chairs or on the table where you would like each student to sit. This will give you the advantage of strategically deciding which students should sit together and avoid having students with distracting behavior sit next to each other. Additionally, you can have students immediately begin an activity when they enter the room by having their name already on the activity paper.

## PREPARING TO TEACH EXPECTATIONS AND BEING CONSISTENT

Consistency is essential when implementing any group, but is of the utmost importance when starting a new group. Be consistent and meet with the students at the same time of day and day of the week as much as possible. This will provide a routine for the students in the group so that they will know what to expect each week. If for some reason the group needs to be canceled, give the students advance notice (if possible) and explain to them when the next meeting will occur. Having the group at the same time and day each week will also help teachers be prepared and plan accordingly.

**Be consistent and meet with students at the same time of day and day of the week.**

Develop a systematic plan for gathering the students from class and returning them back to class after group. Depending on the issues related to development and behavior, you will want to devise a plan that will decrease the transition time between the classroom and group location. For some students it may be appropriate to allow them to arrive to the group on their own. However, other students may need to be monitored more closely and you may want to go to the classroom to pick up and drop off the students.

It is helpful to teach, model, and practice how you would like students to arrive at the group location. For instance, tell the students that they are expected to leave the classroom quietly, line up in single file, walk without talking in the hallway, keep their hands and feet to themselves, and sit down quietly when they get to the group location. Have students practice the expectations as you walk them to the group. In instances where students struggle with the expectations, you may want to model what the behavior looks like, then have them practice again to ensure they understand. Continue providing them with feedback and reteaching the expectation as needed, being consistent for each group meeting.

Also teach, model, and practice what to do when group members enter the meeting room, how to access materials, how to participate effectively in group meetings, and how to exit the group. It can be helpful to develop a list of transitions that will occur during each group session and plan for how you will teach students the expectations for each transition, to avoid wasting time or having lag time that leads to disruptive behaviors. Some examples of transitions that may occur include entering the room and finding where to sit, accessing materials, moving from chairs to the floor, moving from the floor to tables, putting away materials, getting a prize from the prize box at the end of group, ending the group and leaving the room to return to the classroom, or going home for the day. Being prepared to teach students each transition in advance will reduce the amount of time you spend correcting or redirecting students in the group.

## Having a Group Co-Leader

If the opportunity exists, you may decide to have a co-leader for the group. A co-leader can be extremely beneficial to running a successful group. Responsibilities and activities can be divided between the two group leaders. A co-leader can assist with making phone calls, getting students from class for the group, distributing handouts, checking in with teachers, and following up on goal sheets. Co-leaders can also assist with behavior and crisis management during group meetings. It can be helpful to have one leader focus on group content and material while the other leader focuses on group members' behavior. One especially helpful reason for having a co-leader is you can plan for potential crises by having a co-leader remove a student from the group such as for disruptive behavior. The other co-leader can then successfully move the rest of the group forward. Due to limited resources or staffing concerns, it may not be feasible to have a co-leader. However, there are many benefits and it is strongly recommended if the possibility exists.

## Planning and Preparing for Sessions

Prepare for the group sessions *prior* to students entering the group space. If you have a co-leader, meet in advance (if possible) to review content, discuss any possible challenges that may arise during the group, and to be sure all materials are available for group activities. Make copies of all handouts, any homework, and group activities *prior* to starting the group so that all of the materials are ready to go before each session begins. Prior to each session have handouts prepared in piles so that they are easily accessible. If needed, check any video equipment and make sure all other materials are easily accessible and ready for students to use (e.g., pencils, prize box). It is helpful to create a checklist that helps you plan for the group (see Appendix 12 for a sample Planning Ahead Checklist for the child group). Prior planning is imperative to a successful group! Using session time to copy or find materials disrupts the flow of the group and decreases the likelihood that students will remain focused and on-task. There may be things that come up within a group session that you need to attend to or locate (e.g., your chalk breaks as you are writing on the board and you need to find more), but the more you can prepare in advance for the group, the more smoothly your session will run.

> **Prepare for the group session *prior* to students entering the group space.**

## *Evaluating the Group Process*

Obtaining feedback from the students and reflecting on each session can help to optimize the impact of the sessions on student outcomes. At the end of each session, elicit feedback from students regarding what they liked and did not like about the group. This can be done by handing out a brief feedback form (see Appendix 13 for a sample Child Group Weekly Feedback Form) to be completed by each student at the end of the group. The feedback can be completed anonymously if students can read independently, or a group leader can read the questions out loud to the students and they can write down their answers. Another option is for the group leader to have each student share his or her peak/high (favorite part) and valley/low (least favorite) at the end of the group.

### *Reflecting after Each Group Session*

After the students return to their classroom, you (and your co-leader, if applicable) can reflect on any issues that arose related to the session content and any behavioral difficulties that occurred during the group, and brainstorm ideas for improving the next session. For example, you may need to provide new incentives for students or revise the point system for behavior management. You may decide that students need more physical activity in the group and less discussion, or you may need to meet individually with a group member before the next session to discuss concerns. Spending this time reflecting will allow you to make any necessary adjustment(s) to improve the delivery of content and outcomes of the group for students.

Between group sessions you will want to consider touching base with teachers, parents, and group members individually. Make time in your schedule to meet with students' classroom teacher(s), group members (individually), and the students' parents regarding group progress and any issues. The following provides ideas for planning ahead for these between-session meetings.

• *Have a plan for touching base with the classroom teacher.* Keep the classroom teachers informed of the skills students are learning in the group. You may want to provide teachers with handouts from the group and advise on how they could help the students generalize the skills they are learning in the group to the classroom (see Appendix 14 for a sample Session Summary Handout for teachers). Discuss with the teacher only the skills and techniques that students are learning in the group. Specific comments or details shared by the students during group should remain confidential. For instance, you could tell the teacher that the group is working on problem-solving techniques and review the problem-solving steps so the teacher can help the student generalize the skills to the classroom. Do not share information related to specific group discussions or personal disclosures by the group members.

- *Have a plan for touching base with student members outside of the group.* Stop by the classroom or catch students in the hallway to see how they are doing, remind them of homework, or ask them if they were able to use a skill they learned in the group. It may be helpful to meet individually with students to talk about the successes and barriers they have encountered between group meetings.

- *Have a plan for communicating with the parents about how their children are doing in the group.* The group leader may want to send home handouts or other materials on a regular basis that provide information about the content of the child group, student's homework assignments, *positive notes* about how their child is learning and effectively implementing strategies at school, and ideas for how parents can help their children generalize what they are learning in the group to the home (see Appendix 15 for a sample Session Summary Handout for parents). If the child group meets after school and parents come to pick up their children, this is a great time to check in with the parents, review homework, and discuss their child's progress. The skills and techniques learned in the group can be discussed with the parent, but remember to keep specific group member disclosures confidential. For example, you could tell the parent that the group is working on calming-down techniques and explain some of the specific techniques (e.g., deep breathing). The parent can then help his or her child use these skills at home. But do not share information related to specific group discussions or personal disclosures by the group members.

## When Group Attendance Is Low

What happens if only one student or a few students can attend a group session? First and foremost, don't be discouraged. Try to stay positive! You will want to decide whether it's best to have the group session at that time with a limited number of group members or try to reschedule for later in the week. If you choose to hold the group session with a small number of students, implement the group as planned so that it is beneficial to the students who are in attendance.

You will want to brainstorm ways to let the other group members know about the material they missed. One option is to meet with them individually and conduct a shorter session reviewing the group material, or in the next session, members could review the material with the students who missed the previous session. Either way, the missing group members need to receive the information (see "When Students Miss Sessions" below). If you choose to reschedule the group for later in the week, you may still want to hold a smaller group session with those available students so that you can explain the situation and let them know of the rescheduled group session.

INCENTIVES

Another strategy is to award incentives—small tokens of appreciation—to parents. This is a way to increase attendance, participation, or any other behavior that you would like to see increased. Parents can be given incentives for coming to the group on time, for participating in discussions, and completing homework. Incentives also show your appreciation to the parents. Be enthusiastic and have fun with the parents! They often enjoy the small incentives we use with students such as stickers, candy, and pencils. Some parents prefer prizes that they can give to their children as rewards for positive behavior (e.g., small toys, arts and crafts supplies).

Provide incentives at a greater rate at the beginning of a group to gain commitment and increase participation for future sessions. One suggestion is to have a raffle at the end of each session. Distribute tickets to parents who arrive on time or early for the group, or for those parents who stay for the entire group. At the end of the session, randomly choose the ticket(s) and provide rewards to those parents with the winning ticket(s). Prizes for the raffle do not have to be expensive. Small, inexpensive tokens along with a "thank you" are often greatly appreciated. Some ideas for incentives include candles, bath products, lotions, candy, baked goods, snacks, gift certificates to local easily accessible stores (e.g., grocery, coffee, video, movie theaters), games, books, picture frames, baseball hats, balls, and bags. As the group leader you could ask local companies (e.g., Target, Walmart) for donations or purchase them on your own. If a parent does not want an incentive, you could encourage him or her to choose something to take home to his or her child. Another idea is to purchase pencils, pens, erasers, candy, and smaller incentives to give out as rewards for completing homework. This may increase the likelihood that the parents will do the homework if they know that they will be rewarded!

WEEKLY REMINDERS

Another strategy to maintain group attendance is to provide weekly reminders. Make a reminder phone call about 2 days before the next session. If you are unable to reach the parent, call again the next day and confirm with the parent or leave a message. You can also send a reminder flier home (see Appendix 9 for a sample Parent Group Reminder Flier) with the group day, time, session topic, and a list of any incentives (e.g., transportation, food, child care) that will be provided. For example, let parents know if you will be having a raffle. If the school has a newsletter, post a reminder for the group day and time, session topic, and any incentives that will be provided. It is also helpful to inform the students' teachers of the group meeting time so they can also remind parents about group meetings, ask how the groups are going, and encourage parents to attend the groups. If possible, try to be available during arrival and dismissal times at school to personally remind parents about the group and express enthusiasm about their attendance.

Other good ideas are to send home a "thank you" note to those parents who attended a session and a "we missed you" note to those who did not make it to the group. The notes are another way to let the parents know you truly care about them, appreciate their attendance, and want them to continue attending group (see Appendices 20 and 21 for a sample "Thank You" Note to Parent and a "We Missed You" Note to Parent). Parents in past groups have

> **A reminder phone call about 2 days before the next meeting can be an effective way to maintain attendance.**

enjoyed the "thank you" and "we missed you" notes that were sent home to them between groups. They reported that the notes made them feel that the other group members genuinely cared about whether they attended the group, and this made them want to attend the next session.

## PARENT MESSAGE FOLDERS

One final strategy is to create a parent message folder. You can use message folders to write personal notes for parents after each group; parents can then read the notes when they arrive for the next session. For example, you may want to praise parents for completing homework or for their participation in the group. It is beneficial to personalize each message, such as:

> "Thank you so much for participating in the role play. It takes courage to get up in front of other parents and practice skills that we just learned. We really liked how you were able to remain calm, but assertive, when giving a command and how you followed through with praise after [the child] complied."

This message is positive and uses praise to thank the parent for attending the session and doing a wonderful job; it also models behavior-specific praise for parents. Praising parents for completing their homework holds them accountable and lets them know it is being counted in some way. You can also put greeting cards (e.g., birthdays, get well, loss of a loved one, divorce) and gift certificates in the folder. Parents who have attended the groups in the past loved these folders and reported that they looked forward to attending the next session to read the personalized message and find out if there were any other surprises in the folder (see Appendix 22 for a sample Parent Encouragement Form).

## *Evaluating the Group Process*

Obtaining feedback from parents about the group is a useful tool that you can use to make improvements and to ensure that each parent's voice is heard. At the end of each session, elicit feedback from the parents on what they liked and did not like about the group. This could be a group discussion and you could also give each parent a brief feedback form (see Appendix 23 for a sample Parent Group Feedback Form) to be completed at the end of the session. The feedback can be completed anonymously, or if parents prefer, they could write their names on the form. The information on the forms can be used to make changes to the group's process and content based on the parents' feedback. Therefore, we recommend that parents complete the feedback form after every session instead of waiting until the end of the group's course. At the end of this chapter there is a sample role play on how to address a situation where more challenging feedback is offered anonymously by parents in the group (see role-play scenario 1 at the end of this chapter).

> **Obtaining feedback from parents about the group is a useful tool that group leaders can use to make improvements and to ensure that each parent's voice is heard.**

# SUMMARY

Effective organization and planning is essential in implementing successful child and parent groups. Develop a plan of action for all aspects of implementing each group while keeping in mind the potential barriers that could hinder group success. Include all key stakeholders (e.g., teachers, administrators). They can be of great assistance when trying to contact and engage parents. It is important to spend the necessary time planning group logistics such as location, time, and how students and parents will get to and from meetings. Successfully navigating these logistics will help in increasing consistent attendance. By planning ahead, you can ensure that everything is prepared for each group session and also anticipate any potential problems, as well as plan for success. While it can be challenging at times to establish and maintain parents' dedication to attending the group, strategies such as providing incentives during group sessions and reminder notices after group sessions can increase the likelihood that parents will attend and want to come back week after week. Consistency, persistence, and compassion can go a long way when trying to keep group members engaged.

# MATERIALS

The following is a list of materials discussed in this chapter that can support you in planning, organizing, and establishing your group. You will find examples of most of these materials in the Appendices.

- Caregiver Contact Log (Appendix 5).
- Parent Group Reminder Flier (Appendix 9).
- Planning Ahead Checklist—Child Group (Appendix 12).
- Child Group Weekly Feedback Form (Appendix 13).
- Session Summary Handout—Teacher Version (Appendix 14).
- Session Summary Handout—Parent Version (Appendix 15).
- Planning Ahead Checklist—Parent Group (Appendix 16).
- Donation Letter (Appendix 17).
- "Thank You for Donating" Letter (Appendix 18).
- Child Care Permission Form (Appendix 19).
- "Thank You" Note to Parent (Appendix 20).
- "We Missed You" Note to Parent (Appendix 21).
- Parent Encouragement Form (Appendix 22).
- Parent Group Feedback Form (Appendix 23).
- Parent folders.*
- Cards for parents.*
- Meal/refreshments/snacks for group sessions.*
- Incentives/prizes for meeting goals, turning in homework, etc.*

---

*These materials are not included in the Appendices, but may be referenced within this chapter and are also helpful when implementing parent and child groups.

# REFLECTION AND ROLE PLAYS

Here we provide a series of reflection exercises and role-play activities to help you further hone your group facilitation skills.

## *Reflection*

After reviewing this chapter, ask yourself the following questions:

1.  Recruiting parents for group interventions can at times be a difficult task. However, maintaining group attendance poses other challenges. "In what ways do I plan to increase parent involvement and attendance in my parent group?"
2.  "Do I have a procedure if parents or children miss a session? How will I contact them and fill them in on what they have missed prior to the next session?"
3.  "Will I be able to provide child care, transportation, and/or food for my groups?" Brainstorm ways to gather funds or problem solve around these common barriers (e.g., Is it possible to offer the group during school hours so that child care is not an issue?).

## *Role Plays*

After reviewing the reflection questions, apply your understanding of what has been covered in this chapter by responding to the following two scenarios:

### Scenario 1

Feedback was provided anonymously by several group members that material covered in the group would work with "Brady Bunch families" but is not relevant or applicable for their families. Discuss how this feedback can be used to make the group more useful. Discuss how you would address this issue with group members.

EXAMPLE SCRIPTED ANSWER

GROUP LEADER: I really appreciate everyone completing the feedback forms over the last couple of weeks. We really enjoy reading your comments and want to be sure that everyone is getting something out of the group that they find helpful. Our goal is to work together as a team to brainstorm solutions that you may find helpful with your child at home. Over the last couple of sessions, we reviewed the weekly feedback sheets and wanted to bring up something that was written as feedback. Our goal is not to point fingers, but instead discuss some ideas with the group. One of the things that was mentioned was that some of the ideas in our group seem like they are for "Brady Bunch families." Do people feel comfortable sharing what they think about this and whether they agree with this feedback?

PARENTS: (*Some nod their heads; some say "yes."*)

GROUP LEADER: OK. Great. Would anyone like to share their thoughts?

PARENT A: I could see how someone would think that since some of the videos have been warm and fuzzy with easy problems to solve. But a lot of other issues have come up where problems have been more difficult to solve.

GROUP LEADER: Thank you for sharing and for your honesty regarding the videos, role plays, and discussions. Anyone else have anything to add to that?

PARENT B: I've been happy with the material and have found most of it to be rather helpful, especially when we practice using everyday examples.

GROUP LEADER: It's wonderful to hear that you are getting something out of using everyday examples to solve problems. Does anyone have any suggestions for how we can make the content more relevant for your families? Or any advice on what we could be doing differently?

PARENTS: (*Most nod their heads "no."*)

PARENT C: I didn't write that feedback about "Brady Bunch families," but I do have a suggestion. We could try to center the role plays on our personal examples.

GROUP LEADER: That is great feedback and we can definitely use personal examples if people feel comfortable sharing them and using them as role-play scenarios. I can offer this as an option when we are about to start a role play. Does this sound good like a good plan?

PARENTS: (*Everyone nods "yes"; some say "yes."*)

GROUP LEADER: OK . . . great! I'm seeing a lot of people nodding their heads and or saying "yes." I like that we were able to discuss that and come up with some ideas together as a group. If you want to discuss anything further, we can set up a time to meet individually or we can discuss this some more after the group. Thank you all for giving us wonderful feedback. This will not only help us to provide you with what you are looking for in our group but it will help us in future groups.

## TIP

Directly address parents' concerns, especially if they are not verbalizing them in the session and leaving comments on the feedback form. Try not to be defensive when receiving the feedback. Normalize the feedback by saying, "I can understand how you feel. . . ." Ask the group members what could be done differently in the group to make it more helpful or relevant. Encourage the members to always give feedback and that as a group leader, you could meet with parents individually as well. It will be important to ask open-ended questions and use silence if needed so that parents are given time to talk and elaborate on how the group could be more beneficial. Quickly implement the parents' suggestions if possible and then follow up at the end of the group to see if parents found it helpful.

The important thing is to address the concerns, but not push too much. You don't want the person who left the feedback to feel uncomfortable. You also don't want to get too caught up in feedback when there is a lot of group material to cover each week.

### Scenario 2

The parent attends the first group, but does not come to the second session. Walk through the steps you can take as the group leader to reengage this parent in the group.

EXAMPLE SCRIPTED ANSWER

- Step 1: Send a thank you note to all parents who attended the first group.
- Step 2: Send a reminder letter, e-mail, or text to the parents about the second session (based on the parent's preferred method of communication).

- Step 3: If the parent misses a group, send a "we missed you" note (see Appendix 21 for a sample "We Missed You" Note to Parent).
- Step 4: Call the parent and talk to him or her about why the group was missed. Brainstorm any barriers to attending upcoming groups, and see if the parent can come in for a makeup session.

GROUP LEADER: Good afternoon, Ms. Robinson. This is the school mental health clinician, Ms. Smith. How are you?

PARENT: Good. How are you?

GROUP LEADER: We missed you at our last group. I wanted to call and make sure everything was OK.

PARENT: Everything is fine. I had a last-minute errand to run and it took longer than I expected. Sorry, I thought I was going to be able to make it to group.

GROUP LEADER: That's OK. We realize that sometimes things come up suddenly. Is there anything we can do to help out?

PARENT: I can't think of anything right now, but I'll be at the next session for sure.

GROUP LEADER: That's great to hear. I appreciate your dedication to the group. How are things going at home? Were you able to practice any of the techniques we learned in the last group session?

PARENT: I tried using praise a little more this week and it worked well.

GROUP LEADER: That's great! It's wonderful to hear that you are practicing making praise statements. I'd love to hear more about that and fill you in on what we learned in group this week. Do you think we could schedule a time to meet before the next group session?

PARENT: I can stop in when I pick up the kids today from school.

GROUP LEADER: That sounds perfect. Can you come at 2:40 so that we have a little time prior to the end of the school day?

PARENT: Yes.

GROUP LEADER: Great! I'll see you then.

## TIP

If parents are unable to come in for a makeup session, review what was discussed in the group, highlighting the key points and points that the parent may be more interested in. Send any handouts home with the student (if possible). Also, remind parents about the next session by asking them if they plan on attending. For example, "Do you plan to attend the next group?"

- If they say yes: "That's wonderful. We are looking forward to seeing you! Is there anything that you think would get in the way of you attending the next group?"
- If they say no: "I am sorry to hear that. Do you mind me asking why you are unable to attend? [Use silence and give the parent time to speak.] Is there anything that I could do to help?"
- Additionally, you may want to ask specific questions about the parent's work schedule, child care, and transportation to determine whether there are any barriers to attendance.

# CHAPTER 5

# Managing Behaviors in Child Groups

Establishing positive group dynamics and managing behaviors are essential when implementing any group. By being proactive and establishing clear expectations, group rules, and structure, the group leader begins the process of creating a successful group. You will want to act as a "fortune-teller" by anticipating possible group pitfalls and planning accordingly. For instance, what happens if a rule is broken, two group members don't get along, or you're having difficulty engaging a withdrawn group member? Prepare how to best handle these and other potential challenges before they occur in the group. This chapter and the next offer strategies for preventing problems before they happen and suggestions for how to best handle challenging situations when they do occur.

## SETTING GROUP RULES, STRUCTURE, AND LOGISTICS

The first group meeting sets the ground rules, structure, and overall tone of the sessions. Having a consistent format and structure to group meetings is vital.

### *Group Rules*

In the very first meeting, begin by explaining the importance of establishing group rules. Engage the students in developing the rules for their group. Ask the members of the group what rules will help ensure that they have a successful group. Students are typically able to generate rules about being respectful of one another (e.g., don't talk when others are talking, no cursing). You will want to spend a little more time on developing rules with students than with parents, prompting children more because they may not come up with all the rules that should be included. Write the rules on poster board and "hint" at any needed rules that have not already been mentioned by the group members (e.g., confidentiality, how to walk in the hallway to and from the group, having safe hands and feet, one person talking at a time, listening when others have something to say). As students generate ideas for rules, ask the others in the group if they agree, to gain cohesion around the rules. Also ask the students what the rule would look like and how they would know if someone was following the rules. For instance, if a student generates the rule "Don't be disrespectful," ask him or her what "not being disrespectful" would look like (e.g., listening when others are talking, coming to the group on time). Make rules into positive statements of what the students will do in the group. For example, if a student suggests that group members should not laugh at others' ideas, you as the group leader may rephrase it as "Listening and being respectful to the ideas of others." If age appropriate, you may have the students write the rules as they come up with them, or you could create visual signs prior to the next group meeting that represent the rules (e.g., "Raise a quiet hand before speaking" has a corresponding picture that shows a student raising his or her hand with mouth closed). Allow time for the group members to ask questions about the rules and make sure that the group members fully understand each rule and its associated expectation (see role-play scenario 1 at the end of this chapter).

## Establishing Confidentiality

In the first session, it is important to discuss confidentiality with the group members (e.g., "What is said in group, stays in group"). Explain the difference between sharing personal information and general ideas or strategies learned as part of the content of the group. Give plenty of examples and fully explain this rule to the students to ensure they understand. The students will most likely want to talk with their friends, teachers, or family members about what went on in the groups, and that's OK as long as they don't use the names of any of the group members or any specific or personal information. It is also important to discuss the limits to confidentiality. Explain that as the group leader you will need to report child

---

### Confidentiality Tips

- Explain confidentiality in developmentally appropriate terms (e.g., "When we are together in this group what is said here stays here. We do not talk about it with others outside of the group.").
- Explain the limits to confidentiality in developmentally appropriate terms (e.g., "If anyone shares in the group that they are being hurt by someone, if they want to hurt someone else, or if they want to hurt themselves, I have to tell another adult. This is because it is my job to make sure that you are all safe. Does anyone have a question about that?").
- Remind the group members that unfortunately, you do not have any control over group members who share something personal or specific that happened in the group. However, the group members or the group leader may want to come up with a rule that gives a consequence to whomever breaks confidentiality.
- Be sure to discuss the issue of confidentiality whenever a new member (if an open group), or individual outside of the group (e.g., volunteer, intern, school counselor, social worker), attends the group.
- Point out that any volunteer or individual who visits the group to learn how the group is progressing will abide by the group rules regarding confidentiality. If there is going to be a visitor or possible new group member, the group may want to discuss and vote on whether everyone is comfortable with a new person joining the group.

abuse, neglect, and any threat of harming someone else if it is discussed specifically in the group. In addition, if a student discloses that he or she has thoughts of hurting him- or herself, you will need to involve others to protect the student. Make sure the group members fully understand exactly what this means so that they are informed of this rule before a situation arises. Also make sure to review the confidentiality rule and limits to confidentiality over the subsequent sessions to ensure the safety of all group members.

## *Group Structure and Logistics*

Students need to know how the group will function. From the start explain the group's logistics, such as when the group members will be picked up from class, how many times a week the group will meet, the length of the group meetings, what the students will be doing in the group, what is required of them, and any other information that is important for the students to know during the first meeting. It will be important to develop rules and consistent responses for sharpening pencils, using the bathroom, getting a drink of water, and other activities and transitions that can take time away from the group. Without having these clear expectations, you may find that the already short time you have to meet with as a group dwindles as students ask to leave the group to use the restroom or take time away from the group to gather materials. Setting up procedures in advance for how transitions will be handled may help reduce distractions and maximize the time available in the group to cover content (e.g., have students use the restroom and get a drink prior to the group meeting).

## STRATEGIES FOR MANAGING BEHAVIOR

### *The Group Leader as a Fortune-Teller*

The role of group leader includes being able to predict the future. You must constantly be on your toes, ready to tackle any problems that may arise during the group. You can usually predict problems or successes if you have collaborated with the teachers and parents and have built rapport with the students. This will allow you to understand their situations and how they react and behave in certain situations.

Anticipate problems, setbacks, and successes. Think of both positive and negative scenarios when working with students. Have a plan in place for when a student acts inappropriately in the group, such as a procedure for sending a student to "time-out." Also have a plan to praise or reinforce students when they follow the rules of the group. Table 5.1 provides a list of scenarios that you may want to anticipate and suggests a strategy for effectively dealing with each. Tailor the strategies you use to the students in your group and to the school context.

Having rules and structure in place will prevent many disruptive behavior problems. In the next section, we provide additional strategies and group practices that you may find helpful in further preventing and reducing behavior problems.

**You will want to have a plan in place for when a student acts inappropriately in the group and a plan to praise or reinforce positive behavior.**

## TABLE 5.1. Anticipating Problems, Setbacks, and Successes

*Scenario 1:* The group leader is met at the classroom by the teacher, who explains that the child cannot attend the group today because he or she has been misbehaving.

*Possible strategy:* Anticipate that a teacher might take this action. Therefore, at the time the child is recruited for the group, have a discussion with the teacher about the purpose of the group. Explain that attending group is not a privilege, but an important part of the student's learning. The child is attending the group to learn more effective classroom behaviors. Discuss with the teacher that in the past teachers have wanted to use not attending the group as a consequence for misbehavior, but that is not the best action Not attending the group decreases the child's opportunity to learn new strategies. If the teacher later tries to keep the child from the group because of misbehavior, remind the teacher of the discussion.

*Scenario 2:* When the group leader goes to the classroom, the child refuses to leave to go to the group.

*Possible strategy:* The group leader may remind the child that the group only meets on certain days and times. This is the time that they will be meeting. If the child continues to refuse, the group leader can let the child know that it is his or her choice to stay behind, but he or she is welcome to join the group's next session. Leave without a confrontation. The group leader may follow up with the teacher to determine why the child did not want to attend the group (e.g., activity in classroom is fun and the child didn't want to miss out). Problem solve the issue to avoid the child refusing to attend again.

*Scenario 3:* When the group leader goes to the classroom to pick up students for the group, one of the students is clearly upset, refusing to talk on the way to the group.

*Possible strategy:* Don't try to have a discussion with the child to figure out what has upset him or her. Walk the child to the group. Then, offer the child the option of joining the group as a positive participant, or to take a little time in a quiet spot to calm down before joining the group. Quickly engage the child when he or she begins participating in the group. Offer praise and notice that the child was able to calm him- or herself down (e.g., whisper to him or her: "You were able to calm down and join the group. Thanks—you earned an extra point").

*Scenario 4:* During the group, two students are whispering to each other and not engaging in the group.

*Possible strategy:* The group leader should remind the students of the expectation that everyone is a positive participant. When the students begin to participate the group leader can provide them with praise or other reinforcement (e.g., point toward reward). If the students continue to be disengaged, have consequences for not being a positive participant (e.g., lose a point). At the start of next group, make sure the two students are not seated together.

*Scenario 5:* During the group, one student becomes aggressive with another student, hitting the student.

*Possible strategy:* The group leader should intervene to stop the aggression by removing the student either to a time-out spot or outside the group area. Additionally, the student may be required to sit out of group for one session, meeting individually with the group leader instead to set a goal about returning to the group. For instance, the group leader and child may develop a contract that says if the child can reenter the group, is a positive participant, and is not aggressive, then after three sessions he or she can earn a reward.

*Scenario 6:* During the group, a student shuts down, refusing to participate.

*Possible strategy:* The group leader can remind the child that he or she can earn points toward a reinforcer for being a positive participant. Then, praise other students who are participating and give points to them. As soon as the child engages in the group, give him or her a point and offer praise.

*(continued)*

**TABLE 5.1.** *(continued)*

*Scenario 7:* Some group members have been meeting after school and bullying another child who is not in the group. The principal has made you aware of the situation.

*Possible strategy:* At the start of the following session, the group leader can state that he or she has a serious issue to discuss with the group. The group leader can state the facts that were provided by the principal. Next, directly state the problem (e.g., "Members of this group are bullying another student and this is not appropriate. If it happens again, you will each receive in-school suspension"). Then, discuss as a group why this is a problem and what the bullying students could do differently. In addition to this discussion, talk to the victim about reporting the incidents to adults, ensuring that consequences are applied if it continues.

*Scenario 8:* Several group members achieve their goals for the week. In addition, the teachers have noted that they have noticed improvements in the behavior of the students in the group.

*Possible strategy:* The group leader can state that he or she is very proud of the students for meeting their goals. Then, as appropriate, have the principal visit the group briefly to congratulate them on meeting their goals. Send home a note to their parents, letting them know that their child has been working hard and meeting his or her goals.

## Seating

Think about the seating of the group members based on the relationships among them and their individual characteristics and personality (e.g., you may want to sit an oppositional student next to a student who is less oppositional or more withdrawn). Be prepared to switch group members' seats during the group if needed (e.g., if one group member is teasing or touching another).

## Using Proximity

Notice early signs of potential behavior problems (e.g., a student who is not fully engaged and begins to play with objects or talk to peers). When these situations arise make sure you are in close proximity to the identified student (e.g., placing a hand on his or her shoulder or standing between the identified student and the other[s] involved). Use proximity to deter and prevent problems early and keep students engaged and learning.

## Jobs and Helpers

Another way to keep students engaged is to give them jobs or tasks to do throughout the session. This helps group members build confidence, independence, make positive choices, and be closely involved in the group. Jobs also allow for opportunities to praise the student after a task is completed, increasing the likelihood that the student will be helpful in the future. For instance, one student could be the line leader (directing the group to and from sessions), another student could be the timekeeper (timing activities and watching the clock to ensure the group ends on time), and another could pass out materials.

## Superstar of the Group

A potentially reinforcing reward for group members is to be identified as a "superstar." At the end of the group session, select a group member who represented leadership, responsibility, and respect to all throughout the entire group session. Then, you can have this superstar be a special helper for the next group. In addition, you can give him or her a small reward (e.g., a pencil or a sticker). You can keep group members on-task by reminding students throughout the session to try their best to display good behavior and win this award. For example, if students are getting disruptive, you may announce, "Remember, I am looking for students who are following the group rules so that I can give my Superstar award at the end of group. I am noticing that Johnny has his eyes on me and his feet on the floor."

## Ignoring Minor Negative Behavior and Praising Positive Behavior

Some minor negative behaviors can be ignored. This discourages minor problem behaviors by not giving them attention. Paying attention to behaviors (positive or negative) will increase them. Ignore behaviors you want to decrease (e.g., disruptive problem behavior), and pay attention to behavior you want to increase (e.g., following group rules). For example, if a student is tapping his or her pencil over and over again, this behavior should be ignored unless it is causing other students to be distracted. However, there are behaviors that should never be ignored. These are any behaviors that are harmful to others (e.g., aggression, teasing, and bullying). If a student continues to tap a pencil, you can give attention to another student not displaying the behavior and praise him or her (e.g., "Thank you, Kayla, for sitting quietly with your hands in your lap").

During the group you should have more positive interactions with students than negative. Ignoring minor misbehaviors and praising positive behaviors is one way to make this more likely. Any behavior you want to see more of (e.g., positive participation, listening to others, completing homework) should be noticed with praise or other types of positive reinforcement. Positive group behaviors should be praised so that students understand these behaviors are expected and that you want to see more of them. When you give attention to positive behaviors (e.g., participating in the group, completing homework, giving a compliment to another group member) you are increasing the likelihood that students will exhibit this behavior in the future.

## Dealing with Rule Violations

On occasion, students will break a group rule. You must be prepared for how you will respond and have an idea of what the consequence will be. One effective strategy is to develop a list of rule violations and associated consequences. Be sure to develop a comprehensive list that includes a continuum of minor violations to major violations. The students can be informed ahead of time of the consequences and they will know what will happen if a rule is violated. Table 5.2 provides an example of how a group leader may go about predetermining consequences for breaking the rules.

**TABLE 5.2. Predetermining Consequences for Breaking Group Rules**

*Rule violation 1:* Child talks out when the group leader or other group member is talking.

*Consequence:* Remind the child of the rule to listen when others are talking. Ignore additional talk-outs. Give praise and attention to group members who wait their turn to talk.

*Rule violation 2:* Child refuses to participate in a group activity.

*Consequence:* Remind the child of the rule of being a positive participant. Then, remind the child that he or she can earn points for participating. If the child continues to refuse to participate but is not being disruptive, ignore the behavior. When the child chooses to participate praise him or her and give him or her a point. If the child is being disruptive, send him or her to time-out.

*Rule violation 3:* Child teases a group member.

*Consequence:* Intervene immediately by telling the child it is not OK to tease another person. Then, indicate to the child that if it happens again, he or she will lose a point. Then, praise the child who was teased for ignoring the other member and not getting upset.

*Rule violation 4:* Child hits another group member.

*Consequence:* Send the child to time-out. If the behavior happens more than one time, remove the child from the group and do not allow him or her to return for the next session. Meet with the child individually until he or she is able to return to the group and be safe.

*Rule violation 5:* Child is aggressive toward the group leader.

*Consequence:* Send the child to time-out. If the behavior happens more than one time, remove the child from the group and do not allow him or her to return for the next session. Meet with the child individually until he or she is able to return to the group and be safe.

*Rule violation 6:* Child is persistently disruptive and/or aggressive in the group.

*Consequence:* The child may not be appropriate for a group intervention. Meet with the child individually instead. If appropriate, develop a behavioral contract with the child. If the child meets a particular goal and contracts to be a positive and safe group member, allow him or her to return to the group.

## Setting Up Behavior Management Systems

There are many behavior management systems for handling problem behaviors. Choose the best system for handling misbehaviors and be *consistent* with the system. See Table 5.3 for examples of behavior management systems used in various settings. You may find that it's necessary to modify your behavior management systems over time. For instance, in a group that we implemented, we initially used a three-strikes system in which the students were not able to receive a group

**The group leader should choose the best behavior management system for handling misbehaviors and be consistent with the system.**

incentive if they got three strikes. We found that after a student received three strikes there was no incentive for the child to be a positive participant for the remainder of the group. Therefore, we started giving points for positive behaviors that we wanted to increase. Group members were able to spend their points on small rewards. Recognizing positive behaviors

**TABLE 5.3. Examples of Behavior Management Systems**

- *Sticker charts:* Give group members stickers for positive behaviors. They are able to spend these stickers on small rewards; no stickers are awarded for negative behaviors. (see Appendix 26 for a sample Good Behavior Sticker Chart).

- *Daily behavior report cards:* Similar to the sticker charts, the group leader can start a daily behavior report card, where the student would be graded on his or her behavior in the group. Volpe and Fabiano's (2013) book assists leaders in designing and implementing daily behavior report cards to promote positive student behaviors and overcome barriers to learning.

- *Token economy:* Give group members tokens for positive behaviors, for returning goal sheets, returning homework, attendance, and so on. These tokens represent points. Students are able to spend these tokens on small rewards (e.g., school supplies, small toys, computer time, time with preferred adult); no tokens are awarded for negative behaviors. One example is to drop a marble in a glass jar every time someone follows a rule or does something positive (e.g., shares, uses kind words or manners). Often students like the sound the marble makes when it goes in the jar! When the jar is full the group can earn a reward.

- *Incentives:* The group leader may want to tailor the incentives to the group members—sometimes students work harder if the reward is something they want to win. The group leader also can set group goals and individual goals, and provide incentives for both (e.g., prize box for individual goals, pizza party for group goals). Incentives do not have to be costly; the group leader can get the same effect by using nonmaterial items (e.g., extra 10 minutes of recess at end of group, double-point days, play "Simon says"). Keep in mind the following when using a prize box:
  - Make sure to time at the end of the group or set a separate time where group members may spend their points in the prize box.
  - Set a time limit on how long it takes each member to select a prize from the prize box (e.g., use a timer).
  - Lay the prizes out on a table with prices (e.g., prize store) or have a few boxes with small, medium, and large prizes so that the selection process goes more quickly.

- *Strike system:* Group members are given a certain amount of strikes (e.g., three strikes) and then are sent to time-out, back to class, or some other consequence is given.

- *Marking down negative behaviors or broken rules:* Mark down negative behaviors and those group members who have fewer than three (or whatever number the group leader chooses) are rewarded in some way.

- *Response cost:* Remove points from a token economy system when a rule is violated. Be careful not to have students go into debt because the token economy system will become less reinforcing if they determine that they will never be able to earn a reward.

discouraged rule violations because the points earned led to a reward at the end of the session (Stormont, Reinke, Herman, & Lembke, 2012).

## Time-Out

Time-out is a procedure typically used for more severe behaviors, such as hitting another child, destroying property, or persistently refusing to comply. Time-out is an extended form of ignoring in which children are removed for a brief period of time from all sources of positive reinforcement, especially adult and peer attention. This gives the student an opportunity to calm down, reflect on what he or she has done, and consider other solutions (Webster-Stratton, 1999). It also teaches children how to take brief time away to calm down or self-regulate. This is a coping skill that children can use throughout their lives (Webster-Stratton, 1999).

Set up a procedure for time-out before you have a high-intensity problem or a consistent noncompliance issue. For example, you may give the group members three strikes for breaking the rules. If they reach three strikes, then they must go to time-out. You should define what warrants an immediate time-out (e.g., hitting another group member) versus a three-strike system for noncomplying, which will also lead to time-out. It is helpful to review this procedure with group members so they know exactly what to expect if a time-out is warranted.

In time-out, the group member needs to sit quietly for $X$ number of minutes (no talking, crying, yelling, etc.) and calm down (no crying, kicking wall, pounding on desk, etc.) before returning to the group. The rule of thumb for implementing time-out is 1 minute for every year of the student's age, up to 5 minutes, and the last 2 minutes should be quiet, indicating that the child has calmed down and is able to return to the group (Webster-Stratton, 2005). For example, a 4-year-old should be sent to time-out for 4 minutes and a 6-year-old student should be sent to time-out for 5 minutes. Time-out should be very brief and allow time for the student to calm down. Then, immediately give the student a new learning opportunity and praise for successful reentry to the group.

> **Time-out should be very brief. The maximum amount of time a student should be in time-out is 1 minute for every year of his or her age, up to a maximum of 5 minutes.**

## Practicing Time-Out

It is helpful to practice time-out with group members at the start of the group (e.g., the first session, after rules are developed). Students will realize that time-out is nonthreatening and they can learn the procedure before it is needed. It also allows for all group members to practice what to do when one group member goes to time-out (i.e., ignore).

## Time-Out Area

A specific area should be designated for time-out. It is best if the area is away from the group, but visible so you can continue to monitor the student's behavior. Also, it is helpful to have some papers, pencils, and a "cool down" wall thermometer at this area so that the student may visually cool him- or herself down, or write or draw a picture about how he or she is feeling in this moment (see Appendix 24 for a sample "Cool Down" Thermometer).

## Refusal to Go to or Remain in Time-Out

There will be times when a group member may refuse to go to or remain in time-out. In these instances, remain calm and already have a plan in place as to how you will handle this situation. Researchers suggest adding 1 extra minute of time-out (up to 10 minutes) for refusing to go to time-out, refusing to stay in time-out, or acting out during the last 2 minutes of the time-out period (Webster-Stratton, 2005). At 10 minutes, the group member would lose a privilege (e.g., group member could be sent back to class; Webster-Stratton, 2005). By remaining calm, you will help to de-escalate the situation; be sure to add 1 minute at a time at a slow pace that allows the group member time to make a choice. Once a privilege is removed, time-out is over. The main idea is that the group member will quickly learn that it is better to go to time-out in the first place, and will think about this consequence during the next and all future group sessions.

### After Time-Out

In a calm, clear voice without disturbing the group, tell the student that he or she can return to the group. You may want to try to immediately reengage the student in the group by praising him or her for sitting down quietly or asking him or her to do a task. If a student cannot rejoin the group without causing a disruption or a student is continually breaking rules and has been sent to time-out a few times during the group, you may want to either send this student back to class or have an individual session with him or her. If you have a co-leader, you could meet with the student individually at that time or finish the session and meet with the student individually another time.

## Individual Sessions with Group Members

It may be helpful to hold an individual session or a family session if a student is continually breaking rules or having a problem in the group. Sometimes other issues at home or in the classroom may affect the student and the group. Gather additional information from parents about issues that may be contributing to the student's problem behavior. For students who are highly disruptive in the group, another option is not to allow the student to attend the next group meeting as a consequence for his or her behavior. However, removal from the group will only be considered a consequence if the student enjoys the group.

On occasion a student who is referred for a group intervention may not be appropriate for a group. Reasons include having severe disruptive behavior problems that would distract other group members or if the student has severe social phobia or anxiety issues that interfere with the student's ability to participate in the group. If you find that a student is not appropriate, you may decide to continue the intervention individually with the student, adapting the content as necessary.

## ESTABLISHING GROUP EXPECTATIONS

Establish group expectations at the start of the group by giving members an active role within the group. Make sure that the lines of communication with parents and teachers are open and that everyone is on the same page. Have consistent, predictable, and clearly communicated routines. This will ensure child compliance. For instance, goal sheets help to hold group members accountable for their behaviors not only within but also outside the group. Establishing routines such as setting goals on goal sheets and reviewing goal sheets provide structure for maintaining positive behaviors in the group. Homework assists group members in more fully understanding key group concepts and allows them to practice learned techniques and strategies outside the group setting. The following provides information about using goal sheets and homework to establish predictability and generalization of behaviors learned in the group to other settings.

## Goal Sheets

Many students can benefit from learning to set and meet goals. You may want to start a goal sheet with each group member in his or her classroom (see Appendix 25 for a sample Goal Sheet). Discuss possible goals with each group member and select one goal to work on for the week (e.g., staying seated when supposed to be, raising a quiet hand before calling out). Check in with the teacher(s) to obtain feedback on potential goals for each group member. You can have the teacher participate in the process by keeping track of whether the student meets the daily goal.

Tracking goals can also present challenges. For instance, the teacher may forget to fill out the goal sheet, lose the goal sheet, or the group member may lose it. Discuss ways to help students remember to use and track their goals. Brainstorm possible ways to prevent losing the goal sheet with the student and the student's teacher (e.g., put it in a special folder, have the teacher keep it at his or her desk in a special folder). Also discuss ways to remind students to check in with the teacher if the teacher is to sign and validate that the goal is met. Some group members may need to have a goal of simply "returning your goal sheet to the group." Be prepared for some group members to meet their goals while others do not. In groups where students receive points for meeting their goals, feelings of jealousy and anger may arise for students not meeting goals. Be prepared to process these feelings and deal with some group members receiving points and others not receiving points. One way to deal with it is to simply state, "It's OK, you can try again this week."

Ensure that the goals students set are manageable. You would not expect a student who has never turned in his or her homework to suddenly turn in all homework on time for the week. A more manageable goal would be to turn in homework on time 2 out of 5 days, building up to the larger goal over time. Give examples of short-term goals versus long-term goals to help demonstrate small steps toward larger goals. Use the baseline levels of current behaviors of the students in your group to determine what is a manageable goal to increase each student's likelihood of success.

## Group Homework

Many group-based interventions include a homework component. While some students love to do their homework, it is likely that the students in need of group-based intervention will not. You will likely need to think of creative ways to get the group members to complete and return their homework. At the start of each session, determine who completed homework and who needs more motivation (e.g., incentives) to hand in homework. Consider asking group members for their own ideas on how to increase homework completion.

---

### Tips to Promote Group Homework Completion

- Use a different name for homework, such as practice, experiment; give it a try, or challenge.
- Offer points for students who complete and return the group homework on time.
- Offer double points on random days or half points if someone turns in late homework.
- Have a pizza party for a set number of points earned for returning homework.
- Allow some time at the end of the group to start the homework.
- Have a discussion in group about ways to make sure the homework gets completed.
- Create a buddy system among group members. Have the buddies remind one another about the homework, to ask if they completed it, and to make sure to bring it to the group.

---

## Communicating with Parents and Teachers

Be in frequent contact with the parent or guardian and teacher of each group member. To set goals and work on skills outside of the group sessions, it is necessary to involve parents and teachers. This will not only encourage group members to work on their own personal goals and strategies outside of the group, but it will also hold them accountable and set up a system where all adults caring for the group members are on the same page. Involve the teacher and parents early in the process.

Engaging teachers and parents to help remind group members to complete homework will not only increase homework completion but will allow teachers and parents to become aware of the group content. You may also consider offering incentives (e.g., chocolate, flowers, thank you card, small treat) to teachers and parents if they provide reminders. The teachers should be aware of what you are teaching the students in the group so that they can reinforce the students when they use the new skills in the classroom. To make it more likely that teachers become involved, you can develop brief handouts about the session content with some suggestions on how the teacher could encourage the new skills in the classroom setting (see Appendix 14 for a sample Session Summary Handout for teachers).

Similarly, it is helpful to make parents aware of what their child is learning in the group so that they can encourage the use of the new skills at home. Parent briefing notes can also be created that are similar to the teacher briefing notes. This helps keep everyone informed on what the students are learning in the groups, while giving suggestions for how to encourage new skills at home and in the classroom. Parents are also encouraged to help with homework and assist student practice of strategies learned in the group. The involvement of parents promotes positive communication between group members and their family members as group members are able to share what they've learned in the group setting.

**Remember to share successes with teachers and parents. Provide more positive than negative feedback.**

Share the successes of group members with teachers and parents by sending positive notes. Provide more positive than negative feedback to the teachers and parents. Use a 4:1 positive to negative ratio. For many students who are referred to group-based interventions, teachers and parents hear more about the negative behaviors of the students. You have the opportunity to tell them about what is going well with students, giving them reasons to provide students with additional positive reinforcement for their successes. For instance, parents or teachers could share with the student that you mentioned that he or she was really working hard in the group, letting the student know how proud they are of the student. Further, providing more positive than negative feedback to teachers and parents will highlight the effectiveness of the work you are doing with the students (see Webster-Stratton, 2005).

At times you may ask the students to bring home papers or handouts to their parents. Remind parents to ask their children after each session if there is anything that they need to look over and sign. Suggest that parents get in the habit of asking how the group went and what students learned in that session. The more adults ask about what students are learning and encourage students to use the new skills, the more likely are positive outcomes for the student.

## RESISTANCE TO GROUP PROCESS, RULES, AND EXPECTATIONS

There are times when students are resistant not only to the structure of the group but also to the topics presented within the group. It helps to expect in advance that students may resist some of the techniques and strategies used in the group setting. There may be many reasons for this resistance. For example, the group members may not understand the skills they are attempting to learn, may be uncomfortable with other group members, or a lack of social skills may interfere with their ability to participate. If you feel that the student does not understand the skill, you can provide further discussion of the skill, give examples, and ask questions to improve understanding. Another possibility is that the group members may not agree with the techniques being offered. In this case, you may need to discuss their points of view and provide alternative skills to be used in certain situations. If the student lacks social skills to effectively participate in the group, you may consider meeting individually with the student to support the development of skills needed or cover some of this content within the group itself for all to benefit. See Chapter 2 for a list of evidence-based group resources that often cover social skills content. Other possible social skills curricula that you may find useful are the Strong Kids programs (Merrell, Carrizales, et al., 2007; Merrell, Parisi, & Whitcom, 2007; Merrell, Whitcom, & Parisi, 2009), which are brief social–emotional learning curricula designed for teaching social and emotional skills, promoting resilience, strengthening assets, and increasing coping skills of students from PreK to high school.

Group members may seem resistant to content if they become bored with the skills they are learning. Most evidence-based group interventions for children and adolescents are set up to gain and hold the group's attention. But if you notice signs of boredom (e.g., yawning, off-task behavior), consider switching the activity or getting your group members up and moving. Perhaps you need to add creative activities, more interactive segments, or increase the pace of the content. For instance, if you are working on problem-solving skills, have the group members role-play a scenario instead of just talking about it.

Content may also feel less relevant to students if they are struggling with more immediate concerns (e.g., not having enough food at home or having other challenges that feel more pressing to them). You will want to determine the best way to make the content engaging and meaningful to the students in your group. Rather than think students are resistant, think of how you can ensure the group enjoys the experience and develops skills applicable to their individual worlds. Reflect on the possible issues that could be interfering with student participation. Doing so will likely lead to more creative solutions to the problem and lead to better outcomes for students. The following section offers suggestions for how you can address group resistance and in turn increase the likelihood for positive group outcomes.

## Keeping the Group on Topic

It is your responsibility to maintain the fidelity of the intervention by staying focused and on topic so that the content is delivered as it was intended. It is important that all of the objectives, activities, and content for the specific session are completed as originally intended by the intervention developers. Therefore, you may need to redirect group members who repeatedly monopolize the discussion by telling long stories or sharing stories that are not connected to the content of the group session. Similarly, it is critical to address other off-task behavior that interferes with the pacing and delivery of the material.

Come prepared with all materials and have an agenda that you follow while being aware of the session's objective. Starting the group on time, reviewing the session's agenda, and referring back to it are great ways to be sure that all of the necessary content is covered. For instance, if a student begins to discuss a topic that is tangential to the session, refer to the agenda and say something like:

"It looks like we still need to cover a few things today [pointing to the agenda]. I would like to keep us moving along. Perhaps we can talk more about this after today's sessions, Breanna."

## Dealing with Teasing and Bullying

In some groups you may have one or more students who tease or bully (verbal or physical aggression) to intimidate or embarrass group members. These types of behaviors need to be dealt with immediately because they are harmful to the student and to the cohesion of the group. Send a clear message to students that teasing or bullying will not be tolerated. When you become aware of any instance of bullying, you should immediately stop the inappropriate behavior and deliver a consequence for the students involved in line with your behavior management system (e.g., time-out, lose a point). The consequence should occur immediately and be brief. You will then give quick and full attention to the group member who was just victimized. This demonstrates your concern and also communicates that you do not give attention to those who bully. You may want to say something to the victim, such as "You are very brave for not responding to someone who is teasing you," or "Thank you so much for ignoring people who are not being kind."

If one or more students continue to display bullying behaviors, it may make sense to discontinue their membership in the group. You could continue to deliver the intervention in an individual format with these members and develop a plan for how to work with the student on discontinuing any bullying behaviors with others. You may also want to have a discussion with the group about how bullying behaviors are unacceptable. Have them discuss with you how bullying is harmful to others and to the group members. Ask them to generate ideas for how they can handle bullying situations in and outside of the group (e.g., telling the bully to stop, informing an adult, and/or sticking up for the student being bullied). Ongoing bullying should not be tolerated in the group.

Students who are persistently bullied during a group intervention will not benefit from the group and may develop other social behavior challenges as a result. You should be sure to follow up with the victim to determine if the bullying occurs outside of the group, and develop a plan of action for how it can be prevented.

More detailed information on how to identify, prevent, and respond to bullying can be found on the National Association of School Psychologists website (*www.nasponline. org/resources-and-publications/resources/school-safety-and-crisis/bullying-prevention*) and the website managed by the U.S. Department of Health and Human Services (*www. stopbullying.gov/resources*).

## Absent Students

Occasionally, there may be a student who has been missing school and so missing the group sessions. If a group member is missing many days of school, consider calling the parent to determine why the student has been absent. Depending on the explanation for the absences, talk to the parent and the student about what is being missed in the classroom and in the group sessions. Stress the importance of coming to school. It is best to approach this issue in a nonconfrontational way and let the parent know that you are concerned about the student missing so many days at school and that you would really like the student to continue as part of the group.

Problem solve to see if there are ways that you can support the parent in getting the student to school. For instance, we have encountered students who are required to wake themselves in the morning and get to school because the parent works at that time. The student may oversleep and arrive late to school regularly. We have provided these students with alarm clocks, given them a "wake-up call" in the morning, and even gone to their homes to help get them to school each day. A family session may help resolve the problem with missing school. A discussion with the parent(s) could sound something like this:

> "I have been concerned about your child's attendance at school. She has been missing a lot of schoolwork and a lot of important topics in our group. If there's a specific problem that's keeping her from attending school, maybe we could discuss it and work something out. I am here to help. Is there anything that I can do to help her get to school?"

## Students Who Don't Want to Come to the Group

There may be instances in which a student refuses to attend the group session. If a group member refuses to come to the group, you may want to meet with this student individually to see why he or she doesn't want to attend. It could be that the group takes place at the same time as gym and the student doesn't want to miss gym, or there could be something bothering the student about attending the group (e.g., someone teasing him or her, being labeled as "mentally ill"). Talk to this student to problem solve the situation. Through discussion determine what changes can be made so that he or she will attend the groups. Consider if additional reinforcement is required to get a student to come to the group. Sometimes students find other activities more reinforcing than coming to the group. Make sure to have fun in the group and provide incentives, particularly at the early sessions, to get the students willing to attend. You may also want to check in with the student's teacher and parent to see if they have any ideas for why the student may not want to attend the group.

If a student who had been coming to the group refuses to attend, he or she may be upset or unhappy. Something has led the student to be defiant and refuse to come to the group. Trying to convince the student to come in that moment may simply lead to increased noncompliance. One strategy that we have used in the past is to say something like "It is your choice if you want to come to the group or not. If you come, you will earn points that can win you prizes, but if not, you will not earn points." Then, let the student choose to stay or go to the group. If the student decides to stay behind, say something like "I will come for you next week and you are welcome to attend." Follow up with the student later to see why he or she did not want to attend the group. Also, talk later to the teacher to find out how the student is doing in the classroom setting and if the teacher is aware of the reasons behind the refusal.

### Disruptive Students

There may be students in the group whose behaviors interfere with the group. For instance, a student may be a continual behavior problem. After multiple time-out and individual interventions, you may realize that the group setting is not appropriate for this student at this time. If so, have a conversation with the student and the parent to let them know your decision. Students who display highly disruptive behaviors may not be good candidates for group interventions, but would benefit from more intensive supports. Therefore, you should not simply terminate your work with a student who is too disruptive for a group. You could continue to work with the student individually or refer him or her to receive more intensive services. For instance, you may refer this student to the school's behavior support team. A functional behavioral assessment (see Watson & Steege, 2003) could be conducted, which can be used to develop an individualized behavior support plan for the student. You could also discuss the potential for the student to earn his or her way back into the group by exhibiting good behavior in the classroom and during individual counseling.

### Dealing with Questions about the Personal Information of the Group Leader

Students may ask personal questions during the first and subsequent sessions about the group leader (e.g., age, ethnicity, significant others, living situation). Disclosing appropriate personal information helps to build rapport and a positive relationship between you and the group members. However, you will need to be professional in the amount and type of information that you disclose. For instance, the students may be curious as to whether you have children or a significant other. You may want to share this information or keep it to yourself.

Either way, be tactful in what you disclose or how you decline to provide the information. When declining you may want to say something like "I really like that you are interested in me, and I like to get to know things about you, too. But, some things stay private and this is one of those things." It is important to strike a balance between keeping students focused and on pace while remaining sensitive to students' interests (see role-play scenario at the end of this chapter).

> **Disclosing appropriate personal information in response to student questions helps to build rapport and a positive relationship with students, but it requires tactful responses.**

## Challenges to the Leader's Ability to Understand and Help the Group Members

Sometimes, students challenge a group leader's ability to understand their situations and help them. The students may feel threatened, had unsuccessful experiences with professionals in the past, or are feeling misunderstood. There may be cultural difference between you and the students that lead them to believe your experiences are too different from theirs for you to be helpful. It can be helpful to reflect on the differences between yourself and the students, and consider how your culture may influence your interactions with them. Be aware of what biases you have (we all have biases) so that you are able to take the perspective of the student who is expressing doubt about your ability to help. Acknowledge the fact that you and the students may be from different backgrounds and have not had the same life experiences. However, despite this, explain that the group can be helpful. Discuss how the content and skills that the students are learning can be tailored to fit their needs. In some cases, you may want to discuss how the skill can be applied in particular situations that the students face daily, adapting the skill as needed. It can be empowering for the students to understand how the skills you are teaching them can be applied to their specific situation. Let them know that they are the experts of their own lives and you are simply there to share new skills that have been helpful to students in the past.

Students may also feel that you are taking the side of their teacher or parents in a situation. This may make them less likely to disclose information. In these circumstances, first reflect to see whether you are, in fact, taking sides. Is there a more neutral manner you could adopt and be more effective in supporting the student? Perhaps you can be an advocate for the students to the teacher or parents, helping problem solve issues between the two "sides." Talk to the students about how you understand their perspective and that you hope to help them as best you can. Be aware that when students are having a difficult time disclosing information or if they choose to express their emotions by acting out or pouting, it could be due to concerns about whose side you are really on.

## SUMMARY

This chapter has discussed how to manage behavior in child groups. Key strategies for preventing problems are to establish positive group dynamics, group rules, structure, and expectations early on in the group sessions. It is essential to involve group members in creating the rules for their group and to revisit rules as necessary as the group continues. Anticipate possible pitfalls and plan accordingly within your group to prevent problems. The next chapter discusses how these strategies look when managing behaviors in parent groups.

## MATERIALS

The following is a list of materials discussed in this chapter that can support effective group facilitation. You will find examples of most of these materials in the Appendices.

- Session Summary Handout—Teacher Version (Appendix 14).
- "Cool Down" Thermometer (Appendix 24).
- Goal Sheet (Appendix 25).
- Good Behavior Sticker Chart (Appendix 26).
- Rules poster.*
- Incentives list.*
- Stickers for sticker charts and praise statements.*
- Jobs chart for child group if you assign tasks.*
- Superstar of the group award or token.*
- Tokens/chips for token economy.*
- Incentives/prize box items.*
- Strike-system poster or way to record strikes.*

## REFLECTION AND ROLE PLAYS

Here we provide a series of reflection exercises and role-play activities to help you further hone your group facilitation skills.

### Reflection

After reviewing this chapter, ask yourself the following questions:

1. "How will I engage group members in the role plays? How will I make the child feel comfortable participating in role plays?"
2. "What are some things I can do to be proactive with behavior management in my child groups? Do I want to have a superstar of the group and create jobs for my group members?"
3. "How will I handle a student who is aggressive or dominating the conversation? What are some statements I can make to let the child know he or she has been heard, but also keep the group on track and allow for other group member participation?"

---

*These materials are not included in the Appendices, but may be referenced within this chapter and are also helpful when implementing parent and child groups.

## *Role Plays*

After reviewing the reflection questions, apply your understanding of what has been covered in this chapter by responding to the following two scenarios:

### Scenario 1

The students in the group are in the process of setting group rules. One student is misbehaving and coming up with inappropriate rules to gain the attention of the other group members. Try to maintain the focus on setting appropriate group rules while paying attention to the positive group rules that are suggested by group members.

EXAMPLE SCRIPTED ANSWER

GROUP LEADER: Today we are going to set our group rules. Can someone tell me why group rules are important?

GROUP MEMBER: So that we can all be good and follow the rules and learn.

GROUP LEADER: Yes, group rules are very important in our ability to learn and be successful and respectful group members. Group rules are also important so that we can all feel safe and comfortable in our group. I love the way that you raised your hand to share that group rule. Do you think we can start with the group rule of being respectful of others? (*Group members nod.*) What are some other rules that you can think of that we should add to our list?

GROUP MEMBER A: Saying "shut up" when we don't like what another group member says.

GROUP LEADER: Hmmm. I'm not sure that would follow along with our "being respectful of others" group rule that we have on the board already. Maybe we should define this rule further because I'm having a hard time deciding what "respectful" means and what this would look like in our group. How can we be respectful of others?

GROUP MEMBER B: By letting one person talk at a time?

GROUP LEADER: Great answer! That is definitely one way we can show respect. Group member A, would you be willing to help me out and write that answer on the board?

GROUP MEMBER A: Yes. (*Comes to the board.*)

GROUP LEADER: Thank you for helping me. What else can "being respectful of others" mean? How about you, group member C? What does that mean to you?

GROUP MEMBER C: Not saying mean things to other group members.

GROUP LEADER: That's another great point! We can be respectful of others by saying nice things to our fellow group members. These are great ideas. Let's think of some other group rules. . . .

## **TIP**

Notice how the group leader quickly reengages group member A by asking the student to help with a task and redirecting the group to define what respect means instead of reprimanding the group member for saying "shut up" and suggesting an inappropriate rule. Remaining calm and focused is a great skill to have as a group leader.

## Scenario 2

The group leader is introducing a new topic to the group on effective strategies to calm down when you are angry. One student continues to be off-task and asks the group leader personal questions. Try to maintain the pacing of the group and introduce the new topic without completely disregarding the student's interest.

### EXAMPLE SCRIPTED ANSWER

GROUP LEADER: Today we are going to talk about a new topic—calming down when we are angry. Raise your hand if you have ever felt angry. (*Group leader and several students raise their hands.*)

GROUP LEADER: Excellent. I am sure most of us have felt angry at some time in our life. It is OK to feel angry but what is important is what we *do* when we are angry. . . .

GROUP MEMBER A: (*Interrupts.*) Dr. Morgan, do you have any kids?

GROUP LEADER: (*Ignores calling out.*) Remember, if you have a question, please raise a quiet hand. (*Raises hand to model what it should look like.*) Can anyone raise a quiet hand and tell me a good choice we could make when we are angry?

GROUP MEMBER B: When I get really mad at my brother sometimes I go to my room and listen to my favorite music.

GROUP LEADER: That is a great choice and I loved your quiet hand. Can anyone else raise a quiet hand and tell me another good choice we could make when we are angry?

GROUP MEMBER A: (*Interrupts again.*) Derrick said you have a baby named Joe, is that true?

GROUP LEADER: (*To group member A.*) I love that you are interested in getting to know me and I want to get to know you, too. However, you need to raise a quiet hand if you have something to share and we need to get back to our agenda. Let's finish our lesson and then we can take about 2 minutes at the end of the group to share something about ourselves—sound good?

GROUP MEMBER A: (*Nods his head in agreement.*)

GROUP LEADER: Fantastic. Now, who can raise a quiet hand and tell me another good choice we could make when we are angry?

## TIP

Notice how the group leader ignores the calling out and reminds the group of the rule to raise a quiet hand. It is important to ignore negative behavior and give your attention to positive behavior as the group leader did in this scenario (i.e., immediately praised group member B for raising a quiet hand). Maintaining the pacing of the lesson and keeping group members on-task are excellent skills to have as a group leader. However, it is also critical to build strong, positive relationships with group members. Therefore, each group leader will need to think about how much personal information to share with group members. In this scenario, at the end of the session the group leader could choose to share whether he or she has children, how old they are, and so on. The group leader may or may not feel comfortable sharing the name of his or her child but choose to share something else about him- or herself so that group members do not feel as if they are the only ones sharing personal information in the group.

# CHAPTER 6

# Managing Behaviors in Parent Groups

Just like in the child group, it is important to establish positive group dynamics and manage behaviors within the parent group. Although the behaviors will most likely be different from those you may experience in the child group, parent groups can take on their own personality. By being proactive and establishing clear expectations, structure, and ground rules, the group leader begins the process of creating a successful group. You will want to anticipate possible group pitfalls and plan accordingly. Be prepared to handle all potential challenges before they occur in the group. Similar to the previous chapter, this chapter offers strategies for preventing problems before they happen and suggestions for how to best handle challenging situations when they do occur within a parent group.

## SETTING STRUCTURE AND GROUND RULES

The initial group meeting with parents sets the structure, ground rules, and the tone of the meetings. Have the members introduce themselves and share one goal each has for the group. This helps group members to get to know one another and see that many of them share a purpose in attending the group sessions.

Discuss the group's logistics and process. You may want to review the purpose of the intervention, what research has been done on the intervention, and how this group has helped parents in the past. Also discuss the number of sessions, mention any possible visitors, whether the group is closed (no new members) versus open (new members may attend), how the content of the group will progress, and expectations for letting you know about missed sessions. Encourage the parents to be active participants in discussions as much as possible. Share your excitement about the program and welcome them to the group. Also allow time for the group members to express any concerns they have about the group process.

Explain the importance of group rules and allow the group members to come up with their own rules for their group. As the parents develop their list of rules, write them on a poster board that you can display at every group meeting. Be sure to "hint" at any needed rules that have not already been mentioned (e.g., turn off all cell phones, keep confidentiality, starting and ending on time). One rule to include, if it doesn't come up, is to have fun. This sets a positive tone to the group.

## Confidentiality and Limits to Confidentiality

Confidentiality should be addressed in the first group session (e.g., "What is said in group, stays in group"). Explain the difference between sharing personal information and general ideas and techniques. The parents will most likely want to talk with friends, neighbors, and partners about what went on in the group, and that's OK, as long as they don't use the names of any of the other parents or share specific personal information that was said by another parent. Be sure to discuss the limits to confidentiality with the parents. Make sure parents are aware that you are obligated to report child abuse, neglect, and any threat of harming another person if it is discussed in the group. Make sure the group members fully understand what this means and what will happen if a situation arises. For instance, in some states, clinicians are required by law to report parents if they mention that they leave children under the age of 12 alone at home without an adult. Many parents are not aware that this is considered a form of neglect. Therefore, openly discussing what is considered abuse or neglect by law in your state can be very helpful in avoiding challenging situations. Over subsequent sessions you will want to gently remind parents of the need for confidentiality and limits to confidentiality, to protect them as well as their children.

Tell group members that unfortunately you do not have control over their sharing other members' personal information outside the group. However, the group members may want to come up with a rule as to what happens if someone breaks confidentiality. Be sure to discuss the issue of confidentiality whenever a new member or individual from outside the group (e.g., volunteer, intern, school counselor, social worker) attends a session. Point out that any volunteers or individuals who visit the group will abide by the group's rules regarding confidentiality.

> **Be sure to discuss the limits to confidentiality with the parents. Make sure parents are aware that you are obligated to report child abuse, neglect, and any threat of harming another person if it is discussed in the group.**

## Enforcing a Time Schedule and Sticking to Your Agenda

With the first session, start the group on time even if just a few group members are present. As other members arrive, ask them to join the group quietly and respectfully. This sends a message that being on time to group is important. You will want to set this precedent early and praise or reward those who come on time. For instance, you may hand out raffle tickets to parents who arrive on time. Then, at the end of the group, raffle off a few small prizes to those who arrived on time. It is also important to end the group on time. It can be difficult to do this if the group is in the middle of an engaging conversation, but stick to your word and be respectful of the group members' time and other commitments. Consider selecting a parent as a timekeeper for particular tasks to help keep everyone on task and focused.

Having an agenda and sticking to it can keep each session on-task (see Appendix 27 for a sample Parent Group Agenda). Write the agenda for each session in advance. When the parents arrive, begin the session by reviewing the agenda. Each session will include the following elements: open discussion of the agenda; clarifying the goals for the session; debriefing the assignment from the previous week; a brief review of the previous week's skills; the introduction of new ideas and skills, role plays, and discussion; and

> **Start each group on time even if just a few group members are present. This sends a message that being on time to group is important.**

finally, a summary and presentation of the week's assignments. That is a lot to cover in each session! You may also ask the parents if they would like to add anything to the agenda. Once the session begins, refer back to the agenda to keep the session moving along. Use your best judgment on how to handle tangents and refer to the agenda to bring the group back on track. Keep a good balance among each member's needs, the group's needs, and the leader's need to provide new knowledge and teaching. This means that you will want to be both flexible and structured in order to stay on-task. For example, if one of the families has a traumatic or distressing event (e.g., divorce, death of a family member) that occurred that week, you may want to allow time for a brief check-in to see how the parent is doing at the beginning of the group. Another option is to allow each group member (if interested) to provide a brief 2-minute update on their week at the beginning of each group. They could share good news or use the time to "vent" about a stressful situation that occurred that week. One concern is that you must be careful that the "crisis of the week" does not dominate the session, resulting in not getting to the content or new material for the week.

It is your responsibility to maintain the fidelity and integrity of the intervention as developed. It is important that all of the objectives, activities, and content for the specific session are completed as originally intended by the intervention developers. Therefore, you may need to redirect group members who repeatedly monopolize the discussion by telling long stories or sharing stories that are not connected to the content of the group session. Similarly, address other off-task behavior that interferes with the pacing and delivery of the material. Starting the group on time and referring back to the agenda are great ways to be sure that all of the necessary content is covered.

There will be many ideas, reactions, fears, and frustrations voiced at each session. This is the nature of a healthy change process. While you do not want to stifle any member's process, you *do* need to be aware of the group's needs and the agenda demands. Pacing each group through the use of direct time-limit comments, paraphrasing, and summarizing viewpoints is essential. Be aware that each session will have a different dynamic based on the members who are participating and the topic that is being covered. Don't get bogged down on a topic when group members are expressing a clear understanding. You can gauge whether the pace in which you progress through content and discussions is appropriate by monitoring the engagement and understanding of the members. For instance, if you are implementing an intervention that provides multiple examples of a strategy or topic but you find after discussing two examples that the members are clear, move on to the next topic. Otherwise, you may find group members becoming restless and less engaged. At other times, you may find that despite using many examples that you need to spend more time on a topic to ensure members understand. Using your skills as a group facilitator and paying attention to your audience are important in determining the pacing of each group session.

## Setting Goals

As mentioned earlier, parents can be asked to introduce themselves by stating what they hope to gain from the group. Refer to this in introducing the topic of goal setting. Have a discussion with the parents about its importance. Make the parents aware that setting goals and meeting them will allow parents to track their successes. Sharing goals early can create cohesion in the group, as many parents realize they have similar goals and experiences in parenting. Then, at the end of each session parents can be asked to set an individual goal that relates to the content of the session (e.g., Praise my child at least 10 times a day this week). You could have parents track their goals.

> **Begin the first group by asking parents what they hope to gain from participating in the group. Sharing their goals early can create cohesion in the group, as many parents realize they have similar goals and experiences in parenting.**

## Dealing with Questions Regarding Qualifications of Group Leader(s)

You may get questions from parents about your qualifications to be leading a parenting group. If you have no children of you own, parents may call into question your ability to truly know what is most helpful for them. Parents may ask the question directly or be thinking about it without making the issue overt. Therefore, it may be helpful to provide some information about your training and experience working with parents and children.

Disclosing appropriate personal information in response to questions can be helpful in decreasing parent concerns. For instance, it can be helpful to disclose if you do or do not have children at the start of the group. This allows the issue to be brought up right away. Next, discuss the collaborative nature of the group process. It is useful to say that you are not the expert on how to raise the members' children, but the strategies you will be discussing have been very helpful to many other parents. The group leader may say something such as:

> "I've studied [or worked with] _____ and know the techniques that will be used in this group very well. However, I am not the one who is at home, living with your children. I am looking to you as parents to share your experiences and what you have learned as parents, since you are the experts on your children."

This emphasizes the leader as an equal rather than a distanced and aloof expert. This model puts parents in the group on the same level as the leader and is more effective than an expert model. The latter tends to discourage parents as they perceive a large discrepancy between their skills and the group leader's expertise. Also, if you set up the group with you as the "expert," this puts pressure on you to have all of the answers and solve the parents' problems for them. In a more egalitarian group, the room is full of people with shared experiences who can learn from one another.

## Challenges to the Group Leader's Ability to Understand and Help Parents

Sometimes parents may challenge the leader's ability to understand their situation and help them. The parent could feel threatened, could have had a negative experience with mental health professionals in the past, or could simply feel uncertain. For example, if a leader discloses that he or she does not have children, a parent may question whether the leader knows what it's like to be a parent. In response, the leader could reply like this:

> "You know, you're probably right about that. It's hard to know exactly what it's like to be a parent when you've never been one. And I'm going to be counting on you and the other parents to help me understand what it's like for you. On the other hand, I've worked with children and families and studied child behavior. This program has been shown to work for lots of parents. I would like to share this research-supported approach with you. I think we both have contributions to make. Hopefully, we can all learn from each other's experiences."

If you are from a different cultural background than the parents in your group, some parents may feel that you do not completely understand them. It can be helpful to have an open discussion about how your background is similar or different from the group members'. It can also be helpful if you have reflected on the differences in your backgrounds and the inherent biases that you bring to the group. Being aware of your potential biases can help to prevent these biases from interfering with the group process.

## THE GROUP LEADER AS FORTUNE-TELLER: ANTICIPATING PROBLEMS

A group leader should be someone who can "predict the future." You do not want to be caught off guard during the group or find yourself unprepared to handle sensitive or difficult situations. Before beginning a group, brainstorm on your own and discuss with a colleague (or co-leader, if you have one) the possible challenges and worst-case scenarios (e.g., parent attending the group is intoxicated, disclosures of abuse, monopolizing group members, oppositional parents). Come up with a plan that works best for your group. Also, review school, agency, and or state guidelines for reporting abuse and neglect, and be prepared to take action immediately after a disclosure is made. Have a list of referrals prepared to provide to families in need of additional supports.

Consistent with a collaborative model, bring your expertise and knowledge of possible family reactions to bear on the parents' unique situations and experiences. This may include the single parent who is coparenting, the family with several children of differing ages, the mother with a noninvolved father, or the parent with a background of alcohol and spousal abuse. The parents collaborate by bringing their feelings and anxieties to the group to share. To be most effective, you will want to anticipate problems or successes. This can be most easily accomplished by collaborating with the parents, listening to them, and truly trying to understand their situations.

To prevent parents' disillusionment, it's helpful for the leader to predict setbacks in child behaviors, anticipating problems and regression before they occur. The leader can engage in hypothetical problem solving about how parents can handle particular problems should they occur. For example, the leader could prepare families for a child's negative reactions to changing circumstances, or rehearse strategies being learned in group sessions. Parents should be made aware that when they begin planned ignoring for minor behavior problems at home (e.g., tantrumming), the behavior will get worse before it gets better. Parents could think that the strategy is ineffective or think they are doing something wrong if they don't understand that ignoring initially causes the behavior to intensify (i.e., extinction burst). You can discuss the behaviors that can arise for a child after coming home from a week's visit with his or her dad or a child's jealous reactions when his or her stepbrothers or stepsisters come home for summer vacation. When parents have had difficult situations in the past (e.g., child tantrum in the grocery store), you can problem solve with parents to prepare a plan for a more successful experience next time. By mentally rehearsing how they will handle the worst possible scenario, parents' anxiety is reduced because they feel prepared to cope effectively with a conflict situation. Moreover, if the "worst" doesn't happen, they are pleasantly pleased with their progress. You can also prepare parents for regression in child behavior and normalize it by saying something like:

> "Expect and be prepared for relapses. They are part of your own learning process. Your child may test the security of his environment every now and again to see if the rules still hold. Then once he knows his base is secure, he can tackle a new challenge. You know, it's a bit like the old adage 'Two steps forward, one step back.'"

You will also want to prepare parents for the fact that there will be relapses in their own parenting skills. The leader should reassure parents that relapses are normal parts of the learning process. Relapses should be construed as a "signal" that some strategy needs to be implemented; parents can be encouraged to see them as an opportunity to practice or review. It is a good idea to rehearse what they could do when a relapse occurs. For example, they could call a group member; contact you, the leader; practice program exercises again; review strategies; or focus on positive alternatives. Here is an example of what the leader could do to prepare parents for relapses by reframing their interpretations:

> "Parenting is challenging. As you learn new skills you will become more fluent in using them. However, expect that on occasion you might struggle a bit. Perhaps you will snap at your child. Just know that we all need to work on using new skills, particularly in challenging situations."

## Resistance to Change

Behavior change is difficult. Anticipate that parents may not be willing to try new strategies or assignments. Normalize the difficulties that parents encounter. Acknowledge that using new skills in the home can be challenging and that some skills will be more challenging than others. If the difficulty of making behavioral change is not acknowledged, parents may feel that they are inept and incapable of change. Some parents may even become angry for being asked to do assignments that are hard for them or do not fit their personalities. Such feelings will lead to increased resistance. When parents are prepared for these reactions in advance, they are not surprised or anxious when they occur. You can prepare group members for initial discomfort on using a new skill by saying something like:

> "Be prepared to feel awkward when you do this kind of play. Be prepared that you will not want to do it, because it feels awkward. And be prepared for your child not to like it at first. Whenever a family member learns a new behavior, there is a natural tendency for other family members to resist the new behavior and try to revert back to the status quo. In fact, some family members might try to pressure you back to the old way of doing things."

Or:

> "You will probably feel awkward praising at first, especially if you haven't done much of this in the past. You may even feel like your praise sounds phony. So don't wait to praise until you feel warmth toward your child. Just get the words out, even if they are kind of flat. The feelings and genuineness will come later. The more you practice, the more natural it will become."

We have found in past groups that talking about the lack of comfort that the parents experience has been helpful to move them forward toward trying new and seemingly unusual strategies. In addition, preparing them for the negative reaction of other family members can help them to reflect on challenges in the moment.

## Parents Who Dominate the Conversation

In most groups, there will be varying levels of parenting experience, communication skills, and personalities. It is important that you reinforce every parent for sharing ideas so that every member feels comfortable participating. If one or a few parents dominate each conversation, the collaborative nature of the group is compromised. The essential idea behind collaboration is to "empower" each parent. Build on parents' strengths and experiences so that they feel confident about their parenting skills and their ability to respond to new situations. In good group facilitation, those who are not active are encouraged and those who are overactive are redirected with their positive sense of self intact. Simple techniques for redirecting conversations can be employed. You may make statements such as "Good idea, let's hear from someone who has not commented yet today," or "I like the point that you're making. What do other people think?"

If there are parents who are particularly difficult to redirect, a group rule may be initiated, such as "Each member is allowed to make two comments per topic," or "Let's move around the circle so that everyone has a chance to comment."

Rules for equal member participation should be established in the first session. These can include one person talks at a time, be respectful, and do not interrupt. Remember that the role of the group leader is to ensure a smooth and dynamic process. This means that you may need to make direct comments such as "I'm having a hard time hearing everyone. One person at a time, please," or "Freeze! Some good thoughts are getting lost because we are all talking at one time."

If a parent is monopolizing the group by telling long stories or too many stories, the group leader may have to be more direct and say something like "Denise, I am so sorry to interrupt, but I am looking at the time and we are going to have to move on to our next activity so that we can get everything on our agenda completed today. Thanks so much for sharing!"

If you have one or more parents who tend to dominate discussions despite your efforts to redirect them, it may also be necessary to meet with them either before or after the group to express your observations. Have them reflect on this and ask them how you could give them a signal when to allow others to talk. By having this private conversation, the parents may become more aware of the issue and become less dominating. Some people simply don't realize that they are dominating the conversation. You can set up a signal (e.g., "Thanks for sharing, Jenny") that lets this participant know you want others to participate. You may also sit close to this particular member, or move close to him or her when he or she is talking for a length of time. This allows you to more effectively redirect the person.

## Aggressive Parents

Collaboration implies a nonblaming, reciprocal relationship based on utilizing equally the group leader's knowledge and the parents' unique strengths and perspectives. Collaboration also implies respect for each person's contribution and a relationship among group members that is built on trust and open communication. Parents must not be ridiculed for their perspectives, ignored, or criticized for something they have said.

Sometimes a group includes a parent who is critical and verbally aggressive toward either his or her spouse or another parent in the group. In such instances, you need to intervene immediately to stop the bullying pattern—otherwise, the other parent will withdraw and the collaborative nature of the group will be compromised. Find language that is assertive (not aggressive) yet polite, and fits with your style of communication. For example, you may say in a supportive but firm manner, "I need to interrupt you right there," or "Hang on, let's pause there for a minute."

Then explain why you are cutting off the speaker. It is your role as the group leader to model techniques such as constructive criticism and taking responsibility for one's own thoughts and feelings without putting down other people. Rephrasing or offering suggested language can be particularly helpful in these situations. If negative comments or attacking behavior persists, it may be necessary to speak with the group member briefly, in private, before or after the group. Be aware that many members come to the group with relationships, both positive and negative, already established. It may be necessary to negotiate special agreements for interaction while group sessions are in progress (a form of interpersonal mediation among specific members). For instance, when talking privately to a parent who is making negative comments or attacks on other group members, you may say something like:

> "I've been noticing some tension between you and parent A. I will also be talking to parent A about this, but wanted to talk to you first. There are times where you both make comments toward one another that are not always framed in the nicest manner. I just wanted to remind you about our group rules, specifically about having respect for other group members. Do you think while we are in group that you can try to reframe these comments into a more positive light or not say them at all?"

You may mention that you wanted to discuss this individually with each party first, but if necessary, you may also want to hold a small-group meeting with all parents involved to discuss a plan of action of how to respect one another in the group setting. At the end of this chapter there is a sample role play on how to handle a situation where one parent verbally attacks another group member (see role-play scenario 1 at the end of this chapter).

## Parents Who Are Overwhelmed

Parents who feel overwhelmed or stressed by the daily occurrences of family life may appear resistant to some of the parenting ideas promoted in the group. We recommend that you try to understand, work with the "resistance," and confront the issue in a nonthreatening way. You may say something like "You seem to be having difficulty with this new group topic. Can you tell me a little more about your thoughts?"

If you find yourself in a discussion with parents where you are defending parenting strategies or are the only one offering solutions to a problem, then you will likely not make much progress. Ideally, you want the parents to be coming up with ideas about how the strategy will work in their homes with their children. Parental resistance may be the result of life stressors that make it difficult to find the time to do the assignments. The parents may also have unrealistic expectations for behavioral change and are not prepared for the long, hard work involved. You may elicit suggestions from the other parents in the group for using the strategies discussed, despite the challenges the parent is facing. In one group that we were running, a parent was struggling with using strategies with her three children (i.e., giving them positive attention, predictable schedule, time-out). Another group member stated that she had four children and was living in a one-room apartment and then described how she used the strategies. Hearing this from another parent in a similar situation made all the difference. There was nothing that we could have said that would have been as effective. At the end of this chapter there is a sample role play on eliciting solutions from parents who are struggling with using some of the strategies at home due to time constraints and other stressors (see role-play scenario 2 at the end of this chapter).

## *Parents Who Stop Attending Group*

Occasionally, there may be a parent who attends one or two sessions and then stops attending. It is important to contact such parents to determine why they stopped attending. Approach this in a nonconfrontational way and let the parent know that you would like him or her to continue as part of the group. Try to get the parent to come to one more session and then make a final decision. Express concern and invite the parent to rejoin the group with a statement such as:

> "I was concerned that we didn't see you at the group meeting last week. I hope you were finding the meetings helpful and I'd really like to have your input in our upcoming meetings. You've shown some good insights that have been valuable in our discussions. If there's a specific problem that's keeping you from attending, maybe we could discuss it and work something out. . . . [Allow the parent time to respond.] Do you think you could try to come to one more session and then make your final decision about staying in the group or not?"

There are a number of circumstances that could interfere with parent attendance. One involves group-related issues such as being uncomfortable in the group, finding issues discussed not helpful, or disagreement with the ideas presented. Gathering anonymous feedback following each group session may help to identify these types of issues early on and allow you to head them off before the parent leaves the group. Ask parents to leave comments such as this on the feedback form (see Appendix 23 for a sample Parent Group Feedback Form). Or you can have a box or jar located in the group room where parents can leave anonymous feedback or questions they have regarding group content or process. If the parent does offer his or her name when giving feedback or suggestions, follow up with a phone call or individually contact the parent to identify and brainstorm solutions to the problem. Another way to tackle the problem is to bring it up during the next group session by saying something such as:

> "I noticed that a parent dropped a question into the comment box that I would like to discuss today. I want to make sure your voices are heard and that we tackle these issues as they arise so that we are all comfortable and happy with the group content and process. Is everyone OK with us taking the first 5 minutes of group today to review the question that was in the comment box?"

Furthermore, outside influences such as a family crisis, transportation, child care, or monetary issues may impact the parent's ability to attend groups. Again, making contact with the parent to brainstorm solutions to the problem can be beneficial. You may have resources to help provide child care, provide dinners at group meetings, and help with transportation issues that can rectify these issues. If a solution cannot be devised, perhaps a referral to another support group or other agency that can provide the service (despite the identified outside influences) can be provided.

## Predicting Positive Change and Success

Encourage parents to persist with the group and implement the strategies discussed. Parents may find that through the course of the group, their own expectations for positive change will become higher. Express confidence and optimism in the parent's ability to successfully change his or her own behavior and increase the likelihood of positive change in his or her children. As the group leader, you will want to build efficacy among the parents and empower them in using new skills with their child. It is critical that you, as group leader, assume that all parents in the group can learn and use new skills despite life stressors or other challenges they face. For example, you should have the expectation that all parents will complete their weekly homework. We have had parents who are working several jobs and read the required parenting book chapters on the bus on the way to work. Similar to what we tell teachers, having high expectations will lead to positive outcomes, whereas lowering your expectations can be self-fulfilling, undermining the potential of the parents in your group.

> **Express confidence and optimism in the parents' ability to successfully carry out the behavior required to produce positive changes in their child's behaviors. Build self-efficacy among the parents and empower them in using new skills with their child.**

According to Bandura (1977), all psychological procedures are mediated through a system of beliefs about the level of skill required to bring about an outcome and the likely end result of a course of action. Efficacy expectations are thought to be the most important component. Successful treatment will depend on your ability to strengthen the parents' expectations of personal efficacy ("I am able to do").

Devote some time in the group to discussing how other family members can benefit from the group, even if they are not attending sessions themselves. If nonparticipating members of the family are not helped by the participating member to see some possibility of payoff for themselves, they may actively sabotage the participating member's efforts to change. Therefore, work with the participating parents to see how the ideas from the group can be extended in a nonintrusive way to other family members. For example, you may predict that the siblings who previously had been "good" children may regress in an effort to gain attention and to compete for play sessions with the target child. You can then brainstorm ways to utilize the new skills with all the children in the house. While more demanding for the parent, the parent may recognize that it is beneficial to the family as a whole. Predictions should also be made about the nonparticipating parent who may initially be suspicious of the program. However, if the parent continues to consistently use new strategies and they are effective, the nonparticipating parent will follow suit.

## Getting Support for Yourself

Just as parents get tired of the hard work of parenting, group leaders may tire of their hard work. Facilitating groups, especially in the face of confrontations and resistance, can be a formidable task at times and requires a considerable degree of clinical skill. If you are fortunate to know others in your school district or community who are implementing group interventions, you could arrange regular meetings with them. Having a support system in which you can analyze a difficult situation or group problem with other colleagues or a supervisor can be very helpful. It is then possible to brainstorm and problem solve how to reframe an issue in the group, interpret it, or explain it in a different way. These ideas can then be taken back to the group. The added support and objectivity of another person can help immensely to renew enthusiasm and persistence in the face of highly challenging groups.

> **Having a support system in which you can analyze a difficult group situation or problem with other colleagues or a supervisor can be very helpful. The added support and objectivity of another person can help immensely to renew enthusiasm and persist in the face of highly challenging groups.**

Remind yourself that you are capable of making mistakes in your group meetings. Be aware of mistakes, learn from them, be realistic about goals, and don't expect magical solutions. Have frequent conversations with your co-leader or other colleagues that allow time to brainstorm solutions and understand the stressors associated with your role as group leader.

Group leaders should not expect to be perfect the first time they run a group. It is important to be open and responsive to corrective feedback from colleagues, supervisors, and group members. The skills discussed in these chapters may take time to develop and improve with the more groups you facilitate. Therefore, remember to be patient and that being an effective group leader is a process. If possible, seek supervision from colleagues (e.g., other mental health professionals at your organization or school) who have been successful at running groups in the past. You could ask them to co-lead groups with you, sit in on a session (with permission from group members), or you can videotape your sessions and review them in your supervision meetings. Many evidence-based interventions also have fidelity checklists you could complete to be sure you are meeting all of the objectives, activities, and content with integrity.

> **Take good care of yourself by taking time to relax and enjoy life outside of the group. Taking time for yourself will make you more effective in the work you do with others.**

Take care of yourself by taking time to relax and enjoy life outside of the group. Set daily or weekly goals to plan activities that you enjoy (e.g., walks in the park, time with family, time alone with a good book, a night out with friends, bubble bath). For you to be an effective leader, you need to be at your best. Ensuring that you take time for yourself will make you more effective in the work you do with others. Many times we become very involved with the families and children with whom we work. While it is important to be connected, concerned, and empathetic to the needs of those we work with, it can be stressful and can lead to burnout. Reflect on how much time you actively "give" to yourself and monitor when you need to give yourself more time. Then, plan how to use your time, carving out moments to focus on your own well-being.

# SUMMARY

It is important to establish positive group dynamics and appropriately manage behaviors when implementing any group. To begin the process of creating a successful group, you need to set group rules and maintain structure. Involve group members in creating the rules for their group. Anticipate possible pitfalls and plan accordingly within your group to prevent problems. This lays a solid foundation for implementing a successful child or parent group.

# MATERIALS

The following is a list of materials discussed in this chapter that can support effective group facilitation. You will find examples of some of these materials in the Appendices.

- Parent Group Feedback Form (Appendix 23).
- Parent Group Agenda (Appendix 27).
- Rules poster.*
- Incentives list.*
- Stickers for sticker charts and praise statements.*
- Incentives/prize box items.*

# REFLECTION AND ROLE PLAYS

Here we provide a series of reflection exercises and role-play activities to help you further hone your group facilitation skills.

## *Reflection*

After reviewing this chapter, ask yourself the following questions:

1. "How will I engage group members in the role plays? How will I make the parent feel comfortable participating in role plays?"
2. "How will I handle a parent who is aggressive or dominating the conversation? What are some statements I can make to let the group member know that he or she has been heard, but also keep the group on track and allow for other group member participation?"

## *Role Plays*

After reviewing the reflection questions, apply your understanding of what has been covered in this chapter by responding to the following two scenarios:

---

*These materials are not included in the Appendices, but may be referenced within this chapter and are also helpful when implementing parent and child groups.

## Scenario 1

A parent in the group attacks another group member by saying that his or her ideas are stupid. As the group leader, express to the group members that all points of view are valid in this group and that all members should be respected.

EXAMPLE SCRIPTED ANSWER

(*The "attack" was just made and there is some back and forth going on among parents.*)

GROUP LEADER: Hang on a second. There are a lot of people talking at one time and I'm having a hard time following everything. Before we hash this out, I want to remind us of our group rules. Can someone read off rule 2?

PARENT B: "Respect others. All ideas, situations, examples, etc. are to be respected. No idea or thought is stupid."

GROUP LEADER: Thank you for reminding us of that. As we are all entitled to our own opinions, in this group you all took part in developing those rules and you all agreed to abide by those rules. So please let's remember that everyone's ideas are respected and valued so that we can all feel comfortable with sharing. Can we agree on that? (*All parents nod their heads.*)

PARENT A: I apologize for calling your idea stupid, parent C. I just don't think your idea applies here.

PARENT C: That's OK, but I want my idea to be heard. It's what I think and have experienced and I want to share it with the group.

GROUP LEADER: Thank you for apologizing, parent A, and for accepting, parent C. We all don't have to agree with everything everyone says, but we do have to follow our rules of being respectful. Let's give parent A the opportunity to share her idea and then if you have other ideas, parent C (or other parents), we'd love to hear yours too.

## TIP

Remember to try to lead this conversation and always refer back to the rules that the group developed and agreed upon. The goal is to defend the parent who was "teased" and stop this from happening again, but at the same time, you don't want to offend the parent who made the inappropriate comment. Parents will not always apologize like in the example above, but if they can at least agree with abiding by the rules and respecting one another, then you can move on. If the issue persists, the group leader may want to take aside the parents involved after the group session and discuss it further.

## Scenario 2

Parents in the group are struggling with using some of the strategies at home due to time constraints and other stressors. Lead a discussion with the group that will elicit ideas or solutions. Try to avoid discussions that place the group leader in the role of developing solutions or defending the use of strategies.

EXAMPLE SCRIPTED ANSWER

GROUP LEADER: So it sounds like there has been some difficulty using some of the strategies at home that we learned in group due to time constraints and other stressors. Has anyone made an attempt to use the strategies at home? And if so, would you be willing to share with the group?

PARENT A: I can share one attempt. While I was making dinner this week, I happened to see the praise handout from our group on the refrigerator and I decided that this would be a great time to try praising my child for helping out.

GROUP LEADER: Wow . . . that was a wonderful example. Not only did you try out the strategy but you incorporated it into a time when you were still able to complete your task of making dinner for the family. This was excellent thinking. How did it feel to try out this technique?

PARENT A: Pretty good. The kids did what they were supposed to do and seemed happy about the praise, which made me happy. I didn't have too much time and honestly, I'm not sure that I would've remembered had I not seen the praise handout.

GROUP LEADER: It sounds like it went well. That was also a great idea, to hang the handouts on the fridge to serve as a reminder. Does anyone else do this?

PARENT B: I do that, too, and it works well.

PARENT C: I do that, too, but I don't always see them because I'm always running around like crazy taking care of the kids.

GROUP LEADER: It sounds like you are on the right track with hanging them up to help remind you . . . this is terrific. Has anyone else had any success at remembering to try a strategy or finding the time to practice the skill in your busy schedules?

PARENT D: One thing that works for me is practicing the skills while the kids are doing their homework. So when they are doing their homework, I'm doing mine!

GROUP LEADER: Wow . . . another fantastic idea! Thank you for sharing. We realize that everyone is busy and we don't want to burden you with another thing to do, but we also know the success rate of those who practice these skills versus those who don't. It is extremely helpful to practice the skills at home in your own environments. It's like learning to ride a bike. Let's pretend you never rode a bike before, but you really wanted to learn. And let's say that today we came into group and I showed you a video on how to ride a bike, we practiced one time each, and then sent you home with a bike to practice some more. What do you think would happen if you never practiced versus if you did practice?

PARENT B: If you practiced, you would probably learn how to ride a bike and ride it well.

GROUP LEADER: Exactly. And I know that you are all determined to learn these skills and improve the relationship you have with your child. So it's up to you to practice at home. You are all doing a fabulous job so far and we are looking forward to hearing more great ideas on how to practice these strategies at home.

## TIP

Try to elicit ideas from the parents first and then bring other parents in by asking if anyone else has had a similar experience or other ideas of how to "fit it in." Also be empathic because everyone has busy schedules and it is difficult to make time when your schedule is already packed. Finally, try to use an analogy of learning something for the first time or losing weight or running a marathon, and the commitment you need to make in order to do this. Let the analogy be the take-home point, not the starting point in the discussion.

# CHAPTER 7

# Engaging Group Members

Developing rapport, enhancing group cohesion, and building group morale all contribute to the success of a group intervention. Group members need to feel a connection with the group and enjoy coming to the sessions. They should want to be a part of the group and feel included or they may stop attending. Group members often report a predictable level of initial discomfort as groups begin. If the leader does not effectively contain this discomfort, low levels of cohesion can result (Burlingame, Fuhriman, & Johnson, 2001). Group cohesiveness heavily influences group outcomes and greatly influences the course of group therapy (Yalom & Rand, 1966). You can enhance this process by being enthusiastic about the group, building rapport with each group member, making all members feel safe and important within the group, and celebrating group successes. This chapter discusses the essential components of building and sustaining group member engagement. Topics include developing rapport, group cohesion, and increasing group morale to keep group members enthusiastic about attending group sessions.

## CHILD GROUPS

### Building and Sustaining Engagement

Engaging group members from the very start is crucial to the success of a group intervention. The following section provides ideas for ensuring that all group members feel welcome, believe their contributions are seen as meaningful by the group leader and members, and remain engaged throughout the course of the intervention. We explore specific ways to build group cohesion and encourage participation in each group session. First, we look at strategies for increasing member engagement.

### Group Check-In

Taking a few minutes at the start of each group session to check in with individual group members is a great strategy to increase engagement. It can also help address any issues that have occurred over the course of the week since the last session. Incidents occurring between group sessions or right before a group session can interfere with students' ability to focus on the content. For example, a student may come to the group visibly upset by an argument with a peer that occurred 5 minutes before the group begins. It may be difficult to proceed with the group content if this student is upset and focused on the argument.

You may want to block time at the beginning of each session to share difficulties the students may be facing or to check in to see how their week is going. Announce the amount of time allotted for the check-in to appropriately manage time in the group (e.g., first 10 minutes of the session). Ensure that all students have an opportunity to share before moving on to other items on the agenda. Highlight the importance of sharing experiences and supporting one another to build group cohesion.

Usually, a small amount of time at the start of the session is enough for the students to express their concerns and be ready to move on to the content of the session. However, there are times when situations are more serious and students need more than the first 10 minutes of the session. Each situation is different and group leaders will need to decide how to address problems as they arise within the group. It is often a balancing act between allowing group members to share and feel heard, while also maintaining structure and successfully delivering the group content.

Here are four possible ways to address a student's problem at the start of a session while also ensuring that the session's content is delivered:

- *Option 1:* Give the student an opportunity to express his or her concerns for a few minutes. Then, continue with the check-in. When the allotted time for check-in has passed, ask the student if you could continue this discussion after the group and move forward with the agenda for the day.

- *Option 2:* Give the student an opportunity to express his or her concerns for a few minutes. Continue with the check-in. Next, ask the student to write down any other thoughts, feelings, and problem-solving techniques that he or she could use to solve the problem while the rest of the group moves on to reviewing the agenda for the day.

- *Option 3:* Have the student express his or her concerns for a few minutes during group check-in and then have the co-leader meet with the student one-on-one while the group moves on to reviewing the agenda for the day.

- *Option 4:* Allow the student to continue with the check-in, but connect the challenging situation to the day's session content. For example, if you are talking about problem solving, ask the student if the group could use the frustrating incident as an example of how to use the problem-solving steps to develop a list of possible solutions. Together as a group the problem could be identified and potential solutions could be discussed. If the student agrees, the group content would be covered, contributing to the learning of everyone in the group. Hopefully, it would also help the student to feel better about the difficult situation.

The options listed above will help ensure that the student feels heard and supported, while simultaneously moving on with the planned content for that group session.

## Encouraging Group Participation

Engage group members by encouraging participation from all. It may be difficult at times to elicit ideas from a shy group member. However, you will want to include the student and allow his or her ideas to be heard. The following sections discuss three key areas that you may want to focus on when encouraging group members to participate.

### HOMEWORK AND GOAL SHEETS

During each session's check-in, see who has completed their homework and returned a signed goal sheet (see Appendix 25 for a sample Goal Sheet). Have students who completed their homework share what they did at home and then hand it in. Ask those who did not complete their homework to discuss the difficulties that kept them from homework completion and elicit ideas from all group members on how to complete the homework for the next week. Offering group points or prizes for homework completion and returning goal sheets may help group members to remember to complete them each week. Group leaders can also offer a second-chance offer (e.g., smaller prize, bonus points) to those who forgot their homework or left their goal sheet in the classroom.

### ROLE PLAYS

It is fairly easy to get students involved in role playing. You may want to pick names out of a hat to make it fair. However, there are times when it is difficult to get some members involved. If you really want one member to participate who hasn't participated yet, offer to do the role play with him or her and offer support along the way if he or she gets stuck. You could say something like "Come on, I'll do the role play with you and I'll help you out if you get stuck . . . I can whisper ideas in your ear or you can ask for help if needed."

If the student is still reluctant to engage in the role play, then you will want to choose another student who is more comfortable with acting. Have a balance between challenging the student to try the role play and empathy for the fact that it is difficult to get up in front of peers and practice a new skill. The withdrawn student may need to be asked to participate only after other students have "modeled" a few role plays. The group leader can also encourage role playing in small groups, or utilize techniques such as coaching, prompting, and feeding lines to the withdrawn student during role plays. Try to make it as comfortable as possible for the withdrawn student to be in the limelight.

During the role play, make sure you are ready to offer advice and prompts in a subtle, nonthreatening way. After the role play, make sure you first praise the student for being so courageous and then offer feedback to the student beginning with what he or she did really well. Then, allow the group to offer constructive criticism. Make sure that the group is aware of the "actor's" feelings and how difficult it must be to get up in front of peers to practice a new technique. Also be prepared to defend the student if criticisms get too harsh. You may say something like:

"Let's remember that it is really difficult to get up in front of a group of your peers and practice a new technique. So when we are discussing a performance, let's make sure we are offering constructive feedback and that we are aware of student A's feelings while doing so."

If group members feel safe and become more comfortable within the group, they will be more likely to participate.

## GROUP DISCUSSIONS

Make sure that there is active participation from all group members—there may be some who do not like to participate. Allow these members the right to pass. However, you will also want to challenge them to participate and to share their thoughts—for example: "Student A, I noticed that you laughed during that video. Can you tell us what you were thinking when that video was being shown?"

Come up with ways to make sure each student has a chance to participate and feels comfortable doing so. You may use a "talking stick" that is passed around the group; each participant contributes one at a time when holding the stick. You may also want to state at the beginning of the group that you are providing points for positive participation. Then, define what positive participation looks like (e.g., providing an answer when asked a question, raising a hand to offer a suggestion when talking about a new skill). Another idea is to set a goal for each member to contribute at least three times during the group. Provide a reinforcer for those who meet this goal. Another strategy for engaging the withdrawn student is to give him or her an administrative task (e.g., passing out materials or acting as a timekeeper for a group activity). Make sure to acknowledge even the slightest comment made by the student and praise any efforts made in a nonchalant way. For instance, you may say something such as "Thanks so much for handing out those papers, Malik. You sure are a good helper. I couldn't have done it without your help!"

If one student is dominating the conversation, you may want to praise that student for ideas and input, and then direct attention to those who are not participating and try to get them involved—for example: "We have heard a lot of great ideas from you, student B. Thank you for sharing those with us. Are there other ideas that other group members want to share with us?"

If some students are particularly difficult to redirect, a group rule can be developed. For instance, each member is allowed to make two comments per topic or that comments move around the circle so that everyone has a chance to comment. Remember the role of the group leader is to ensure a smooth and dynamic process, which means that you need to enforce the rules. If situations arise where a rule is being violated and students are talking over one another, you may need to make direct comments such as "It is difficult to hear everyone. One person at a time please," or "Freeze! Some good thoughts are getting lost because we are all talking at the same time."

You can use other techniques to ensure that students have an equal amount of time to contribute to the session. For instance, create popsicle sticks with the students' names on them. Pull a stick out of the cup and the student whose name is pulled can comment. Continue to pull the sticks until each student has had the chance to contribute. Another idea is to have a ball or other soft object that represents the "talking piece." The members can pass or toss the ball only to a member who has not yet had the chance to participate. In another strategy, have students write down their answers in their notebooks or on small white-boards. All the students then hold up their answers at the same time. Be creative, but fair!

## Building Group Cohesion

Developing and supporting group cohesion is an important aspect of effective group facilitation. Students who feel connected to you and one another will be more likely to share experiences, successes, and challenges they face throughout the sessions. Further, they will be more engaged and participate more actively in role plays and discussions. The following sections provide ideas for building group cohesion.

### Communication Systems

Establishing a communication system in the group helps group members to feel connected with you and with one another. One suggestion is to have a folder for each student in the group. You may have the students write their names on the folder and decorate it during the first meeting. The folder can hold important documents (e.g., reminder of the rules, goal sheets). Then, you can place the folders on members' chairs to find when they enter the room for group. You may want to write personal notes for the folders that offer specific feedback from the week before. You may also use the folders to keep a record of the homework that the students have completed, how often their goals were met, and track other success experiences. This type of information helps monitor the progress of group members (see Chapter 9).

Other helpful ways to build group cohesion include having group members' sign and send a "we missed you" note to a group member who was absent. You can also send birthday or holiday cards to the members in your group and announce birthdays or special occasions at the beginning of a session. Of course, be sure to ask the group member beforehand to ensure that he or she is comfortable with this information being shared with the group.

### Buddy System

To help build group cohesion, you can assign each group member a "buddy" from the group. Group members can check in with their buddies at least once a week to remind each other of homework and help each other work on their goals. You can discuss in group what it means to be a buddy and how to be a helpful buddy. You can switch the buddies around at regular intervals so that everyone gets to have a variety of buddies before the group sessions end. You may also want to encourage the use of the buddy system by offering rewards to those who use it!

### Icebreakers

Icebreakers are activities that quickly allow group members to get to know and feel comfortable with one another. Icebreakers are most important in the first session but you can do them throughout group sessions. The following provides some icebreaker ideas:

- *Interview your partner*: Encourage each student to interview the person sitting next to him or her and then introduce this person to the group.
- *I am famous*: Tape note cards with famous people's names written on them on each student's back and have the students go around the room and ask "yes" or "no" questions until they figure out whose name is on their back.
- *Stepping-stones*: Group members must devise a way to get from one area to another by utilizing stepping-stones (e.g., brown paper bags, carpet squares, newspapers) and by following these directions—You may only cross the "lava" with the magical stepping-stones; the stepping-stones only work when there is human contact with them at all times; and if any group member falls into the lava, the whole group must start over.

## PARENT GROUPS

### *Building and Sustaining Engagement*

Similar to the child group, it is important to engage parents at the very beginning of the group process. The following provides ideas for increasing member engagement, ensuring that all group members feel welcome, and see their participation in this group as meaningful.

### *Group Check-In*

One strategy to make the group content relevant is to allow parents time at the start of each session to briefly discuss their experiences and challenges since the last session. Group check-in can be a way to assess whether additional time needs to be spent on other issues or if the group can move forward with the planned agenda for the day. For example, a parent may come to the group late because he or she had a really difficult time getting a child dressed and ready for school. The parent may need some time to share his or her frustrations and gain support from parents who have similar challenges getting their children ready for school. It can be difficult to move forward with new material when a parent is frustrated and needs time to vent.

Announce the amount of time allotted for the check-in (e.g., first 10 minutes of the session). All parents should have an opportunity to share before moving on to other items on the agenda. Highlight the importance of sharing experiences and supporting one another to build group cohesion.

Sometimes parents need more time than the check-in allows. Group leaders will need to decide how to address problems as they arise within the group. At the end of this chapter there is a sample role play of how to handle a situation where a parent is monopolizing the group time by discussing an issue that occurred yesterday (see role play scenario 1 at the end of this chapter).

As discussed under "Child Groups," there are four possible ways to address a parent's problem at the start of the group while also ensuring that the group content is delivered as intended by the intervention developers:

- **Option 1:** Give the parent an opportunity to express his or her concerns for a few minutes and then ask if you could continue this discussion after the group. Move forward with the agenda for the day.

- **Option 2:** Have parents pair off and check in with each other for a small amount of time (3 minutes). Circulate around the room during this time to be sure any serious issues are addressed, either within the pair or individually with this parent after the session is over.

- **Option 3:** If you have a co-leader, have him or her meet with the parent one-on-one while the group moves on to reviewing the agenda for the day.

- **Option 4:** Connect the issues raised by the parent to the session's agenda. For example, if you are talking about problem solving, ask the parent if the group could use the frustrating incident to develop a list of possible solutions.

These options help ensure that the parent feels heard and supported, while simultaneously moving on with the planned content for that group session. You need to prevent a problem from taking over the group session while also addressing the issues of the group.

## Teaching Relaxation Strategies

Sometimes parents may come to sessions feeling overwhelmed with home assignments or their daily life stressors. If this is the case, you may want to teach some relaxation techniques. You could light candles and play calming music while taking parents through a muscle-relaxation or deep-breathing activity. You could also discuss using self-talk to reduce stress. For instance, parents could identify a statement to say to themselves when they are feeling overwhelmed or stressed (e.g., "I can do this"; "Calm down, it will be fine"). Then, when feeling overwhelmed during group, they can use the self-talk statement to calm down and continue with the session. It can also be fun to give parents a candle or soothing bath products that they can use at home to help them relax. Group members love to receive gifts and it will encourage them to practice relaxation at home. Group members who feel relaxed can more fully engage in the group process.

## Encouraging Group Participation

Encourage participation from all members of the group. Group discussion, active role plays, and homework are important components of group interventions. Some parents eagerly engage in these learning behaviors while others do not. You will want to make every member comfortable with the idea of participating. One way to do this is to use an icebreaker in the first session to help familiarize the parents with one another (see Table 7.1 for icebreaker ideas for adult groups). Have group members wear name tags and learn their names so that you can readily call on them. You may also want to have parents pair up with a buddy so they begin to get comfortable with each other. You can assign pairs, dividing up couples or family members so that they can meet new people. Allowing members time to build rapport with one another will decrease the discomfort of actively participating.

Be a little assertive in getting parents involved, but don't force anyone to do anything they don't want to do. You will want to have the right balance between encouraging some-

**TABLE 7.1. Adult Icebreaker Activities**

*Icebreaker 1:* Meet and Greet (15 minutes)

*Description:* Have group members turn to a parent they do not know. They then interview each other to find out what they do for a living, where they grew up, how many children they have, and other information of interest. Finally, each member introduces the other to the whole group, sharing the information he or she has learned.

*Icebreaker 2:* Three People

*Description:* Have each group member meet at least three other people in the group and find out one interesting fact about each of them.

*Icebreaker 3:* I Am Famous

*Description:* Write famous people's names on index cards and tape them on each parent's back. Have parents go around the room and ask "yes" or "no" questions until they figure out the name on their backs.

*Icebreaker 4:* Candy Color (15 minutes)

*Description:* Have group members each choose one Jolly Rancher (or another type of candy that has multiple color options). Ask each group member to go around and introduce him- or herself. Depending on what color Jolly Rancher group members have chosen, they are to respond to the following:
*If the parent chose red:* "What is one activity that you really enjoy doing with your child?"
*If the parent chose green:* "What is one movie your family could watch during a family movie night?"
*If the parent chose blue:* "What is one book that you really enjoy reading to your child?"
*If the parent chose purple:* "What is one game that your family could play during a family game night?"

*Icebreaker 5:* Family Strengths (10 minutes)

*Description:* Have the group members introduce themselves to the group and name one strength they think represents their family. Start by introducing yourself and then giving an example of a family strength (e.g., "I feel that my family communicates well by the way we can talk through issues and figure out the best way to solve problems and share feelings").

*Icebreaker 6:* What Makes Me Unique? (15 minutes)

*Description:* Ask group members to think of a unique quality or interesting fact about themselves (e.g., "I have a twin sister"; "I have five kids"; "I have gone skydiving"). Then have them write it down on an index card, not showing anyone. Shuffle the index cards and hand them back out to each group member. As you pass out the index cards, make sure that no one receives his or her own index card. If members do receive their own, give them another card and reshuffle theirs into the pile. Ask group members to move around the room introducing themselves to other group members and trying to find the person whose index card they have. Parents then introduce themselves to the whole group and share their interesting fact or quality.

---

one to do something and making someone do something! To make it more likely that everyone will participate, during group discussions you can:

- Call on a parent who is raising his or her hand. There are usually a few parents who will raise their hands so you may want to begin with them since they seem comfortable enough with the group to participate.
- Call on a parent who is not raising his or her hand. Be aware of the personalities in

the group. You do not want to scare someone who is not ready to participate. Remind parents that participation is completely voluntary but you would love to hear what they think!

- Respond to a facial expression or nonverbal communication from a parent. For instance, you may say, "Parent A, I noticed that you just smiled when parent B made that comment. Can you tell us what it was that made you smile?"
- Go around in a circle and allow each member to respond, making everyone aware that they are allowed to pass.
- Give stickers to group members who participate. Yes, even adults like stickers!
- Encourage parents to have fun in the group. You will want to model enthusiasm so that parents do not feel nervous or anxious about the role plays.

The following sections discuss three key areas that you may want to focus on when encouraging parents to participate.

## HOMEWORK

During each session, check in to see who has completed his or her homework. Have the parents who completed their homework share what they did at home and hand in the assignment. Have parents who did not complete their homework discuss the difficulties that got in the way of homework completion for that week. Elicit ideas from these and the other parents on how to complete the homework for this week.

It may be helpful to arrange parents in pairs to review their homework. If there are parents who did not complete their homework, pair them with a parent who did so that the noncompletor can get ideas for making time for homework. Encourage the completion of homework each week—that is how the parents practice techniques between sessions. Offering incentives such as candy or small toys to be given as gifts to their children are often helpful in encouraging parents to complete their homework.

## ROLE PLAYS

It is often difficult to get parents to volunteer for role plays, but one idea is to start by asking for volunteers. Explain that you will be there to assist them if they get stuck and that the group is here to learn, so there is no right or wrong way of doing the role play. If no one volunteers, choose someone from the group who is fairly outgoing and suggest that he or she help out in the role play:

> "Tishawna, you did an amazing job with your homework this week. I'd like to role-play this scenario with you as the parent and Deshawn as the child. Let's give Deshawn some direction on how to act as your child acted in this situation, while you act out exactly what you did while completing your homework. I'll be here to help out and pause us as needed."

Or:

"Maggie, I really like how you put that. You were specific and offered praise right when it was needed to keep your child on track. Come on up here and let's show the group how this simple specific praise statement can be used while playing with your child. I'll be the child and I want you to say the same praise statement that you just said while I play with these blocks."

During role plays the group leader can:

- Begin by doing the role play with the co-leader (if you have one). One group leader is the parent and one is the student.
- Before the role play is announced, say, "Devon, why don't you come up here with me?"

Then, just start getting the materials ready and announce what Devon will be doing for the role play. Sometimes it is easier for a parent to first play the role of a child. Often after the first role play other parents will feel more comfortable once they see how easy it is to participate. Here are some additional suggestions:

- Split the members into smaller groups and conduct smaller role plays where everyone has to take on a character.
- Provide direction by fully explaining what it is that the parent(s) will be acting out in the role play. You may also want to review key points and techniques and ask the parents to specifically try a technique that has been discussed.
- Make sure that you are close by the participant. If he or she gets stuck or you want the parent to try something else, you can whisper in his or her ear and offer advice.

Have a balance between challenging parents to try the role play and empathy for the fact that it is difficult to get up in front of peers and practice a new technique. During the role play, make sure you are ready to offer advice and prompts in a subtle, nonthreatening way. You may need to pause the role play to further clarify or highlight something important that came up. Be prepared to take the blame if the role play did not go as well as you would've liked. For example, ask a parent to use fewer questions and more descriptive comments during a role play in which she is playing with her child. If she then starts to ask many questions, you may say:

"Let me pause you for a second. I don't think I was very clear on the directions. That was my fault. Let's pretend that you are not allowed to ask any questions. Instead, use only descriptive comments about what your child is playing and how she is engaging with you. You can use this list of comments as a guide if you'd like."

Even if you felt like you were clear in stating the directions for the role play, group members may understand concepts and ideas in different ways. By taking the blame, you take the pressure off the parent, allowing him or her to feel more comfortable in trying again.

After each role play, thank the "actor(s)" for being brave enough to act out a scenario and use the techniques. You may want to encourage clapping so that the entire group joins in a round of applause. Consider giving parents who participate in role plays a small reward (e.g., sticker, candy, small gift). We use a small basket of treats, stickers, pencils, and pens that we hold out for parents to choose from after they complete the role play.

Then, offer feedback to the parents beginning with what they did really well. Ask the group what the participants did well. Allow the group members to praise the participants, but watch out for criticism! If you find a member being critical, you could say something like "Remember, we are starting with what they did well." Next, ask the parents in the group to add any other constructive feedback. You may want to clarify that constructive feedback is feedback in which you mention an area for improvement and add what they could do differently in a noncritical manner. Also, make sure the group is aware of the actors' feelings and how difficult it must be to get up in front of their peers. Be prepared to defend the parent actors if criticisms get too harsh. You may say something like:

> "Let's remember that it is really difficult to get up in front of a group of adults and practice a new technique, so when we are discussing the performance, let's make sure we are offering constructive feedback and that we are aware of parent A's feelings while doing so."

At the end of this chapter there is a sample role play on how to handle a situation where a group member criticizes another group member for his or her role play. It offers suggestions on how to protect the parent and increase the likelihood that he or she will engage in role plays in the future (see role-play scenario 2 at the end of this chapter).

You may also want to start a discussion about what would have happened if the parent in the role play had done something differently. You may say something such as "What would have happened if parent A [parent] decided to ignore parent B [child] in this role play? Do you think parent B [child] would have acted the same way?"

This offers another idea of how to act out a technique without making the actors feel uncomfortable or hurting their feelings.

It can also be helpful to have the parents reflect on how the "child" in the role play felt when the "parent" used a strategy. This helps the group think about how what they do as parents makes their children feel. Many parents find it very enlightening to think about how their behaviors impact their children. For instance, following a role play in which one parent practiced child-directed play with another group member, you could ask, "So, as the child, how did you feel when Candice was playing with you like that?" In response, the parent is likely to say that she felt important, and that her ideas were good.

## GROUP DISCUSSIONS

Try to have all group members actively participate. You will want to allow quieter group members the right to pass. However, you will also want to challenge them to participate and share their thoughts—for example: "Parent A, I noticed that you were nodding your head when you were listening to parent B's comments. Can you tell us what you were thinking when you were listening to parent B?"

For a parent who rarely participates, try approaching that parent before or after the group. Briefly share your observation that the person seems reluctant to participate and express your concerns in an empathic, respectful, and caring manner. Determine if there is a way to adapt the group process or your facilitation style to encourage the parent's participation. For example, the group leader may say:

"Monique, we really appreciate you coming to group every week and that you are always on time. We would love to have you share some of your great ideas and the wonderful things you do with Terrell at home. Do you feel comfortable participating in the group? Or is there anything we could do to make you feel more comfortable?"

At times, the simple act of talking with the parent and addressing the concern helps to alleviate his or her reluctance. Awareness of who is and is not actively participating in each session is a sign of good facilitation. Make a mental note about how each group member reacts to the group process. Various techniques can be used to engage the withdrawn parent during the session. For example, you can give the parent an administrative task such as passing out materials or acting as timekeeper for the session. Be sure to acknowledge even the slightest of comments made by a parent and follow up with the use of open-ended questions such as "What you just brought up is important. Tell us more about what you did."

If one parent is dominating the conversation, thank the participating parent for his or her ideas and input, and then direct attention to those who are not participating as much and try to get them involved—for example: "We have heard a lot of great ideas from you, parent B. Thank you for sharing those with us. Are there any other ideas that other group members want to share with us?"

When parents share great ideas the group leader may want to write them down on the board, praise, and give parents credit for their ideas. Consider rewarding the parent with a sticker, or naming the idea after the parent (e.g., Kelly's principle = We see more of what we pay attention to)—for example: "That is such an important concept, parent A. We are going to add your name and concept to our list of core ideas. Great thinking, parent A!"

If more than one parent is talking at a time, refer back to the rules and remind the parents to talk one at a time so that everyone is heard. As with child groups, you could use a talking stick (or other object). It can be passed from one group member to another, ensuring that only one person is talking at a time. After group discussions, thank all the parents for participating and have the group clap for themselves.

## Building Group Cohesion

Having a group in which parents are comfortable and connected to one another will increase engagement in the group and make it more likely that parents will be positive participants. Your role as group leader is to develop and support group cohesion. Some ideas for helping parents to feel comfortable, safe, and supported follow.

## Communication Systems

Establishing communication inside the group helps parents to feel connected with the group leader and the other group members. Just as suggested in the child groups, you may want to have a folder for each parent in the group, placed on his or her chair when parents enter the room for the session. Each parent can find his or her folder, get food and a drink (if offered), and take a seat. You can use the folders to assign seating. You can place important documents and other items you want to share with the parents (e.g., cards, notes, certificates) in the folder. You can provide the parents with specific feedback from the week before by placing a note in the folder about their successes and progress (see Appendix 22 for a sample Parent Encouragement Form). You may also want to track homework completion and progress on goals in the folder.

It is also a good idea to establish communication between group members and yourself outside of group sessions. One suggestion is to send a one-page newsletter home by mail or with the students that highlights relevant issues, common problems, and information that can be used in the home. You could send it at regular intervals (e.g., weekly, monthly, or every other month). You could send group members holiday cards and birthday cards. If you are interested in sending cards to individual group members, include a section on information sheets that solicits dates for birthdays and anniversaries and all contact information (i.e., phone, cell phone, work numbers, and addresses). You could announce birthdays or special occasions at the beginning of the sessions, if you've checked beforehand to ensure that group members are comfortable sharing this information with the group. Last, it can be helpful to send a "thank you" note to each parent who attended the group session that week and a "we missed you" note to those parents who were not able to attend the group (see Appendices 20 and 21 for a sample "Thank You" Note to Parent and a "We Missed You" Note to Parent).

## Buddy System

Another strategy for building group cohesion is to organize a parent buddy system; pair up members of the group to be buddies during the week. You could develop an activity that identifies similarities among group members and have parents pair up with each other based this activity. For example, parents could be paired based on their child's homeroom teacher.

Buddies can remind each other about group meetings, encourage each other to complete homework, try out new strategies, vent feelings of success and frustration, get clarification of a particular skill, and provide ongoing support. Encourage the buddies to communicate during the week with each other. The relationship could also lead to opportunities to carpool or share child care. Have group members write down contact information they are willing to share with each other during the first or second group session to facilitate the buddy system and a phone tree (see below). Once you have gathered this information, type it up and provide it to the members at the next group meeting.

## Phone Tree

You can develop a database with group member information (e.g., telephone number, address, child's homeroom, e-mail address) and organize a phone tree to pass along pertinent group information. The phone tree should be used to share information related to the group and other relevant school information. For instance, if a group has to be canceled at the last minute, the group leader could call the first parent on the phone tree and ask that parent to call the second parent and so on until all parents have been reached. Be sure that group members are comfortable with the information that is being shared. State that the information is for group member use only and should not be shared with individuals outside of the group. You and the co-leader need to share your information as well.

## Icebreakers

Icebreakers provide an opportunity for parents to learn about one another and become comfortable sharing in the group. To help group members get comfortable you may want to begin the group with an icebreaker that is not too difficult. You will want to use a simple icebreaker that allows the parents to meet one another and begin becoming comfortable with the group. You can do this throughout the group. However, it is most important to get the parents comfortable with one another at the start of the group. See Table 7.1 for a list of adult icebreaker activities.

## Social Activities

Finding ways for group members to interact socially can build group cohesion and provide additional support for parents. You could ask the group if they want to have a periodic social segment where refreshments can be shared (e.g., a potluck, baked goods, snacks and drinks). If a meal is routinely provided prior to group sessions, a special potluck dessert and coffee could be organized. Other possibilities include holiday celebrations, organizing an end-of-year party, celebrating birthdays or special occasions among group members, and a closing banquet with the presentation of certificates. Other friends and family could be invited to the banquet to celebrate the commitment and hard work of group members. During the banquet parents can be presented with awards for perfect group attendance or other group accomplishments.

In addition, you could encourage group members to plan activities independently outside of the group if interested. However, be cognizant that some group members could feel left out if cliques appear to form among group members. If this occurs, encourage the inclusion of everyone in activities outside of the group to the extent possible. Take aside clique members and have a discussion with them about the affect the clique may be having on the group, and facilitate the group in a way that ensures equal participation among all members.

# SUMMARY

The key to keeping group members coming to each session is developing and maintaining rapport, group cohesion, and group morale. This chapter provided suggestions for how to develop group cohesion and engage students and parents throughout the group process. As the group leader, it is important that you are not only enthusiastic about the group but that you also build rapport with every group member, making him or her feel safe and important within the group, and to celebrate group successes!

# MATERIALS

The following is a list of materials discussed in this chapter that can support you in engaging group members. You will find examples of most of these materials in the Appendices.

- "Thank You" Note to Parent (Appendix 20).
- "We Missed You" Note to Parent (Appendix 21).
- Parent Encouragement Form (Appendix 22).
- Goal Sheet (Appendix 25).
- Stickers.*
- Box of cards for birthdays and other events.*
- Postage.*
- Materials for newsletter.*
- Group folders.*
- List of potential icebreakers (Table 7.1).*
- Parent contact list used for buddy calls.*
- Talking piece (if needed for taking turns speaking).

# REFLECTION AND ROLE PLAYS

Here we provide a series of reflection exercises and role-play activities to help you further hone your group facilitation skills.

## *Reflection*

After reviewing this chapter, ask yourself the following questions:

1. "What strategies will I use to increase group member participation and engagement?"
2. "What can I do as a group leader to make sure group members feel included in the group?"

---

*These materials are not included in the Appendices, but may be referenced within this chapter and are also helpful when implementing parent and child groups.

## *Role Plays*

After reviewing the reflection questions, apply your understanding of what has been covered in this chapter by responding to the following two scenarios:

### Scenario 1

A parent is going on and on about an issue that occurred yesterday and is monopolizing the group time. Find a way to acknowledge the parent's feelings while keeping the group on track.

EXAMPLE SCRIPTED ANSWER

PARENT: I just couldn't wait to get to group today and tell you about what happened yesterday at my house. You wouldn't believe it. I came home from the store and I was in a great mood. I unpacked our groceries and my mother came in to tell me that the neighbor was asking to borrow our lawn mower last week. My mother, of course, told her she could use it and they apparently cut their lawn and put it back, and when my son went to use it this weekend, it wouldn't turn on. I was really angry because it had been working just fine prior to the neighbor's using it. So I went over there and told the neighbor. And you'll never guess what she said. She said, "Well, your son must have broken it when he went to turn it on because it worked fine when we were using it." I was fuming! She had no right to accuse my son and she probably broke it and was just hoping that someone in our family would use it soon so she could switch the blame to us.

GROUP LEADER: Wow! That sounds like a really frustrating situation.

PARENT: (*Interrupts.*) Yes. It was really annoying. Can you believe she had the nerve to accuse my son and not take any responsibility? I mean, does she really think that he broke it just from turning it on? I've lent things to her in the past and she always seems to return them in bad condition or not at all, and I have to go banging on her door to get them. I decided to not lend anything to her again and then my mother goes and lends out our lawn mower and goes against my rules again.

GROUP LEADER: It sounds like you made a good decision to think about lending items to her in the future and I'm sure that was frustrating to have your mother go against your wishes. Maybe we can talk about some ways to handle future instances with your neighbor and your mother after the group, but we have a pretty full agenda today so I want to make sure we cover everything. Would it be OK to review the agenda?

PARENT: Sure. Sorry, I was just venting!

GROUP LEADER: It's not a problem. Sometimes we need a little time to vent. We are actually going to talk a little bit about making sure that everyone is on the same team when setting rules with your children, so this may somewhat apply to other instances, too. (*Directs everyone's attention to the agenda and begins to review.*)

## TIP

Always try to empathize with the parent and allow a small amount of time to vent. Sometimes group leaders build that time into the beginning of the session while parents are getting settled. If you choose to do this, it is important to stick to the time allotted for settling into the group and to the agenda throughout the group. This will help to keep group members and yourself on-task!

## Scenario 2

A group member makes fun of another group member for doing something during a role play. How can you put an end to the teasing, protect the parent or child from feeling bad, and increase the likelihood that he or she and others will engage in role plays in the future?

### EXAMPLE SCRIPTED ANSWER

GROUP LEADER: OK, so it's time to practice using assertive techniques to get out of a tough peer pressure situation. You each have a scenario on your slip of paper that describes a peer pressure situation, and we have a list of assertive statements and techniques to use as a guide while acting out the situation. Marcus, it looks like I picked yours first. (*Smiles.*). Are you ready to use your Hollywood acting skills and be my acting assistant?

PARENT A (MARCUS): Sure. (*Agrees.*)

(*The group leader and student act out the role play using the list of assertive statements as a guide.*)

GROUP LEADER: Great job, Marcus! Let's give Marcus a round of applause for being our first actor of the day! And I really like how everyone else paid attention and was watching closely for how Marcus chose to get out of the peer pressure situation. Who can tell me which technique he used?

PARENT B: He used "Make a joke, use humor" to get out of the situation, but it was stupid and not funny.

GROUP LEADER: I just want to remind you all of our group rules that we are to be supportive of each other . . . it's difficult to get up in front of peers and act out a scenario and you will want the same support when you are up here. Marcus was very brave to go first and he chose one of the harder assertiveness techniques. So who can tell me in a supportive way, what statement Marcus chose to use?

PARENT B: He used "Make a joke, use humor" to get out of the situation.

GROUP LEADER: Yes. Excellent observation! Can anyone tell me something good he did with his eyes?

PARENT C: He kept his eyes on you.

GROUP LEADER: Yes! You are right, he had great eye contact. (*Processes role play some more.*).

GROUP LEADER: Thank you, Marcus, for acting out "Make a joke, use humor" perfectly, and thank you to our audience for paying attention to which assertiveness technique he used. You all make great detectives! OK. . . . let's see who's next?"

## TIP

If the group member who was the target of the teasing quickly reacts, stay calm and try to focus on the group rules and protecting the group member who was teased. The group leader in this mock role play chose to ignore the group member who made the comment and makes a general comment to the group while praising Marcus for being brave. If the teasing persists or if this does not "solve the problem," the group leader may want to take the two group members aside to discuss further while the co-leader continues with the group. If there is no co-leader, the group leader could ask to talk to both members after the group to discuss this further.

# CHAPTER 8

# Abuse, Neglect, Crisis Situations, and Suicidal Ideation

As group members begin to feel safer and more comfortable in the group setting, sensitive issues, such as suicidal ideation and abuse, can surface. These sensitive issues may not only affect your relationship with group members but they can also affect relationships among group members, challenging the group dynamics and process. If a group member shares an instance of abuse, this is not only difficult for the group member to share but it can also be traumatic for other group members. The group process will change for at least that session. Group leaders need to be able to handle such serious occurrences within the group setting while maintaining the group's integrity.

The purpose of this chapter is to make you consider in advance how to effectively handle situations such as disclosure of child abuse or neglect, suicidal thoughts, or a desire to harm someone. We provide examples of protocols for assessing and reporting suicidal ideation and disclosure of abuse in this chapter and in the Appendices, but you should also follow the policies and procedures outlined by your agency, school district, and state. Serious issues can arise within any group; preparing for them in advance is crucial.

## CHILD GROUPS

### *Abuse and Neglect*

Familiarize yourself with the definitions of abuse and neglect prior to beginning any group intervention. It is important that you (and your co-leader, if applicable) review the policies and procedures for reporting abuse and neglect in the state in which your group is being run. For instance, in many states, a group leader is required by law to report the incident within 24 hours of a disclosure.

> **Be familiar with the definitions, policies, and procedures for abuse and neglect in your state.**

As noted earlier, inform group members about the limits of confidentiality during the first group session. Revisit confidentiality and its limits in subsequent group sessions. This includes informing student group members that if they should disclose being physically harmed by an adult, you are required by law to report these disclosures. You may want to provide examples or use wording that students will understand, such as "If you tell me that an adult has done something to hurt you, then I will need to keep you safe by telling your family or another adult."

## Physical Punishment

Physical punishment is a discipline technique that has been used for generations across ethnic and socioeconomic groups. Do not be surprised if a group member discloses information about being physically punished. Families may be using this technique as a form of discipline. Physical punishment itself is not necessarily a form of abuse. It is important that you listen carefully to what is being disclosed. Many children use typically explosive language because that is the language their parents and other members of their community use. For example, parents may say they "beat" their children and students may report that they "got beat" last night. This term may lead you to conclude that abuse is taking place. However, the term "beat" is used freely by many to describe the act of physically hitting a child without the use of significant force that would result in some type of injury. If you are unsure, simply ask the student to describe what they mean by "got beat" last night. Don't assume. If a student reports something that you believe to be reportable, consult with your supervisor, co-leader, or other colleagues to determine whether the incident is indeed something that should be reported. When sharing information with colleagues, share only general information to determine the need for reporting, and only share this general information when necessary. See the next section if a report is warranted.

> **Inform group members about the limits of confidentiality during the first group session and revisit confidentiality and its limits in subsequent sessions.**

## Suspicion of Child Abuse and Neglect in Child Group

There are times when you may have a strong suspicion that child abuse or neglect is occurring, but the student has yet to disclose specific, clear information. In situations like this, you may want to have an individual session with the student and assess the situation further. You will want to remind the student of the confidentiality rule and its limits so that he or she is aware that you may have to report something if abuse or neglect is disclosed. You will not want the student to feel tricked into disclosing abuse or neglect. If the student describes a reportable incident, then tell him or her that you will need to share this information with other adults, but that you would like the child to be involved in these conversations. At a minimum, explain who you will be talking to and exactly what you will tell the person. The more that you can include the student, the better, so that he or she does not feel you are "telling on him or her" for disclosing the information.

## Reporting Abuse or Neglect

If you have received information that a student has been injured physically in some way, has been sexually abused, or that neglect is occurring at home, then action is needed. Be sure to speak individually with the student immediately after the group. Do not attempt to discuss the issues during the group. If there is a co-leader, you may want to take the student out of the group and meet individually while the co-leader continues with the group.

Carefully consider the information that has been shared with you prior to involving the parents. Depending on the circumstance and considering the safety and well-being of the student, you will want to involve the parent(s) to the greatest extent possible. In some instances, you may feel that reporting should be made without informing the parent beforehand. For instance, the abuse may involve the parent, be severe, and place the student in greater harm from the parent. However, we recommend involving the parent as much as possible if the collaborative relationship developed during the counseling process is to remain intact. You will want to inform the parents that you will need to report the disclosed incident. Have a frank discussion with them about the likely consequences associated with reporting the incident. If the parents are not directly involved in the abuse incident, you will want to inform them of what the student has shared with you. You may want to have the parents present when you call child protective services (CPS) and immediately provide them with information following the call.

If the parent was involved in the incident, it can be helpful to have him or her make the call to CPS while you are present. Be sure to talk to the agency yourself, expressing concerns about the incident and providing the necessary information, including information about the student being in the group and whether or not you have an ongoing counseling relationship with the parent (i.e., parent group). If the parents are not comfortable making the call, make the call in their presence and provide them with immediate feedback as to the result of the call.

You will also want to let the school principal and other relevant individuals know that you've reported an incident. There could be police involvement at the school (e.g., the police may come to the school to question the student). However, be cautious about what is disclosed; only relevant individuals need to be made aware of the overall situation. Share with others only what they absolutely need to know to keep the student safe.

## Crisis Management

Students occasionally may experience a personal crisis and are not able to benefit from the group. For example, the student may have a serious health problem, a death in the family, substance abuse in the family, divorce, or marital problems in the family. Students may become more oppositional or withdrawn because of such serious issues going on outside of the group. It would be appropriate to offer empathic statements such as "It sounds like a difficult situation and I'm proud of you for attending the group, even though you are going through this tough time."

These problems may require more intense intervention than can be provided at the group level. You may need to assess whether this student is still appropriate for the group setting and determine if you can provide more intensive services or choose to refer the student to an outside mental health agency. Think about having individual or family sessions with the student separate from the group. Ask the student if it would be OK to bring his or her parent into an individual session. A phone call can be made to the student's parent to discuss a meeting date and time. During the family meeting you may want to discuss the student's group progress and the difficulties that are occurring in the group. During this time you may want to discuss alternative counseling options and provide referrals for service. See Table 8.1, which provides strategies for recognizing and responding to students in crisis.

## Preparing a List of Referral Resources

An effective group leader will expect that crises will arise during group interventions (i.e., "being a fortune-teller") and be prepared with a comprehensive, up-to-date list of community resources. Prepare a list of referral resources prior to beginning any groups. Be sure that all phone numbers are accurate; do not give out phone numbers to referral resources that you have not contacted yourself. If you do not currently have access to a referral list, talk to other clinicians at the school, in your agency, or community to see if they have access to resources. You can also utilize the Substance Abuse and Mental Health Services Administration (SAMHSA) Behavioral Health Treatment Services Locator, discussed in greater detail later in this chapter. Your agency or school district may have already developed a list of resources. You can search the Internet for potential referral resources; some areas have help lines that you and families can access to determine appropriate referral services. Referral resources can also be obtained by calling the parents' insurance provider. In fact, for families that have an insurance provider we have often had them pull out their insurance cards and call the number on the back to request the names of agencies that are covered for the needed services. You can offer to contact the referral for the

**TABLE 8.1. Handling Crisis Situations**

- *Crisis cues.* A number of cues can help you identify group members in need of more intense services or outside referrals. They may approach you either before, during, or after the group about a serious personal problem. You may notice changes in the way a student interacts with the group (i.e., withdrawing, teasing other group members, becoming more oppositional, etc.). If the student is giving cues during a group session that are disruptive to the group process and the goals for that day, then it will be necessary to intervene.

- *Disclosure of crisis circumstance.* If the student discloses information pertaining to a crisis occurring outside of the group, support the group member. Make a supportive and empathic statement that acknowledges the difficulty of the situation and offer individual attention after the group is over. If this happens during the session, redirect the group to the agenda and the task at hand. If the student persists, tell him or her you can meet after the group to discuss this further. (If a co-leader is present, you or the co-leader can meet with the student individually while the group continues.) You may also want to make a statement to the group about how difficult it is to come to school to learn while difficult situations are occurring at home.

parent or to be present while the parent makes the call. This helps make the process less intimidating for the family member and may make it more likely that the resource will be utilized by the family.

## Suicidal Ideation

A student may discuss thoughts of suicide during a group session. It is your duty to follow all safety precautions and assess whether the student is at imminent risk of suicide. Depending on the seriousness of the statement and the student's intent, you may need to stop the group and send the other group members back to class. If a co-leader is present, he or she can run the group while you further assess the student. Group members may be scared, upset, or confused. If a co-leader remains with the group, he or she can facilitate further discussion and process members' feelings and thoughts surrounding the suicidal statement, or you can process it with the group later. The top priority is to make sure the student who made the suicidal statement is safe.

You will want to assess whether there is imminent danger of suicide. Find out if the student has a *plan* (e.g., when, where, how), if the student has *access to the method* described (e.g., pills, weapon), and if the student has *intent* to complete the plan (see Appendix 28 for a sample Suicide Assessment Form). Note that the protocol below and the assessment form in the Appendices are valid but basic suicidal assessments. More intensive assessments and protocols for assessing suicidal ideation are available for use by mental health clinicians or other qualified professionals. If you do not feel qualified to make the assessment, seek assistance from a mental health clinician or other qualified professional.

If you assess there is an *imminent danger* (e.g., student has a plan, has access to the method described, and has intent to complete the plan), seek immediate assistance through hospitalization. Be familiar with the procedures at the hospitals in the surrounding locale so that you can quickly and efficiently get the student the help he or she needs. For example, you will want to know the names and phone numbers of the local hospitals. We recommend that you consult with your supervisor, colleagues, or other mental health professionals to be sure you are following the appropriate policies and protocols for your agency, school district, and state. An example protocol is provided in Table 8.2.

> **If a student reports thoughts of suicide, it is your duty to follow all safety precautions and assess whether the student is at imminent risk of suicide.**

If the *danger is not imminent,* a first step is to have the student sign a safety contract (see Appendix 29 for a sample Safety Contract). Next steps include notifying parents, notifying the teacher and principal, continuing to meet with the student individually, and assessing whether more intense services are needed (e.g., day program, crisis response unit). An example protocol in Table 8.3 covers these steps in more detail. As you or another counselor continue to meet with the student, it is important to assess the student's suicide risk level on an ongoing basis. For example, over the next few weeks following the first incident, a "check-in/check-out" procedure may be utilized to determine whether the student is safe and the suicidal thoughts have subsided.

**TABLE 8.2. Example Protocol after Imminent Suicide Risk Assessment**

- *Make sure the child is safe and being watched at all times!* If you are making the plans for keeping this child safe, have another adult in the room to watch the child. The main goal is to keep the child safe at all times. Someone should meet with the child and review a safety contract (see Appendix 29 for a sample Safety Contract). Ensure that the child understands the contract, and have him or her sign it.

- *Contact the parents or guardians.* Notify the parents about what happened, explain your concern and plan of action, and recommend that the parents take the child to the hospital emergency room. You can ask the parents to meet you at the school (or location of the group). If you cannot get in touch with the parents, leave a message for the parents to call you, and then call the school police or 911.

  *Note:* Share details of the situation with the parents in the event that they are not aware of it or its severity. Also, talk with the parents about ways to keep the child safe at home and to monitor the child. For example, if the child states that he or she plans to use a kitchen knife to hurt him- or herself or others, share this with the parents and develop a plan to remove all knives from the home.

- *Contact the principal and mental health counselor (if applicable).* Make sure the principal is aware of the situation. This is particularly important if a police car or other emergency vehicle is coming to the school. Tell the principal briefly what happened and the protocol that is in place. Also contact any counselors who are involved in this child's case. If the counselor is off-site, make sure to contact him or her once the child is safely at the hospital.

- *Inform classroom teachers and school staff (if applicable).* It may be helpful to inform the student's teacher(s) or other school staff about how they can help support the child in the classroom. As an example, if a child is homicidal or suicidal and exhibits disruptive or aggressive behavior due to being bullied, make sure the teacher and staff are aware of the bullying and how it is triggering the student's behavior. The teacher and staff can monitor the students accused of bullying.

- *Once parents or police arrive, recommend that the parents take the child to the hospital emergency room.* If you are willing, offer to follow in your own car. If the parents are not available and you called the police, explain the suicidal ideation and assessment to the police and have them take the child to the nearest hospital emergency room. It is helpful if you follow the police in your own car. Continue to try to get in touch with the parents.

- *Call the hospital emergency room if time permits.* If there is waiting time (e.g., waiting for the parents to arrive at the group location), it is helpful to call ahead to the hospital emergency room, give background information, and let them know you are on your way.

- *Bring case information (if accessible) and document everything!* If the group leader is also the clinician, gather important information, such as suicidal ideation assessment, recent case notes, and a psychological evaluation if it's recent and accessible. If there is time, you could also type a one-page summary of the child's current treatment, diagnoses, and the specific behavior that resulted in the child being sent to the hospital. Include specific examples of suicidal ideations or statements. This is helpful to the hospital in the event that the child or parents do not share this information. Make sure you document everything that happens. If you are unable to go to the hospital emergency room, make sure you follow up with the parents to make sure services are in place.

- *Hospital staff makes a decision.* At this point, the hospital staff will review the case and make a decision as to whether the child needs to be hospitalized or if another course of action is better. If the student is not admitted to the hospital or if there are no beds available, the hospital staff and group leader may want to discuss other appropriate options, such as a day hospital, crisis counseling, wraparound services, and individual or family counseling at school or in the community. The hospital can assist in locating these programs, but it is also helpful if the group leader is knowledgeable about such programs in the area.

- *Provide referrals.* Once the child is discharged from the hospital, the group leader can provide referrals for the family. The group leader will want to work with the hospital staff and if possible, obtain copies of any evaluations and the discharge summary. This information can help the child transition back to the group and school.

*Note.* Remember to review the policies and procedures outlined by your school district, agency, and state, as these take precedence over what is offered as an example here.

## TABLE 8.3. Example Protocol after Nonimminent Suicide Risk Assessment

- *Sign a no-suicide contract.* A contract should be signed between the leader and the student that identifies three people the student can talk to if he or she feels upset (e.g., depressed, angry) or thinks about harming him- or herself or others. The contract should also state that the student will call 911 or a crisis hotline number if the three people cannot be contacted. The last sentence should read, "By signing this contract I promise not to hurt myself." Remind the student that you have to discuss this with his or her parents because that is one of your duties as the group leader. Remind the student about the limits to confidentiality. You may want to say something such as "Remember when we created our group rules and we discussed that everything that we say in group stays in group? Well, do you remember what I said about when I would have to break this rule in order to protect your safety?" Hopefully, the student will remember the limit to confidentiality, but if not, remind him or her of this rule, explaining it carefully so that the student does not feel threatened by you sharing this information with his or her parents. (See Appendix 29 for a sample Safety Contract.) Emphasize that you are doing this because you care about the student and want to keep him or her safe!

- *Contact the parents.* Notify the parents of the situation, and explain your concern and plan of action. Make sure the parents are aware of the situation. Give the parents information about what to do if their student is suicidal, such as calling a crisis hotline number or 911. Discuss possible options to treatment and offer brochures and handouts about suicide. Also, make sure the parents are aware of the signed contract, and know the three people who the student chose to talk to if he or she has suicidal thoughts again.

  *Note:* Share details with the parents in the event that they are not aware of the situation or the severity of the situation. Also, talk with the parents about ways to keep the student safe at home and monitor the student. For example, if the student thinks about using a kitchen knife to hurt him- or herself or others, share this with the parents and develop a plan to remove all knives from the home.

- *Notify the teacher and principal (if applicable).* It may be helpful to inform the student's teacher(s) or other school staff about how to support the student in the classroom and at school. For example, if a student is homicidal or suicidal and exhibits disruptive or aggressive behavior due to being bullied, make sure the teacher and staff are aware of the bullying and how it triggers the student's behavior so that the teacher and staff can monitor the students accused of bullying.

- *Contact the student's counselor.* If you are not the student's counselor and the student has one, contact the counselor and notify him or her of the situation. You can ask the counselor what type of activities or techniques may be helpful and practice these with the student. The student's group and individual counseling should be consistent and not contradict each other. With increased repetition and practice, the student is more likely to use the skills.

  If you are also the student's counselor, continue individual counseling over the next few weeks. You will want to introduce evidence-based skills and techniques to treat a case of this nature and continue to assess for suicidal ideation. For example, you may want to develop a "check-in/check-out" system with the student for at least the first week. The student may enjoy this additional attention and it is an opportunity to reiterate that you care about the student, as well as confirm that he or she is safe (e.g., Is the student still able to keep his or her promise about not hurting him- or herself or others today?). During these next few weeks, the group leader should also continue to assess for suicide ideation. Furthermore, you may develop a plan to give the student a "pass" to leave class and talk to an adult he or she identified in advance, in the building, if he or she is having thoughts of self-harm during the school day. The student should be praised for communicating and expressing feelings to the identified adult.

*Note.* Remember to review the policies and procedures outlined by your school district, agency, and state, as these take precedence over what is offered as an example here.

After an initial suicidal threat has been assessed as "not imminent," more intensive services may be needed if:

- The student continues to report having suicidal thoughts.
- The student remains distressed following repeated attempts by you and other adults to be helpful.
- The student becomes increasingly isolated, unkempt, irritable, or disconnected.
- The student's behavior reflects increased hopelessness.
- The student withdraws from treatment within your setting.
- You feel your services as a counselor or group leader are no longer helping the student.

It is also helpful to discuss future treatment with a supervisor to best plan for services for the student. At the end of this chapter is a sample role play on processing a suicidal assessment of a child with a supervisor based on what was reported in a group session (see role-play scenarios 1 and 2 at the end of this chapter).

If more intensive services are not needed and services continue within the school setting, it is crucial to keep lines of communication open with the parent, counselor (if it is not you), and the teacher. Staying in touch with the parent can assist you in making a plan for the student's future course of treatment. It is helpful to know if anything is happening at home and whether the suicidal thoughts are happening outside of school. If you are not the student's primary counselor, you will want to stay in close communication with the counselor, especially if the student is continuing in the group setting. Also, stay in close contact with the teacher to be aware of events happening within the classroom and to develop a plan if the student needs immediate attention or a break from a stressful situation. For instance, you may develop a plan to offer the student a "pass" to leave class to talk to a specific adult in the building if the student is having thoughts of self-harm during the school day. Have plans like this in place prior to another incident.

## Essential Resources for Assessing Suicidal Ideation and Further Treatment Options

In this section, we offer a selection of Internet-based resources for learning more about assessing and treating suicidal ideation. Remember to review the policies and procedures outlined by your agency, school district, and state, as they may be able to provide resources specific to the locale in which you practice.

The *National Association of School Psychologists* (NASP) is committed to working to prevent suicidal behavior of children and youth within the school setting. There are many resources on their website (*www.nasponline.org/resources-and-publications/resources/school-safety-and-crisis*) for preventing suicide, determining risk factors, assessing for suicide, and providing appropriate treatment. The website also offers a section of handouts for parents and educators along with articles for principals that can assist in the prevention and treatment of suicide in the school setting. And finally, NASP offers a list of programs and support for counselors working with students who experience suicidal thoughts.

The *National Suicide Prevention Lifeline* (*www.suicidepreventionlifeline.org*) is a wonderful resource that can be offered to students when they are not within the school setting. For instance, this lifeline phone number (1-800-273-8255) can be written into a contract between the student and the counselor to help ensure that the student is safe at home and in school when not in the presence of adults. Having multiple courses of action that a student can follow when not in the presence of an adult is essential when planning for the student's continued safety. Also included on this website is pertinent information on getting help, to be used by the student with Internet access, if age appropriate. It can also be used by a counselor, group leader, or other adult when offering services to a student who has had or is having suicidal ideations. It offers suicide prevention resources, crisis center information, and best practices for assessing suicide risk.

Another helpful suicide prevention resource is the *Suicide Awareness/Voices of Education* (SAVE) website (*www.save.org*). It offers information on prevention, intervention following a suicide or suicide attempt, coping, and depression. The website is geared toward older students. However, it can be utilized by counselors, group leaders, and other adults when working with suicidal students or students in distress. Printable handouts, booklets, and brochures are offered, as well as links to other suicide prevention websites.

The *Suicide Prevention Resource Center* (SPRC) offers an abundance of resources for counselors, group leaders, and other adults when working with students and preventing suicide within the school setting and other settings (*www.sprc.org*). Links to important articles and other library resources, the Best Practices Registry, and suicidal prevention basics are offered within the site and can assist adults who work with suicidal or distressed students.

Last, the *Substance Abuse and Mental Health Services Administration* (SAMHSA) offers a Behavioral Health Treatment Services Locator (*www.findtreatment.samhsa.gov*) where one can search more than 8,000 mental health treatment facilities and programs. This can be utilized by counselors, group leaders, and other adults when trying to locate more intensive services for a student outside of the group setting. Once a location is selected, the locator lists the facility name, address, and phone, as well as provides a summary of the services offered within this facility.

The resources listed here are just a few of the more easily accessible resources available in the ever growing field of suicide prevention.

## Processing after a Group Member Leaves/Is Taken Out of the Group

If a group member leaves or is removed from a group, you will want to make sure you process this with the remaining group members. If the student needed to be removed from the group, you will want to explain why this happened and whether the removed member will be offered the chance to return or has permanently left the group. If a group member transfers schools, leaves voluntarily, or is taken out of the group by a parent, you will also want to process this with the group members and explain what it will mean for the group.

The group leader may want to say something like "As you all know, Dylan is transferring to another school and we will be losing him as a group member. I wanted to make sure we talk about this change and share any thoughts or feelings about Dylan leaving."

In discussions with the group members, you will also want to think about whether it is appropriate to add another member to the group or leave the group as is. Every group member should have a chance to process the situation and share feelings.

# PARENT GROUPS

The topics of abuse, neglect, and other crises can be extremely difficult for leaders to manage within parent groups. Prepare ahead of time for these topics to come up so you know how you will address them. Furthermore, always consult a supervisor or colleague if an issue arises and you are unsure of how to handle it. You can always reschedule the content of a group session, if need be, to address a situation that occurs within the group.

As noted earlier, inform group members about the limits of confidentiality during the first group session. Revisit confidentiality and its limits in subsequent group sessions. This includes informing the group members of possible scenarios in which you would be obligated to report suspected abuse, and what you would need to do if a person discloses thoughts of suicide or harming others. This can be done in a nonthreatening and transparent manner that indicates you are supportive and collaborative in nature.

## Abuse and Neglect

### Physical Punishment

The use of physical punishment as a behavior management strategy may be a topic that comes up. Many evidence-based parenting support programs directly discuss the use of physical punishment and alternative strategies (e.g., The Incredible Years Parenting Programs). The use of physical punishment as a discipline technique is not a method advocated by current parenting groups. However, it is likely that some parents may be using this technique as a primary form of discipline. You will want to revisit confidentiality and its limits when discussing "spanking," "physical punishment," and time-out. Clearly define what constitutes abuse and neglect. Inform parents that if they disclose information about physical abuse or neglect, you are required by law to report such incidents. Many parents are unaware of the laws and what is reportable. Use the group to educate parents about these issues. If you discuss the use of corporal punishment without reminding parents of your duty to report, you may find yourself in a difficult situation and reporting a lot of experiences to CPS. As mentioned under "Child Groups," many parents describe what they do to their children by using language such as "beating," "whooping," or "knocking around." However, these terms may be used by many parents to describe the act of physically hitting a child without significant force that would result in injury. If you are unsure, simply ask the parent to describe what he or she means by "giving my child a beating." Don't assume. If a parent then reports something that you believe to be reportable, consult with the co-leader, a supervisor, or other colleague for clarification and agreement if needed.

## Time-Out versus Spanking

Be prepared to facilitate a healthy discussion regarding physical punishment and to effectively present alternative discipline methods for parents to consider. You will want to make parents feel comfortable talking about their experiences with spanking. Child discipline is a sensitive and personal subject. However, discussion is beneficial and helps parents realize that there are ways to discipline a child besides physical punishment. The parents cannot learn about the pros and cons of each technique if the group leader avoids or tiptoes around the subject. The group leader may want to say something like:

> "We are now going to discuss the pros and cons of 'time-out' versus 'spanking.' I want to remind everyone that what is said here is confidential, but I am obligated to report instances of abuse. However, I want everyone to feel comfortable discussing this topic. I will give you some examples of when I would have to report something to child protective services. But, first let's discuss ways that we can feel comfortable sharing personal experiences while staying within the confidentiality and nonreportable guidelines."

The group leader will then begin trying to elicit ideas from the parents (e.g., using the term "spanking" instead of "beating," keeping references general as in "some parents"). The group leader may also want to let all parents know that this is a sensitive subject and if any parent feels that he or she has something to report or discuss further, he or she can meet with you individually.

Parents who have relied upon corporal punishment, such as spanking, for a long time may be resistant to the idea of trying something new. In keeping with the collaborative model, as the group leader you will need to explore and problem solve the reasons for the parent's viewpoint in a respectful and nonjudgmental way. Listen carefully and understand parents' preference for spanking as legitimate. You will want to explore and problem solve the reasons for this viewpoint with nonjudgmental questions such as:

> "How does your child feel about it?"
> "How does it affect your relationship?"
> "Do you ever feel you lose control when you spank?"
> "What do you see as its advantages?"
> "Are there any disadvantages?"
> "How did it affect your relationship with your parent when you were spanked as a child?"

You may be tempted to engage in a one-on-one dialogue with the parent who first speaks about physical punishment. However, a discussion that engages all group members will be much more powerful. Parent feelings will be validated and you will be able to better assess the most productive avenue for discussion.

Explain the alternative approach, time-out, and ask questions similar to those for spanking: "What don't you like about it?"; "What are its disadvantages?"; and "Are there any advantages?"

Notice that the questions are open-ended and in the form of "What do you think?" or "How does your child feel?" rather than "Why not?" These questions serve to clarify the parent's feelings, thoughts, and experiences surrounding any resistance, and to facilitate problem solving and collaboration.

This topic tends to quickly draw everyone into the debate. It is helpful to organize the discussion by listing the advantages and disadvantages, and short- and long-term consequences for the child and parent, on a whiteboard, large poster paper, or blackboard. At the end of this discussion, you can summarize all the ideas that have been generated, clarify misperceptions, and add your own interpretations if they have not already been covered. Some points you can present are listed in Table 8.4.

> Asking parents open-ended questions about the issue can help to clarify their feelings, thoughts, and experiences surrounding the resistance and can facilitate problem solving and collaboration.

Following the discussion, invite the parents to consider a short experiment during which they try time-out, keep records, and discuss and evaluate the experience with the group. Do not address any parent's continuing skepticism or resistance by direct confrontation or lecture on why time-out is right and the parent is wrong to use spanking. Rather, engage in a process of gentle persuasion through open, honest communication. Explore the reasons for the resistance, followed by looking at the advantages and disadvantages of spanking versus time-out. This is a values-

**TABLE 8.4. Example of Discussion with Parents about Physical Punishment versus Time-Out**

| Spanking/physical punishment | Time-out |
| --- | --- |
| Quick; may get short-term gain. | Long term, future oriented. |
| Child may externalize blame to the parent rather than focus on his or her own behavior. | The child is more likely to develop an internal sense of conscience (he or she has to deal with his or her behavior during time-out). |
| Models hitting and violence. | Models self-control. |
| The child feels pain. | The child may be upset, but there is no physical pain. |
| The child could get hurt. | The child does not need to feel pain for consequences to be effective. |
| It could get out of hand if the parent is too upset. | It allows the parent and child to "cool off." |
| The child may not understand the reason behind being spanked. The child may begin to think that whenever the parent is mad, Mom or Dad may "hit," which in turn may cause the child to do this in similar situations when he or she is mad. | The child will understand why he or she is in time-out if a clear and specific explanation is given (e.g., "You just hit your sister and broke one of our family rules. You will now need to go to time-out"). |

clarification and problem-solving exercise that helps clarify feelings and experiences surrounding the issue. This joining strategy is more likely to result in a gradual change in parents' perceptions and behaviors, especially if conducted in the context of a supportive relationship. Ideally, you want the parents to come to the conclusion themselves that time-out is a better choice. Get parents to tell you the reasons that may sway them. For instance, you may ask them, "What are some reasons to use time-out rather than spanking?"

Be careful not to judge or criticize parents who spank their child. This could cause parents to feel uncomfortable sharing and be less honest in future discussions. The overall goal is to increase the number of tools in the parent's tool kit and improve the likelihood that they will use more positive parenting strategies (e.g., praise, positive reinforcement) and less negative and punitive strategies (e.g., spanking). At the end of this chapter there is a sample role play on how to have a discussion with the group about the pros and cons of physical punishment versus time-out (see role-play scenario 3 at the end of this chapter).

> **The overall goal is to increase the number of tools in the parents' tool kit and improve the likelihood that they will use more positive parenting strategies (e.g., praise, positive reinforcement) and less negative and punitive strategies (e.g., spanking).**

## Suspicion of Child Abuse and Neglect in Parent Group

Parents should feel safe to speak freely without the fear that they will be reported to CPS. However, a situation may arise where you have a strong suspicion of abuse or neglect but there has not been clear parental disclosure. This situation may require your action. Review your agency, school district, and state policies and procedures for reporting abuse and neglect. *In many states, you are required by law to report the incident within 24 hours of the disclosure.*

If you receive information that a child has been injured physically in some way by the use of physical punishment, is being sexually abused, or neglected, you will need to take immediate action. Be sure to speak with the parent immediately after the group. Do not attempt to discuss the issues during group (see role-play scenario 4 at the end of this chapter).

## Involving Parents When Reporting Abuse or Neglect

Depending on the seriousness of the situation, use the following guidelines for reporting abuse or neglect. As with child groups, we recommend involving the parents so that the collaborative relationship developed during group can remain intact.

1. Inform the parent that you will need to report the disclosed incident.
2. Have a frank discussion with parents about the likely consequences of reporting the incident.
3. If possible, have the parent make the call to CPS while in your presence. Be sure that you talk to the agency yourself, express any concerns about the incident, and provide information about the frequency with which the parent attends group sessions.

4. If the parent is not comfortable making the call, make the call in his or her presence and provide the parent with immediate feedback as to the result of the call.

5. Involve the principal as necessary, such as if the police will be coming to the school to question the parent or child. Be cautious about what you disclose; make only the principal or other relevant school personnel aware of the overall situation.

## Crisis Management

Occasionally, a parent may be experiencing a serious personal crisis (health problems, loss of job, death in the family, marital problems, substance abuse) that compromises their ability to participate in the group. A parent could be too uncomfortable with the group setting to participate fully, or their child may require more intense outside intervention. If situations such as these arise, a referral to the school or community-based organizations may be appropriate. Referral sources can include school psychologists, counselors, or social workers; community agencies; physicians; or mental health clinics.

### Utilizing Outside Referrals and Resources

A number of cues can help you identify parents in need of outside referrals. They may approach you before or after the group and disclose information about difficult circumstances. You may see a noticeable change in the way the parents interact with the group (i.e., withdrawing or becoming curt or harsh with other group members). If a parent's behavior is disruptive to the group process and the session's goals, it will be necessary to intervene. For example, a parent may repeatedly bring up his or her marital problems during the group. Support the parent by making a supportive and empathetic statement that acknowledges the difficulty of the situation. It will then be necessary to redirect the group as a whole to the agenda and task at hand. If the parent persists in discussing the situation, tell him or her you have some ideas that may help and ask to discuss them briefly during the break or after the session. This would also be a golden opportunity to make a global statement to the group about how difficult it is to be an effective family member and parent.

At the break or after the session, engage briefly in small talk to put the parent at ease, and then bring up the referral in a nonthreatening manner: "Have you ever thought about counseling?"; "Here, in the community, there are a number of good agencies that I can give you information about."

Have a comprehensive and up-to-date list of referral resources readily available as described earlier for child groups. Make sure any phone numbers are current; you don't want to give out incorrect information to a family member during a time of crisis. You can also utilize the SAMHSA Behavioral Health Treatment Services Locator (discussed earlier in this chapter). Parents with insurance coverage can be encouraged to contact their provider for referrals to needed services. It is always a good idea to offer to contact the referral for the parent or to be present while the parent makes the call. This may make it more likely that the resource will be utilized by the family.

## *Dealing with Parents under the Influence of Alcohol or Drugs*

A parent may come to the group session obviously under the influence of alcohol or drugs and not be able to participate in an effective way. He or she may not be able to speak clearly or coherently, smell strongly of alcohol, have trouble with motor control, and be disruptive to the group. You will need to address this with the parent but it is a difficult situation because the intoxicated parent may not be in a position to appreciate a discussion about this disruption of the group process. Still, if the parent is highly disruptive and does not respond to your attempts to redirect this, you may need to take a break and speak with the parent privately. You may need to ask the parent to leave the group in a nonjudgmental manner by saying something such as:

> "The fact that you are here tonight tells me that you really care about your children. I would like you to continue with us next session and take the rest of this evening off. I am concerned that you may not be able to benefit from the group tonight. I will contact you during the week to talk more so that we can figure out a way for you to be able to join us next time."

Make sure that the parent does not drive him- or herself home. Call a taxi or help arrange for a friend or family member to take the parent home. When contacting the parent during the week, begin with supportive statements such as "I am calling you as I said I would because I'd really like for you to be a part of the group. I was concerned during the last session that you may not have been able to benefit from the group."

Allow the parent to reply. If the parent does not offer any information, continue with nonaccusatory probes:

> "You seemed rather disoriented and I was concerned that you might be experiencing health or other problems. [Again, allow the parent time to respond.] If you do feel that you are in need of assistance, there are good agencies here in the community that I can give you information about. . . . I would like for you to join the group next week . . . between now and then I encourage you to contact the agencies we talked about [or, if the parent did not want the information], or to take some time to think this over. . . . If you would like to talk about this further, please let me know."

If this parent comes to the group intoxicated again, it would be necessary to have a more direct conversation about the parent's substance use, and how it affects the group. You may want to develop a behavioral contract with the parent in which he

**Be sure the parent does not drive him- or herself home. Call a cab or help arrange for a friend or family member to take the parent home.**

or she agrees to come to the group sober. Make it clear that the parent may not be able to attend the group in the future if he or she arrives under the influence of substances. Circumstances may appear extreme enough that as the group leader you may feel the parent should not return to the group until certain issues are resolved (e.g., the parent seeks treatment for substance abuse). It is up to the group leader's discretion and the safety of the group and its members.

## SUMMARY

This chapter provided information on how to deal with potentially sensitive process issues, such as crises, suicidal ideation, and disclosure of abuse. While we offer an example of a protocol for assessing and reporting suicidal ideation and disclosure of abuse, make sure you follow the policies and procedures outlined by your agency, school district, and state. These take precedence.

## MATERIALS

The following is a list of materials discussed in this chapter that can support you in handling crises and other sensitive process issues within your groups. You will find examples of most of these materials in the Appendices.

- Suicide Assessment Form (Appendix 28).
- Safety Contract (Appendix 29).
- List of suicide and abuse hotline numbers.*

## REFLECTION AND ROLE PLAYS

Here we provide a series of reflection exercises and role-play activities to help you further hone your group facilitation skills.

### *Reflection*

After reviewing this chapter, ask yourself the following questions:

1. "Do I know the current procedure for reporting incidents of abuse and neglect in my state? How can I maintain a relationship with the parent if I have to make a report?"
2. "What is my plan of action if a parent or a child discloses physical abuse within the group? How will I appropriately handle the situation while maintaining group cohesion?"
3. "How would I handle a group member who came to the session intoxicated? How would I process this with the intoxicated group member at a later time?"

---

*These materials are not included in the Appendices, but may be referenced within this chapter and are also helpful when implementing parent and child groups.

## *Role Plays*

After reviewing the reflection questions, apply your understanding of what has been covered in this chapter by responding to the following four scenarios:

### Scenario 1

During a child group discussion on coping thoughts and what students think about when they are really angry, a student reports, "I get so mad that I just want to kill myself." Discuss how you would follow up with the student after the group session is over regarding these self-harm statements.

EXAMPLE SCRIPTED ANSWER

GROUP LEADER: Can I talk to you for a minute after group?

STUDENT: Sure.

GROUP LEADER: I wanted to check in with you about the comment that you made in group that you sometimes get so angry that you want to kill yourself. When do you think these thoughts?

STUDENT: Sometimes when the boys are messing with me, hitting me in the back of the head. I get so mad and I think I just want to die.

GROUP LEADER: That must be really hard. I am sorry to hear that they are being so mean to you. When is the last time you had that thought?

STUDENT: Last week, when the boys were messing with me on the playground.

GROUP LEADER: Have you ever thought about how you would hurt yourself?

STUDENT: I sometimes think I would just jump off of the school building.

GROUP LEADER: How would you jump off the school building?

STUDENT: I don't really know how I would do it. I just get so angry and I want them to stop.

GROUP LEADER: That must be so frustrating!

STUDENT: It is. I try to tell them to stop but they will not leave me alone. They do it at school, after school, and at football practice.

GROUP LEADER: Wow. I can see why you get so angry. You can't seem to get away from them when they do it at school and in the neighborhood, and even when you are at football. Have you ever told anyone about what they are doing?

STUDENT: No.

GROUP LEADER: Who are some people that you would feel comfortable telling when the boys are messing with you?

STUDENT: Well, my mom, uncle, the principal, Mrs. Smith, you, my teachers . . .

GROUP LEADER: Great. You have a lot of adults here at school that care about you! What I am going to do while we are talking is start making a list for us of people you can talk to when you get really angry and start having these thoughts. (*Completes the "My Supports" section on the Safety Contract form [see Appendix 29]*). I am really sorry this is happening at school. I really care about you and want to keep you safe. I want us to complete this safety contract together. This is an agreement between you and I that if you have any thoughts of hurting yourself or anyone else while you are at school, you will tell one of the adults we just discussed. If you are at home, you will tell your mom or uncle. I have listed all of the people you feel comfortable talking to on this form. Would you be willing to sign your name here (*pointing to the form*) that you will tell someone if you have these thoughts about hurting yourself again?

STUDENT: Yes. (*Signs the form.*)

GROUP LEADER: I am really glad you felt comfortable sharing this with me today. Is there anything else you think I could do to help with the situation with the boys?

STUDENT: No. I try to tell my teachers, but they don't do anything. The boys always do it when people are not around.

GROUP LEADER: Would it be helpful if I explained what is happening to your teachers and asked them to watch out for the boys messing with you?

STUDENT: That would be great. Thanks!

GROUP LEADER: Do you remember in the beginning of the group when we talked about that big word, confidentiality?

STUDENT: Yes.

GROUP LEADER: We talked about how what is said in group, stays in group, except if a student says they are being hurt or want to hurt themselves or others. This is because I care about you and want to keep you safe. Would you be OK if I talked to your mother about what is going on with the boys?

STUDENT: That would be fine.

GROUP LEADER: Great. So I am going to talk with your teachers about what is going on with the boys so they can watch out for them hitting you on the back of the head. I am also going to call your mom and let her know about what the boys are doing, how it makes you really angry and frustrated, and that sometimes you think about hurting yourself when this happens. Does that sound good?

STUDENT: Yes.

GROUP LEADER: Wonderful. I am going to give you a copy of the safety contract to take with you back to class and then I am going to call your mom. Thanks again for being so brave and sharing this with me today.

## TIP

Complete the Safety Contract (see Appendix 29) and the Suicide Assessment Form (see Appendix 28). If a student had a more specific plan for hurting him- or herself, you would ask the follow-up questions about when the student plans to do it, how he or she plans to do it, and does he or she have access to the method (e.g., gun, knives). It may be necessary to call the parent several times during the day before reaching him or her. Agencies, school districts, and states have different procedures, so it is best that you refer to your state laws and program rules, but you may not want to let the child leave school until you have informed the parent. It may also be necessary to send the child to the emergency room, depending on the severity of the situation.

### Scenario 2

To follow up after your discussion with the student in scenario 1, process what you would want to highlight and confirm with your supervisor or a colleague to be sure you have covered everything in your suicide assessment and the "Immediate Intervention Procedures" from the Suicide Assessment Form (see Appendix 28).

EXAMPLE SCRIPTED ANSWER

GROUP LEADER: Hi. I know you are very busy, but do you have a few minutes?

SUPERVISOR: Sure, is everything OK?

GROUP LEADER: Yes. I had a student disclose thoughts about wanting to hurt himself in group today and I wanted to share it with you to make sure I did everything correctly.

SUPERVISOR: Absolutely. It is always great to discuss these situations to make sure we cover everything. Was the student able to contract for safety?

GROUP LEADER: Yes. The student reported that boys at school were messing with him and hitting him in the back of the head. They are doing this when adults are not around. The student is frustrated because they bother him at school, in the neighborhood, and at football practice. He gets so angry that he sometimes thinks he wants to die. I asked him if I could talk to the principal about this, as it appears that he is being bullied. He agreed to this. I also completed the suicide assessment form and he reported that he has thought about jumping off the roof of the school. However, he does not have a specific plan for how or when he would do it.

SUPERVISOR: Great work. Was he able to identify adults he feels comfortable talking to if he has these thoughts in the future?

GROUP LEADER: Yes. He was able to quickly identify his mother, uncle, the principal, me, and his teachers.

SUPERVISOR: Excellent. Did you call his parent?

GROUP LEADER: Yes. I reviewed confidentiality with the student and reminded him that this was one of the exceptions to confidentiality. He gave permission for me to call his mother. We also discussed that it would be helpful for me to talk to his teachers so they are aware of the boys bothering him at school. I gave him a copy of the safety contract to take with him that has all of his identified supports listed and the hotline numbers.

SUPERVISOR: Great work! I can't think of anything else. Sounds like you covered everything. You may want to touch base with the student tomorrow or the next day you are at school to see how he is doing and whether he has had any self-harm thoughts.

GROUP LEADER: Sounds good. Thanks for your help!

SUPERVISOR: Anytime. You are doing an excellent job with suicide assessments. However, it is always best practice to check in with a supervisor or colleague to make sure there isn't anything else we could do to help keep the student safe. Keep up the great work!

## Scenario 3

A parent in the group states that there is nothing wrong with physical punishment. In fact, the person's parents used physical punishment, and she sees no problems with it. Have a discussion with the group about the pros and cons of physical punishment versus time-out.

EXAMPLE SCRIPTED ANSWER

GROUP LEADER: This is definitely a reaction I get from parents at times, especially since people have been raised differently over the years. Let's have a discussion about the pros and cons of physical punishment versus time-out. I'd like to record our responses in a chart and really get a feel for both sides of the issue. (*Creates a chart on the board, similar to Table 8.4.*)

I'm going to start with a few discussion points. Let's start to fill in this chart, while we talk about pros and cons. Let's start with short-term versus long-term response. Is spanking a short-term or long-term response?

PARENT: Short term.

GROUP LEADER: Yes. It's a quick, short-term response. It stops the behavior for the time being, but it can often be based on parent frustration rather than child behavior change. What about time-out? Is this also short term, or are you teaching a technique here?

PARENT: I guess teaching a technique, which would take some time to accomplish.

GROUP LEADER: Yes. You are building up a long-term, future-oriented response that will hopefully decrease the likelihood that the behavior will occur in the future. Which one models self-control and which behavior models, at times, loss of control, and at times, hitting and violence?

PARENT: Time-out models self-control and spanking models violence and loss of control.

GROUP LEADER: If time-out is introduced correctly, for example, if an adult is calm and collected when offering time-out, then yes, it does model self-control. Spanking models violence and at times, loss of control if the adult is reacting in anger.

The group leader should continue the discussion surrounding spanking versus time-out and add to the chart as the parent further processes the ideas. The group leader should try to cover the key points listed in Table 8.4. Once all ideas are in the chart, the group leader will want to talk about pros and cons.

GROUP LEADER: What are you noticing about most of the items listed under spanking/physical punishment versus what is listed under time-out?

PARENT: Spanking a child doesn't seem to be good and time-out seems to be a better technique. Although time-out doesn't work for my child.

GROUP LEADER: Yes, I'm noticing the same thing . . . there are a lot of pros in the time-out category and a lot of cons in the spanking category. Although spanking will often stop the behavior immediately, research has not shown it to have long-term effects. For example, students will often continue to do the undesired behavior because they don't link it to the spanking. Time-out takes more time and can be challenging to implement, but it has proven to be effective in the long term. Though, I have heard before that time-out doesn't work for some families and it has for others. We are going to further discuss the procedure of time-out and how it can be used effectively. I ask that you just keep an open mind and think about the way you have been implementing time-out in the past. See if there are any new strategies that can be helpful in implementing this challenging technique in the future.

**TIP**

Remain calm and collected and refer back to Table 8.4 as necessary. The group leader will want to allow the ideas to come from the group members and help them come to their own opinion on spanking versus time-out by reviewing the advantages and disadvantages of both. Let all ideas be heard, but also remind the group members of the limits to confidentiality.

## Scenario 4

The parent group members are participating in a discussion regarding time-out versus spanking. As the group leader, you have reminded the group members about confidentiality and its limits. However, one parent makes a comment about a past instance of abuse.

EXAMPLE SCRIPTED ANSWER

GROUP LEADER: As we look at our list, we've generated many benefits to using time-out and we have also listed some pretty serious risks and consequences of using spanking or other forms of physical punishment. Does anyone have anything to add regarding how to successfully utilize the time-out procedure to provide a consequence for a negative behavior that you do not want to see repeated?

PARENT A: I've used time-out when my child misbehaves and it really works. I have seen the benefits while he is in time-out and the behavior that we were using it for has decreased significantly.

GROUP LEADER: What was the behavior that you used time-out for?

PARENT A: My son has been having a problem with taking things from my daughter when he wants something that she has. At times he has knocked her down as he grabs something so hard from her hands. So we have been using time-out to try to decrease this behavior and also try to teach him other ways to handle his frustration.

GROUP LEADER: This is really great. It sounds like you have identified a problem, taught some prosocial skills, but also provided a consequence when you see this behavior. Time-out is a wonderful technique to use in this situation. Great work! Anyone else have anything to share? Positive situations or challenges with using time-out?

PARENT B: I have not found time-out to be that successful. Oftentimes, my child will kick and scream and I basically have to drag him to time-out. Then he throws tantrums while in time-out and one time he even kicked a hole in the wall. My boyfriend at the time came home and beat him for that one. I mean, he can't kick holes in our walls and needed to be taught a lesson.

GROUP LEADER: It sounds like you've had a more challenging time with time-out in your house and that your child reacts in a more aggressive manner. It also sounds like your boyfriend used a physical punishment approach, which can cause more severe consequences and harm to your child in the short term and long run. The use of the term "beating" concerns me a little as this can mean different things to different people.

PARENT B: Yeah. I wasn't happy about him doing that, especially because I have my own set of rules in our house. He basically came home from work and spanked my son.

GROUP LEADER: That can be tough when you have a set of rules set in your house and then another adult comes in and applies his or her own strategies. Do you think you and I can talk about this further at the end of the group? As you know, our confidentiality limits help to protect children from harm and offer assistance so that they remain safe. I'd just like to discuss this further with you to assess your feelings regarding this instance and make sure that you and your child are safe.

PARENT B: Sure. I'm probably making it out to be more than it was and shouldn't have said that, but it has been really tough to use the time-out strategy with my son and I need some help.

GROUP LEADER: This is really incredible of you to be able to admit the challenges in your household. Sometimes it's difficult to tell others, especially a whole group, that things are difficult at home and that some strategies aren't working. I appreciate your honesty and now we can begin to tackle difficult time-out scenarios and what happens when time-out doesn't work as we planned. Believe me, you are not the only parent in this world that has struggled with using the time-out procedure! In fact, we struggle with it at times when we use this strategy with children in our child groups. It doesn't always go perfectly, and kids sometimes do throw temper tantrums. So it's good to plan for these instances, too, and have some strategies in our back pockets to use when these more challenging instances occur. With a show of hands, have others had difficulties at times with time-out? (*Multiple parents raise their hands.*)

PARENT B: I'd appreciate the help, and it also is nice to know that I'm not the only one.

GROUP LEADER: This is perfect timing because in our next group session we will be discussing time-out in more detail and plan for those times when time-out isn't working. For instance, what do we do if a child refuses to go to time-out? What if the child leaves the time-out area? What if the child is not quiet for the time allotted? We will discuss all of these issues and set a plan for how you handle it as a parent.

## TIP

The group leader will still want to meet with this parent after the group to further discuss the "beating" by the boyfriend to make sure the child was not abused or in harm's way presently. From the way the parent further described the instance, it sounds like the boyfriend used an open hand to spank the child. Although this may have caused harm to the child, it may not be reportable in most states. Still, it is good to cover all bases and make sure the child was not harmed. It also sounds like the boyfriend is no longer in their lives, but it will be helpful to plan for a situation like this in the future. Remember to learn and follow your state laws on reporting abuse. You can always call CPS or the services that protect children in your state and ask whether this instance would be reportable or not. They can provide further assistance as to what steps to take no matter what the outcome.

# CHAPTER 9

# Data-Based Decision Making and Planning for Termination

Matching the intervention to the needs of the students is vital when selecting an evidence-based group intervention. A student with social phobia would be less likely to benefit from a group intervention on anger management skills than a group that specifically targets social phobia. Not only is it important to identify and select an appropriate group intervention at the start of your group, but it is also vital to continuously assess whether this group intervention is meeting the needs of your group members. In this chapter, we discuss how to effectively identify and select measures to identify students for group participation based on their needs. We also explain how to use data to monitor the progress of the students in your group and determine whether students are improving as intended. Finally, we discuss group termination. Allowing time to plan for the end of the group will result in many positive benefits for group members (Keyton, 1993). Each group member will have a different response to the group ending and show a variety of emotions. Therefore, it is helpful to begin talking about group termination early and plan accordingly.

## USING DATA TO IDENTIFY STUDENTS IN NEED OF SUPPORT

Effective use of data and measurement depends on a careful planning process that starts with asking important questions, selecting the right tools for answering these questions and finally using those data to make informed decisions. Align your measures or the existing data with the risk factors that the group intervention targets. If you plan to run group that targets anger management, identify students with anger issues. If you plan to implement a group for at-risk depressed teens, identify students who report depressive symptoms. In other words, don't place a student into an existing group because the teacher had concerns and thought a particular student could use your help. Work toward matching the services you provide to the identified needs of the students in question. There are a number of ways to go about determining the needs of the students with whom you work. Initially identifying students in need of additional supports may involve the use of existing data, a systematic schoolwide or caseload-specific screening process, or a less formal process based on teacher reports and school records (see McIntosh, Reinke, & Herman, 2010). The following provides a brief review of these options.

## Existing Data

Many schools gather several forms of data that can be used as indicators of the need for additional student support. For instance, most schools gather office disciplinary referrals (ODRs), or documentation of significant problem behaviors in the schools. This information may be referred to as incident forms, discipline tracking forms, or behavior log entries. They tend to be indicators of externalizing problems in students. ODRs are readily available data and provide information about problem behavior intensity and frequency. They can be used to determine which students are consistently presenting with behavioral challenges. To a certain extent, data on suspensions may also be helpful if used in conjunction with ODRs. This is because suspensions that typically occur for severe behavior do not provide information on lower-level behaviors, which could be used to predict and prevent problems. Other readily available data that schools gather and can be used are reports on latenesses and absences from school. Students with higher rates of tardiness or absences could be further assessed to determine whether they would benefit from a group-based intervention. Your school may gather other data that could indicate risk among students. Use these data as your initial screening and then gather more specific information. See Chapter 2 for more details on keeping school staff informed of group interventions and obtaining data to determine student needs.

## Teacher Rankings

Another method that can be used alone or in conjunction with existing data is teacher rankings of students. For instance, you may ask all fourth-grade teachers in your school to rank the top 10 students in their classrooms with regard to externalizing problems (see Appendix 4 for a sample Teacher Nomination Form). Then, cross-analyze the information with existing data such as ODRs or suspension data. In selecting potential students for a group, consider the severity of their behaviors reported by the teacher. You may not want the top two students identified; they may struggle in a group setting because their behaviors may warrant more individualized attention. Keep in mind that teachers are much better at identifying students with externalizing problems such as disruptive behaviors, impulse control, and attention issues than internalizing problems. Therefore, use teacher ranking with caution when attempting to identify students who would benefit from interventions targeting anxiety or depression. At the end of this chapter there is a sample role play on how to discuss student rankings with a teacher for inclusion in a group setting (see role-play scenario 1 at the end of this chapter).

## Schoolwide or Caseload-Specific Screening Processes

Schools can use multiple gating systems to identify students who may benefit from additional supports. These are systems of progressively intensive measures to identify students at risk for negative outcomes (Lochman, 1995). Multiple gating measures include a series of stages. The first stage (or gate) involves a relatively inexpensive screening that is conducted schoolwide. Only students identified at this stage progress to the next stage, which includes more intensive screening. At each stage, the assessment becomes increasingly more expensive and time-consuming, but fewer students are assessed.

There are several multiple gating systems commercially available that utilize behavior rating scales to identify students in need of additional supports, including the *Systematic Screening for Behavioral Disorders* (SSBD) rating system (Walker & Severson, 1992), the *Social Skills Improvement System* (SISS; Gresham & Elliott, 1990), and the *Behavioral and Emotional Screening System* (BESS; Kamphaus & Reynolds, 2008). These measures typically assess multiple domains of social–emotional and behavioral functioning in children, such as internalizing, externalizing, and social problems.

For its first gate, the SSBD uses teacher rankings of students on externalizing and internalizing problems. Those students who are in the top five for externalizing and the top five for internalizing problems move on, and the teacher completes a brief measure to determine whether the student exhibits behaviors that are at risk in comparison with other same-age students. Those who are identified as at risk are then observed to determine whether the behaviors are truly significant and warrant intervention. Students who have behaviors that are in the at-risk range are good candidates for a group intervention matched to their presenting problem.

The SISS and BESS begin by having teachers and parents rate students on a brief measure of externalizing, internalizing, and social problems. Older students may be asked to self-report on their behaviors as well. Next, teachers and parents of students with elevated risk are asked to complete a more comprehensive measure to determine whether the students' behaviors are truly in need of additional support. Those students who garner reports from teachers or parents of symptoms in the at-risk to clinically significant range can be offered supports based on the severity and identified risks. Using multiple sources for your data will increase the likelihood that you will correctly identify those students at risk while ensuring that you target your intervention to the identified area of need.

Another option is to assess students who are already part of your current caseload and obtain consent from parents to assess additional students in order to determine whether they qualify for a group intervention. You may already have a group intervention in mind and are looking for appropriate candidates for the group. For example, say you have two students on your caseload who have anxiety symptoms and you think it would be beneficial to implement the Coping Cat group intervention. You have two potential members, but you would like to find more members for this group.

First, select the group intervention you will be leading (see Chapter 2 for more details on selecting an evidence-based group intervention); in this instance, Coping Cat. Then determine the best screening measure to use in order to assess whether the students on your caseload or within a specific group (e.g., first graders) would be a good fit for the group intervention. Selecting and identifying an appropriate screening tool for a group intervention can be challenging. Carefully research or consult your supervisor or other colleagues to see what screening tools they have used for the same area. Review these forms while thinking about group content and dynamics. If you are planning on implementing Coping Cat (Kendall & Hedtke, 2006), then you may want to use the Screen for Child Anxiety Related Disorders (SCARED; Birmaher et al., 1999) measure to assess for anxiety symptoms.

There are commercial screening tools that cost money to obtain (e.g., the Beck Depression Inventory; Beck, Ward, Mendelson, Mock, & Erbaugh, 1961) and there are free, publicly accessible screening tools (e.g., the Center for Epidemiological Studies Depression Scale for Children [CES-DC]). It is easier and cheaper to access the free screening forms. However, you will want to make sure that these tools are from a reputable source, that they actually measure what it is you are trying to assess, and that they will assist in appropriately selecting students for your group. If they do not meet these requirements, or if you are looking for assistance in using a screening tool and you have the funds to purchase measures, then you may want to look into the purchase of screening tools. Commercial screening tools (e.g., the Behavior Assessment System for Children [BASC-2]; Reynolds & Kamphaus, 2004) can be extremely helpful by offering a scoring system, options to generate reports, and a company that backs the product and can provide consultation or troubleshooting advice as needed.

As a school-based group leader, you may not have access to funds to support your group interventions, and so finding a free screening tool may be the way to go. Table 9.1 includes a selection of screening tools that are valid and easily attainable. We include summaries along with website addresses, where you can locate these tools and learn more about their use. Below, we list three reliable websites where you can locate a variety of screening tools for use within your own practice.

• *SAMHSA*, a reputable government agency, offers a list of free screening tools on their site (*www.integration.samhsa.gov/clinical-practice/screening-tools*). These screening tools can be used to assess students for group inclusion in an array of topic areas: depression, drug and alcohol use, bipolar disorder, suicide risk, and anxiety and trauma. They state any rules and requirements while using the tool (e.g., must be licensed to offer screening).

• The *Anxiety and Depression Association of America* is a nonprofit organization dedicated to the prevention, treatment, and cure of anxiety, obsessive–compulsive disorder, posttraumatic stress disorder, depression, and related disorders. The organization also offers a list of free screening tools on their site (*www.adaa.org/living-with-anxiety/ ask-and-learn/screenings*). Most of the screening measures are based on the *Diagnostic and Statistical Manual of Mental Disorders* of the American Psychiatric Association or other reputable sources. They offer the scales directly through their website with the references listed below the scales.

• The *University of Maryland's Center for School Mental Health* has complied a list of assessment measures for clinicians to use in the school setting that help assess symp-

## TABLE 9.1. A Selection of Free Screening Tools

Screening tools for depression

*Patient Health Questionnaire (PHQ-9)*

This is the most common screening tool to identify depression. It is available in Spanish as well as in a modified version for adolescents.

Adult version: *www.integration.samhsa.gov/images/res/PHQ%20-%20Questions.pdf*
Adolescent version: *www.integration.samhsa.gov/images/res/8.3.4%20Patient%20Health%20Questionnaire%20(PHQ-9)%20Adolescents.pdf*

*Depression Management Tool Kit*

This measure was created by the MacArthur Foundation Initiative on Depression and Primary Care. It can be utilized in other settings, but it's intended to help primary care clinicians recognize and manage depression. Not only is this a screening tool but it also provides education to patients about depression, provides tools for treating depression, and assists in monitoring patient response to treatment.

*www.integration.samhsa.gov/clinical-practice/macarthur_depression_toolkit.pdf*

*Center for Epidemiological Studies Depression Scale for Children (CES-DC)*

This depression scale for children is a 20-item self-report depression inventory. The CES-DC can be used with children and adolescents ages 6–17.

*www.brightfutures.org/mentalhealth/pdf/professionals/bridges/ces_dc.pdf*

Screening tools for suicidal behaviors

*Columbia–Suicide Severity Rating Scale (C-SSRS)*

This questionnaire is used to assess for suicide. It is available in multiple languages (116) and various professionals can administer the scale (mental health training is not required to administer). It can be used in the school setting.

*www.integration.samhsa.gov/clinical-practice/Columbia_Suicide_Severity_Rating_Scale.pdf*

*Suicide Behaviors Questionnaire–Revised (SBQ-R)*

This questionnaire assesses suicide-related thoughts and behaviors. The 14-item and four-item scales were developed for use with adults, but subsequently have been studied and used with adolescents.

*www.integration.samhsa.gov/images/res/SBQ.pdf*

Screening tools for anxiety

*Generalized Anxiety Disorder 7-Item Scale (GAD-7)*

Often used in conjunction with the PHQ, this seven-question screening tool facilitates complete assessment for whether anxiety is present. This scale can be used with adults and adolescents.

*www.integration.samhsa.gov/clinical-practice/GAD708.19.08Cartwright.pdf*

*(continued)*

**TABLE 9.1.** *(continued)*

*Revised Children's Anxiety and Depression Scale (RCADS)*

This 47-item scale is designed to assess depression and anxiety in youth from grades 3 to 12. The RCADS includes subscales of separation anxiety disorder, social phobia, generalized anxiety disorder, panic disorder, obsessive–compulsive disorder, and major depressive disorder. The scale is also available in a parent version as well as in several languages.

User guide: *www.childfirst.ucla.edu/RCADSGuide20110202.pdf*
Child version: *www.childfirst.ucla.edu/RCADS%202009.pdf*
Parent version: *www.childfirst.ucla.edu/RCADS-P%202009.pdf*

*Screen for Child Anxiety Related Disorders (SCARED)*

This 41-item measure is designed to screen for anxiety disorders in children ages 8 and older and is available in both a child self-report and parent versions. It measures general anxiety, separation anxiety, social phobia, school phobia, and physical symptoms of anxiety.

Child form: *http://psychiatry.pitt.edu/sites/default/files/Documents/assessments/SCARED%20Child.pdf*
Parent form: *http://psychiatry.pitt.edu/sites/default/files/Documents/assessments/SCARED%20Parent.pdf*

*Spence Children's Anxiety Scale*

This screening tool is a 45-item self-report measure of anxiety for children and adolescents. The Spence includes subscales for the following: panic/agoraphobia, social anxiety, separation anxiety, generalized anxiety, fear of physical injury, and obsessions/compulsions.

Child version: *www.scaswebsite.com/docs/scas.pdf*
Parent version: *www.scaswebsite.com/docs/scas-parent-qaire.pdf*

Screening tools for posttraumatic stress disorder

*Traumatic Events Screening Inventory for Children (TESI-C)*

This PTSD scale is a 15-item clinician-administered interview that can be utilized for children and youth ages 3–18. It assesses a child's experience of a variety of potential traumatic events including current and previous injuries, hospitalizations, domestic violence, community violence, disasters, accidents, physical abuse, and sexual abuse.

*www.ptsd.va.gov/PTSD/professional/pages/assessments/assessment-pdf/TESI-C.pdf*

*Child PTSD Symptom Scale (CPSS)*

This scale is a 26-item self-report measure that assesses PTSD diagnostic criteria and symptom severity in children ages 8–18. It includes two event items, 17 symptom items, and seven functional impairment items.

*https://www.aacap.org/App_Themes/AACAP/docs/resource_centers/resources/misc/child_ptsd_symptom_scale.pdf*

*(continued)*

**TABLE 9.1.** *(continued)*

Global screening tools

*NICHQ Vanderbilt Assessment Scales*

This measure can be completed by parents and teachers and can be used to assess for high frequencies of symptoms associated with attention-deficit/hyperactivity disorder in children ages 6–12. The parent measure has 55 items and the teacher measure has 43 items. The scale also includes screening questions for commonly coexisting conditions, including oppositional defiant disorder, conduct disorder, and anxiety disorders.

Parent measure: *www.multicare-assoc.com/pdfs/NICHQVanderbiltParent.pdf*
Teacher measure: *www.jeffersandmann.com/client_files/file/JMA_Vanderbilt-Teacher-Informant.pdf*

*Parent/Teacher Disruptive Behavior Disorder Scale*

This screening tool for disruptive behavior is a 45-item scale that can be filled out by parents or teachers. It assesses symptoms associated with attention-deficit/hyperactivity disorder, oppositional defiant disorder, and conduct disorder.

*http://ccf.fiu.edu/for-families/resources-for-parents/printable-information/dbd.pdf*

*Strengths and Difficulties Questionnaire (SDQ)*

This brief 25-item behavioral screening questionnaire for children and adolescents ages 3–17 includes a parent form, teacher form, a modified form for parents and teachers of nursery school children, and a self-report form for youth ages 11–16. The SDQ assesses the following five domains: emotional symptoms, conduct problems, hyperactivity/inattention, peer relationship problems, and prosocial behavior.

*www.sdqinfo.org/py/sdqinfo/b3.py?language=Englishqz(USA)*

*Brief Problem Checklist (BPC)*

This screening tool is a 15-item questionnaire of internalizing and externalizing problems among youth ages 7 to adolescence. It offers both child and parent versions and is designed for repeated periodic assessments of clinical progress among children with a wide variety of problems.

Child version: *www.childfirst.ucla.edu/Brief%20Problem%20Checklist%20-%20Child.pdf*
Parent version: *www.childfirst.ucla.edu/Brief%20Problem%20Checklist%20-%20Parent.pdf*

toms for clinical disorders (*http://csmh.umaryland.edu/media/SOM/Microsites/CSMH/docs/Resources/ClinicalTools/Summary-of-Free-Assessment-Measures-And-Google-Doc-Link-to-Measures-Saved.pdf*). Or search the Center for School Mental Health site for "Clinical Resources" and "Free Assessment List." They provide a thorough summary of screening tools that are available for free, can be printed out, and are listed in the following behavioral areas: global clinical measures and disorder-specific clinical measures, including anxiety, depression, attention-deficit/hyperactivity disorder, posttraumatic stress disorder, and suicidal behavior.

These three websites offer great lists and summaries of current free screening tools along with links to these tools.

Once you have identified a group intervention and screening tool, you will need to obtain consent from parents in order to assess specific students, or follow the procedure outlined above for using multiple gating measures schoolwide. If you want to use a screening tool for a parent group, you will need to discuss this with the potential group members to be sure that they understand the screening and selection process. Remember that screening tools and rating scales do not produce a diagnosis. These tools help identify potential causes of a person's emotional and behavioral difficulties and assist group leaders in selecting members for a specific group intervention. Symptoms suggestive of suicidal or harmful behaviors warrant immediate attention. (See Chapter 8 for more information on handling suicidal behaviors and managing crises.) Once you have obtained consent, you may proceed with administering the measure and assess for potential group inclusion.

## PROGRESS MONITORING STUDENT OUTCOMES FOR GROUP MEMBERS

Now that you have selected your group members using data as described above, effective group-based interventions include ongoing progress monitoring of relevant student outcomes. The purpose of ongoing progress monitoring is to (1) verify whether or not a gap exists between current and expected levels of performance, (2) ascertain the magnitude of that gap, (3) elaborate specific strategies to reduce the gap, and (4) monitor the effectiveness of those strategies. Data gathered as part of this process can consist of student self-report, teacher report, and observations of the student using the skills learned in the group intervention. For the data to be useful for progress monitoring, the measure(s) utilized need to be sensitive to change and indicate the malleable risk or protective factors targeted by the intervention. For instance, if you are running a social skills group to teach students effective peer communication skills, you will want to (1) observe the students where they would need to use the skills (e.g., playground, cafeteria), (2) ask teachers whether they have seen an improvement in the student's communication with peers, and (3) ask the student to evaluate his or her use of the skills.

Other data that may be overlooked are goal sheets or behavior monitoring forms that many interventions use to reinforce student behaviors outside of the group (see Appendix 25 for a sample Goal Sheet; also see Figure 9.1 for examples of completed goal sheets that can provide data for progress monitoring). You can use these forms to track how a student progresses over time. Teachers or parents can be asked to fill out these goal sheets on a daily basis and return them to you. You can then review the data to determine where progress is or is not being made. You may even want to graph student progress over time, share the graph with students, and encourage them to set goals for themselves in specific areas of need (e.g., staying calm and in control during reading).

Figure 9.2 provides an example of how you could track and share progress monitoring data with the students in your group. Using this example, the group leader may pull the student aside to review the data, showing him or her how much better he or she was doing by following directions and being safe in the classroom. Then, set a goal with the student

<u>Good Behavior Monitoring Form</u>

Date: 12/12

Reward Chosen: Legos

Number of "agrees" from teacher needed to earn reward: 8

| Content Areas | Behavior Goals | Student's Rating | Teacher's Rating |
|---|---|---|---|
| Morning Activity | Be Safe. | ☺ ☺ ☹ | Agree  Disagree |
| | Follow Directions. | ☺ ☺ ☹ | Agree  Disagree |
| Calendar | Be Safe. | ☺ ☺ ☹ | Agree  Disagree |
| | Follow Directions. | ☺ ☺ ☹ | Agree  Disagree |
| Work Stations | Be Safe. | ☺ ☺ ☹ | Agree  Disagree |
| | Follow Directions. | ☺ ☺ ☹ | Agree  Disagree |
| Guided Reading | Be Safe. | ☺ ☺ ☹ | Agree  Disagree |
| | Follow Directions. | ☺ ☺ ☹ | Agree  Disagree |
| Silent Reading | Be Safe. | ☺ ☺ ☹ | Agree  Disagree |
| | Follow Directions. | ☺ ☺ ☹ | Agree  Disagree |
| Math | Be Safe. | ☺ ☺ ☹ | Agree  Disagree |
| | Follow Directions. | ☺ ☺ ☹ | Agree  Disagree |
| Specials | Be Safe. | ☺ ☺ ☹ | Agree  Disagree |
| | Follow Directions. | ☺ ☺ ☹ | Agree  Disagree |

Teacher's Signature: Miss S

Date: 12/12

**Good Behavior Monitoring Form (Morning-I)**

Date: 3/2

Reward chosen: Legos

Total Points needed to earn *Morning* reward: 6

| Content Areas | Behavior Goals | Student's Rating | Ms. Teacher Rating | Points |
|---|---|---|---|---|
| 1. Specials | I was safe. | Yes  No | AGREE  disagree | 1 |
| | I stayed calm & in control. | Yes  No | AGREE  disagree | |
| 2. Reading | I was safe. | Yes  No | AGREE  disagree | 1 |
| | I stayed calm & in control. | Yes  No | AGREE  disagree | 1 |
| 3. Writing | I was safe. | Yes  No | AGREE  disagree | 1 |
| | I stayed calm & in control. | Yes  No | AGREE  disagree | |
| 4. Band/Stations | I was safe. | Yes  No | AGREE  disagree | |
| | I stayed calm & in control. | Yes  No | AGREE  disagree | 1 |
| TOTAL | | | | 6 |

| INTENSITY 1 (CIRCLE) | INTENSITY 2 (CIRCLE) | | INTENSITY 3 (CIRCLE) | INTENSITY 4 (CIRCLE) | WHY AM I ANGRY? |
|---|---|---|---|---|---|
| VERY HIGH | VERY HIGH | | VERY HIGH | VERY HIGH | Students calling me names |
| HIGH | HIGH | | HIGH | HIGH | Students annoying me |
| MEDIUM | MEDIUM | | MEDIUM | MEDIUM | Teacher bothering me about homework |
| LOW | LOW | | LOW | LOW | Getting extra homework because of the rest of the class' behavior |
| VERY LOW | VERY LOW | | VERY LOW | VERY LOW | |

Teacher Signature Miss S

Parent Signature: _____

Notes: _____

**FIGURE 9.1.** Examples of goal sheets that provide data for progress monitoring.

for the number of points he or she wants to earn each day for the coming week, have the student tell you what he or she will do to be successful (e.g., "I will remember to use my coping thoughts when I feel upset, to stay safe"), and let the teacher know that the student is really working toward meeting a new goal each week.

Figure 9.3 shows how a group leader could develop a simple chart that students can keep in a folder to color in and track their own progress based on their goal sheets over time. As in the prior example, goals can be set to improve progress over time. At the end of this chapter there is a sample role play on how to use the data from a student's goal sheet as a guide in reviewing this student's progress with him (see role-play scenario 2 at the end of this chapter).

Progress monitoring data give you important information about what strategies promoted by the intervention are being generalized to other settings—which is what really counts toward making positive improvement in the lives of students in your group. Progress monitoring information can be used to support specific students in the group who are struggling. For students who are progressing slower on some aspects of the intervention, you may choose to review the skills in the group and perhaps hold additional individual meetings with the students to review and practice the skill. Continue monitoring the skills to see if they begin to translate into the classroom or other settings. If some skills are more challenging for the majority of students in the group, you may consider slowing down the pace and adding additional practice opportunities during group sessions.

Progress monitoring data can also guide your understanding of the contextual factors that may inhibit skills transfer for students in your group. Use direct observation as well as self-report to understand the challenges or barriers for the students in using the

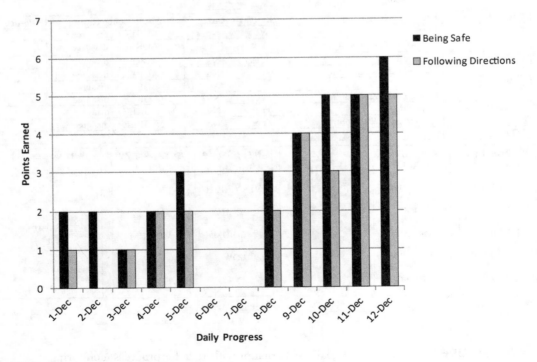

**FIGURE 9.2.** Example of tracking data to monitor progress and motivate students.

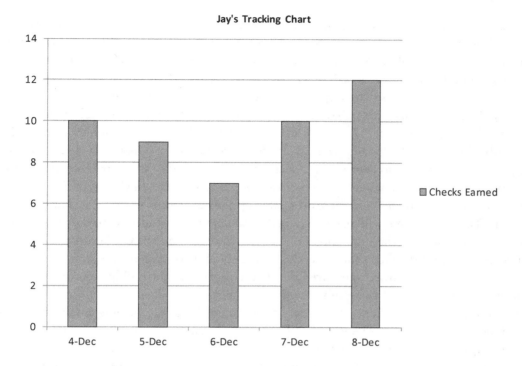

**FIGURE 9.3.** Example of a form used to track student progress using goal sheet data.

new skills they are learning. Perhaps there are contextual factors that limit the likelihood that they can exhibit the new behaviors. For instance, in schools where students do not feel safe, they may be less likely to use a skill that makes them vulnerable to becoming a victim. Imagine that you are asking students to walk away from confrontations as part of a problem-solving training curriculum. In some contexts, however, a student who does not stand up for him- or herself when bullied by other students is more vulnerable; walking away from confrontation may even increase the likelihood that others will use aggression. Your role is to consider these contexts and how the interventions and skills you are teaching may or may not translate into the students' daily environments. Meet with teachers and other school personnel to have them encourage students to use the new skills. This can be as simple as having a teacher prompt and reinforce a student to exhibit a new skill, or as complex as working with school faculty and staff to improve schoolwide encouragement of positive behaviors.

## USING PREGROUP AND POSTGROUP DATA IN DETERMINING STUDENT OUTCOMES AND WHEN TO TERMINATE SERVICES

Use data to determine when students have progressed to the point they are no longer in need of additional supports. This is an evidence-based practice. It is important for you to know beyond your professional judgment that a student has benefited from the group intervention and no longer needs services. Therefore, prior to your first session, gather data on the current functioning of the student on important variables that are likely to be impacted by the group intervention. You may have already gathered this information through a thorough screening process or by using available school data. Many clinicians will also gather information using a broad standardized measure that can assess multiple domains across externalizing problems, internalizing problems, and adaptive behaviors, such as the BASC-2 (Reynolds & Kamphaus, 2004), the *Child Behavior Checklist* (CBCL; Achenbach, 1992), or the publicly available *Strengths and Difficulties Questionnaire* (Goodman, 1997; see *www. sdqinfo.org*). Other options are rating scales that specifically target social–emotional risk and protective factors, such as the *Social Emotional Assets and Resilience Scales* (SEARS; Merrell, 2011). Many of these measures offer options to gather parent, teacher, and child reports. These measures will give you information about how students are doing across multiple domains prior to the implementation of the study. If you are not familiar with how to correctly interpret the data that you collect using standardized measures, you should obtain proper training. The broad measures discussed above are not highly sensitive to change within a short period of time and therefore are not sensitive enough to use for progress monitoring. However, when it is time to discontinue the group or determine who should continue with a group intervention, implementing the same measure(s) will give you information about whether the student has improved enough to terminate services. Use this data in conjunction with your progress monitoring data to determine who needs additional supports and who has met all goals for improvement.

Tables 9.2 and 9.3 provide an example of data used by a clinician to determine areas of improvement over the course of an anger management group intervention for a student who exhibited high levels of aggressive behavior. Areas that fall into the "clinically significant" and "at-risk" ranges have been highlighted both prior to the start of the group and at the end. Notice there are other areas of concern for this student at the start of the group, including problems with attention, anxiety, and depression. Often students who need additional supports present with problems in multiple areas. Determining the areas that need the most support will require that you gather information from multiple sources, including the teacher, parent, and student.

Prior to the group intervention, both the parent and teacher reported concerns in the domains of hyperactivity, aggression, conduct problems, depression, and attention problems. The teacher reported more significant concerns on several of the domains than the mother. However, ratings gathered at the end of the group intervention from the teacher and the parent indicate that concerns related to the aggression and conduct problems have diminished. Further, the teacher and parent also report improvement for the student with regard to symptoms of depression. However, a few concerns remain. For instance, the teacher continues to report concerns with hyperactivity and attention problems. The mother concurs with the teacher's continued concerns with attention problems. This information can be used to evaluate whether the group intervention (which, in this case, targeted aggressive behavior) was helpful to the student and whether other concerns remain that would benefit from additional attention. Based on the report of the teacher and the mother, it appears that the student has made significant improvements in the areas of aggressive behavior and conduct problems, but would benefit from additional supports for inattention.

**TABLE 9.2. Example of Pre–Post Data to Determine Improvement and Need for Additional Support**

| BASC clinical scale | Parent rating prior to group | Parent rating at end of group | Teacher rating prior to group | Teacher rating at end of group |
|---|---|---|---|---|
| Hyperactivity | 64 | 54 | 78 | 65 |
| Aggression | 60 | 40 | 70 | 42 |
| Conduct Problems | 62 | 48 | 69 | 48 |
| Anxiety | 59 | 58 | 55 | 55 |
| Depression | 63 | 43 | 74 | 45 |
| Somatization | 36 | 30 | 43 | 53 |
| Attention Problems | 67 | 66 | 66 | 64 |

*Note.* Data are expressed as *T* scores: ≥70 = clinically significant; 60–69 = at risk; <60 = normative.

**TABLE 9.3. Example of Student Self-Report Pre–Post Data**

| | Self-rating prior to group | Self-rating at end of group |
|---|---|---|
| **BASC clinical scale** | | |
| Attitude to School | 50 | 50 |
| Attitude to Teachers | 65 | 45 |
| School Problems | 73 | 48 |
| Locus of Control | 62 | 51 |
| Social Stress | 52 | 48 |
| Anxiety | 61 | 55 |
| Depression | 61 | 45 |
| Sense of Inadequacy | 58 | 48 |
| Attention Problems | 71 | 65 |
| Hyperactivity | 65 | 60 |
| Inattention/Hyperactivity | 70 | 62 |
| | | |
| **BASC adaptive scale** | | |
| Relations with Parents | 38 | 45 |
| Interpersonal Relations | 37 | 50 |
| Self-Esteem | 28 | 38 |
| Self-Reliance | 50 | 52 |

*Note.* Data are expressed as *T* scores: For the clinical scale, ≥70 = clinically significant; 60–69 = at risk; <60 = normative. For the adaptive scale, ≥30 = clinically significant; 30–40 = at risk; >40 = normative.

Table 9.3 provides information from the student's self-report pre–post group intervention. From this data we can see that the student demonstrated improvement across several areas of concern. However, similar to the parent and teacher perspectives, the student continues to self-report problems with inattention and hyperactivity. Therefore, the group leader may want to either continue to meet with the student in a group format with a focus on supports for students with inattention and hyperactivity, meet with the student individually, or provide a referral for additional supports in these areas. While many groups have a limited number of sessions or last for a brief period of time during the school year, it is important to evaluate whether students in your groups continue to need additional supports with the original referral concern or others that have yet to be addressed.

## DATA-BASED DECISIONS AND PARENTING GROUP OUTCOMES

Data can also be used to make determinations about outcomes for parents in parenting groups. As the group leader, you can use pre–post measures to evaluate the progress parents have made in using new skills at home and in their own lives. These pre–post measures should measure important factors related to the group content. For instance, if you are running a group to support effective parenting practices, you will want to identify a measure of parenting. You can find appropriate measures from websites such as the California Evidence-Based Clearinghouse, which provides a list and links to relevant assessment tools (see *www.cebc4cw.org/assessment-tools*). When determining which measure to use, ensure the measure is valid, in that it is measuring what it says it is measuring, and that it is relevant to meaningful outcomes associated with the parenting group. This will allow you to make a determination of whether you should provide additional services or a referral to a family. At the end of this chapter, there is a sample role play on discussing the progress of the parents in the parent group with a supervisor using pre–post measures to make determinations about overall group outcomes (see role-play scenario 3 at the end of this chapter).

## TERMINATING THE GROUP

When terminating a group it is important to evaluate the progress and ongoing needs of the parents in the group. Some members may have made wonderful progress, learning and applying new skills into their own lives, while others may continue to need support. If a group is ending, be sure to evaluate where each member is and how to offer additional support to those with additional needs.

### Terminating the Child Group

Members have grown to know one another, shared many experiences and challenges together, and celebrated successes. Most students will be sad about the group ending because it was a safe, comfortable place where they could gain support, learn techniques, and obtain feedback, while creating lasting relationships with other group members. Making determinations about when to terminate a group should include some review of data to make sure that group members have made enough progress to warrant ending a group (see Chapter 7). You have the option of continuing the group if needed. Even if a specific program calls for a total of 10 group sessions, you may find that the particular students in your group would benefit from additional review of material or extensions on certain topics. Alternatively, progress monitoring data may indicate that your group has progressed more quickly than expected in the intervention curriculum. If so, you may decide to end the group early. As discussed earlier in this chapter, use data to inform your decisions about how the group is progressing, who in the group may need additional services, and when to terminate a group.

Once you decide when to terminate the group, begin discussing it a few sessions in advance so that the students are aware of the end nearing. You will want to process feelings about the group ending, future plans, review what students have learned, and talk about what happens after the group ends.

You may want to involve the students in planning an end-of-the-group party. If you have the resources, serve food and drinks at the party. Make sure that they will be able to attend the party at the specific date and time, and ask them what kinds of food and drinks they would like. Hand out invitations so that they are formally invited to the party. The most important thing about the celebration is making it all about the success of the group. You may want to ask all students what they learned from coming to the group, what techniques they will most likely continue to use, and what they liked about the group.

It can also be nice to have an awards ceremony. A certificate can be given out to each student who completed the group and other awards may also be given out (e.g., perfect attendance, best participator; see Appendix 31 for a sample Certificate of Completion). Parents and teachers can be invited to the ceremony to make the celebration even more special. Group members can choose to put on a performance based on what they learned in the group or you can share specific qualities about group members that made them an integral part of the group. Group members often enjoy performing for their parents and teachers, which in turn often makes their parents and teachers proud of the effort they put into the performance and into the group.

You can also ask the members of the group to fill out a feedback form, sharing what they liked, did not like, and what they think should be changed in future groups (see Appendix 30 for a sample Final Group Feedback Form). You can incorporate the suggestions into future groups. The feedback form shows that you respect your group members and value their opinions.

Last, a week or two after the group is over, you may want to check in on the students and see how they are doing. Ask them if they are still utilizing the techniques taught in the group. Encourage them to use the techniques and offer praise and support. You can also check in with their teacher(s) and parent(s) to see how students are doing, and remind the adults to continue to reinforce the use of skills the students learned in the group.

## *Terminating the Parent Group*

The termination of a group can be an effective way of reinforcing the work that has already been done. It is your obligation to inform the members that the group will be terminated on a given date. Your termination date will be based on the data that you've collected within and outside of the group to determine whether the needs of the group have been met. Allowing time to plan for the end of the group will result in many positive benefits for group members (Keyton, 1993). Each group member will have a different response to the group ending and show a variety of emotions. Therefore, it may be helpful to begin talking about group termination early and plan accordingly. Be sure to give reminders well in advance that the group is ending. Also, reinforce the accomplishments that the group has made upon wrapping up the session. Consider encouraging members to continue meeting despite the formal ending of the group or to stay in contact with one another as supports. As you discuss termination, you will need to discuss any feelings of frustration, sadness, anxiety, or rejection. Allow group members to "work through" their feelings and also discuss their successes and accomplishments. Review what members have learned, and talk about what happens after the group ends. Group members will have different emotions about the group ending. Be sensitive to all feelings. You may want to meet with a group member individually if needed to further process feelings regarding group termination. As you start to review the outcome data, you will be able to better plan for group termination and in turn be sensitive to the feelings of group members. At the end of this chapter there is a sample role play on how to handle a situation where a parent is having a difficult time with the group ending (see role-play scenario 4 at the end of this chapter).

If an ongoing group has to be terminated suddenly because of some unexpected event, such as illness, obligations that have a higher priority, or transfer of position, you should inform the group members at the beginning of the last session. Under no circumstances should you wait until the last few minutes of a session to say, "We have to terminate our sessions unexpectedly; this is the last session." This will frustrate and upset the group members. They will not be able to "work through" feelings of frustration, rejection, anger, and so on, that may be precipitated by a sudden termination of the group. It may negate much of the constructive work that has gone on in the previous sessions.

Group members generally handle separation as well as the leader is capable of handling it. If you are willing to separate and give the group members the recognition that they deserve (i.e., recognize that they will be able to separate without difficulty), then you will reinforce the capability of the members to handle the responsibility of separation. You may want to celebrate at the last session with a small party or a potluck. It is also a nice gesture to provide the group members with a certificate that demonstrates their success in completing the group (see Appendix 31 for a sample Certificate of Completion).

## SUMMARY

This chapter provided information on using data to select students for group interventions and evaluate outcomes. We listed websites for free screening tools to be used in the assessment and selection of group members. Existing information, such as goal sheets, as sources of data can be very useful in determining where to focus additional attention. Data can help you to determine whether each student's behavioral goals have been met. We also discussed progress monitoring to evaluate students' use of newly learned skills in settings outside of the group. You can use these data to evaluate the barriers to using new skills, including those in students' daily context outside the school. Collecting and utilizing data to improve student outcomes is as important as selecting an appropriate evidence-based intervention. Finally, we discussed the importance of preparing group members for the end of group meetings.

We hope this book provides the growing population of school-based mental health clinicians with a practical step-by-step guide to locate, plan, implement, and maintain effective parent and child group interventions. Often it is difficult for practitioners to translate theory into practice. This is especially true for many evidence-based interventions that lack details on how to effectively implement these programs in real-world school settings. This unique book provides the necessary link between these two areas of training and practice.

## MATERIALS

The following is a list of materials discussed in this chapter that can support you in using data to identify group members, monitor group progress, and determine group termination. You will find examples of these materials in the Appendices and in the figures located within this chapter.

- Teacher Nomination Form (Appendix 4).
- Goal Sheet (Appendix 25).
- Final Group Feedback Form (Appendix 30).
- Certificate of Completion (Appendix 31).
- Examples of completed goal sheets that provide data for progress monitoring.*
- Examples of tracking data to monitor progress and motivate students.*
- Form used to track student progress when using goal sheet data.*

## REFLECTION AND ROLE PLAYS

Here we provide a series of reflection exercises and role-play activities to help you further hone your use of data in making decisions regarding group recruitment, monitoring, and termination.

---

*These materials are not included in the Appendices, but may be referenced within this chapter and are also helpful when implementing parent and child groups.

## *Reflection*

After reviewing this chapter, ask yourself the following questions:

1. "How can I use existing school data and teacher rankings to select students for my group intervention? Specifically, how can I identify students whose needs match my chosen group intervention? How can I involve school staff in assisting in the group selection process without allowing their opinions to heavily sway student inclusion within the group?"
2. "How can I use a goal sheet in making decisions regarding a group member's progress within the group? How would I relay this information to the group member?"
3. "What is my plan of action for terminating my group intervention? How will I appropriately handle group members' feelings while basing my decisions on the outcome data?"

## *Role Plays*

After reviewing the reflection questions, apply your understanding of what has been covered in this chapter by responding to the following four scenarios:

### Scenario 1

You are meeting with a teacher to discuss her rankings of students within her class using the nomination form in Appendix 4 as a guide. Be sure to explain to the teacher that you will consider the rankings, but you will also consider group dynamics when choosing members for the groups (e.g., you may not want the teacher's top-two problem students in the group, because their behaviors may warrant more individualized attention).

EXAMPLE SCRIPTED ANSWER

GROUP LEADER: Thanks so much for meeting with me, Mrs. Morgan. As we discussed, I was hoping to get your input on students in your class who may benefit from my new anger coping group.

TEACHER: That is so great. I am glad you contacted me. I definitely have two students in my class that need additional support.

GROUP LEADER: Excellent! Let me tell you a little more about the group, and then it would be great if you could complete this nomination form. (*Hands the teacher a copy of the nomination form.*) Please read this list of behaviors that are bulleted at the top of the page. It includes behaviors such as threatens or bullies others in order to get his or her way, and gets other kids to gang up on somebody that he or she doesn't like. Next, rank order the students in your class according to the extent they exhibit these behaviors. The student who exhibits the greatest degree of these behaviors is ranked first and so on until 10 students [or as many students who apply] are rank ordered.

TEACHER: Great. I can easily think of a few students. (*Starts completing the nomination form. The group leader will want to wait patiently and give the teacher time to think about students who would be appropriate for the group.*)

GROUP LEADER: Thanks for taking the time to meet with me and complete this form. We find that teachers are the best nominators, since they spend so much time with students. I am also going to meet with Mrs. Jones and Mrs. Smith to see if they have students that would be appropriate for the group. I will be looking for a total of six students to participate in the group and we will want to have a mix of students so that we have a range of coping skills. For example, I would not want to have six students with severe anger problems in a group together. We want to have a balance of students so that they can learn positive coping skills from one another. Does that sound good? Do you have any additional questions?

TEACHER: It sounds great. I am crossing my fingers that a few of my students are in the group!

## TIP

Find a time when the teacher has a few minutes to complete the nomination form, such as before or after school, or during his or her planning time. If possible, it is beneficial for the teacher to complete the form while you are there so that you can explain the rank order to the teacher and answer any questions. Make sure teachers understand that you may not be able to include all of the students they nominate in the group and that you will be selecting a balance of students.

## Scenario 2

You receive a goal sheet back from the teacher of a group member (see Figure 9.1 for an example of a goal sheet that provides data for progress monitoring, dated 12/12) and are meeting with the group member to review his progress using this data as your guide. How would you review this data with the student?

### EXAMPLE SCRIPTED ANSWER

GROUP LEADER: Hi, Terrell. How's your week going?

STUDENT: Things are good. I played basketball today in gym!

GROUP LEADER: That's great. I know you love basketball. I wanted to talk for a few minutes and review your goal sheet. Is that OK with you?

STUDENT: Sure, my teacher said I am improving.

GROUP LEADER: Excellent. I love to hear that. Let's take a look at your goal sheet. (*Hands the student a copy of the goal sheet from 12/12.*) You needed to earn eight "agrees" from your teachers. How many did you earn?

STUDENT: Twelve.

GROUP LEADER: That is correct. You had 12 agrees. So, did you earn your reward?

STUDENT: Yup! I sure did.

GROUP LEADER: Nice job! I am so proud of you. (*Offers a high-five to the student.*) Yesterday you had 10 agrees, so it's great that you increased to 12 agrees today. It looks like you had two "disagrees" for following directions. Tell me what happened during Calendar and Guided Reading today.

STUDENT: I was calling out answers.

GROUP LEADER: What are you supposed to do when you have an answer to the teacher's question?

STUDENT: Raise a quiet hand.

GROUP LEADER: Yes. Raise a quiet hand and sit quietly until the teacher calls on you. Overall, you are making lots of improvements and your teacher told me you are really working hard on your goals. For tomorrow, let's focus on raising a quiet hand and not calling out. Is there anything you can think of to do instead of calling out the answers?

STUDENT: One thing I was trying was to count to 10 inside my head while I waited for the teacher to call on me.

GROUP LEADER: That is a good strategy. How about you try that tomorrow during Guided Reading and Calendar when you want to call out an answer?

STUDENT: OK.

GROUP LEADER: I will let your teacher know that you are focusing on raising a quiet hand and not calling out. Tomorrow we will meet at the end of the day to review your progress. Keep up the great work!

STUDENT: Thanks!

## TIP

It is important to celebrate successes but also to review all parts of the goal sheet to challenge the student to use similar strategies to earn positive marks throughout the day. If a student does not meet his/her goal, review the goal sheet with the student and discuss the new goal for the next week. You may want to make the goal easier to accomplish the next week. Then as the student meets the goal, increase it slowly each week, making it more and more challenging. Although you may feel as though this is a setback, you will find that meeting the needs of the student will provide for future success.

## Scenario 3

You are meeting with your supervisor to discuss the progress of the parents in your parenting group using pre–post measures to make determinations about overall group outcomes.

### EXAMPLE SCRIPTED ANSWER

GROUP LEADER: Thanks for meeting with me. I wanted to see if we could use this time to look over the pre and post measures of the parent group to determine if there were positive outcomes from the group.

SUPERVISOR: Sounds good. Remind me what measures you used.

GROUP LEADER: We used the Behavior Assessment System for Children [BASC-2; Reynolds & Kamphaus, 2004] parent, child, and teacher reports, which were administered at the beginning of the group and the end of the group. I have an example of some of the results. (*Provides the supervisor with Table 9.2.*) I have a similar chart for each student with the $T$ scores for hyperactivity, aggression, conduct problems, anxiety, depression, somatization, and attention problems based on teacher and parent report. I highlighted the $T$ scores that were in the "at-risk" and "clinically significant" ranges. There is a column for prior-to-group and end-of-group $T$ scores. What are your thoughts?

SUPERVISOR: This chart is very clear and organized, which makes it easy to understand the data. I like that you have parent and teacher report. How about the student report data?

GROUP LEADER: For each student we made a chart with the $T$ scores pregroup and end of group. The $T$ scores that are in the "at-risk or "clinically significant" range are highlighted. (*Provides the supervisor with Table 9.3.*) As you can see for this student for the BASC clinical scale, five of the highlighted $T$ scores were in the normative range. The three remaining highlighted scores were reduced but remained in the at-risk range. For the BASC adaptive scale, two of the three highlighted $T$ scores were in the normative range at the end of the group. The self-esteem $T$ score improved from the "significant risk" to "at-risk" range. From this data we can see that the student demonstrated improvement across several areas of concern. However, similar to the parent and teacher perspective, the student continues to self-report problems with inattention and hyperactivity. Therefore, we may want to either continue to meet with this student in a group format with a focus on supports for inattention and hyperactivity, meet with the student individually, or provide a referral for additional supports in these areas.

SUPERVISOR: This chart looks great. Did you have a parent evaluation form?

GROUP LEADER: We had a final parent group feedback form. (*Provides the supervisor with Appendix 30.*). Questions included "How important was it for you to attend this group?" "How helpful was the group for you?" and "How confident are you that you can use the new skills you learned in the group?"

SUPERVISOR: This is excellent. It would be great to enter all of these responses into a database so that you make a summary. For example, nine out of 10 parents reported the group was very helpful. Then, you can also summarize the questions at the bottom about what parents liked best about the group and what they liked least about the group.

GROUP LEADER: Sounds good. At our monthly meeting I can bring the results for the teacher, parent, and student BASC data as well as the summarized Final Group Feedback Form.

## TIP

To measure outcomes, use pre–post instruments related to the group content. Consult with your colleagues or supervisor to identify appropriate pre–post measures. As discussed in this chapter, it is important to have objective evidence that a student has benefited from the group intervention and no longer needs services.

### Scenario 4

A parent states that she is having a hard time with the group ending next week. Process this issue and discuss feelings regarding group termination and outlets of support outside of the group.

EXAMPLE SCRIPTED ANSWER

PARENT: Can I talk to you for a minute about group ending next week?

GROUP LEADER: Sure!

PARENT: I'm having a hard time thinking about the group ending. This group has been really supportive and I've learned so much since starting the group. I'm just afraid that if the group ends, that I won't have anyone to turn to for support and that I'll lose these skills.

GROUP LEADER: So, it sounds like you are concerned with not having a system of support and losing the skills that you have gained once the group ends?

PARENT: Yes. I really just wish it wasn't over yet.

GROUP LEADER: This is a common feeling that most people experience at the end of a group. Often-times we form ties with group members, we have common experiences from which we all can learn, and the group becomes part of our everyday lives. It is good to be in touch with these feelings and begin to prepare for what comes next after the group is finished.

PARENT: So, what does come next after the group is finished?

GROUP LEADER: There are many options and often they depend on what supports you have outside of the group and what you find beneficial to meeting your goals. Are there people that you can turn to when issues arise or who are supportive of you and your family?

PARENT: I have a couple people who are supportive and whom I can turn to, but I just really liked the group members and knowing that we could lean on each other for support and guidance.

GROUP LEADER: It sounds like you have a couple supports outside of the group, which is great, and it also sounds like you really valued the relationships that you gained in the group. I think you may be on to something. In the past, group members have kept in touch and continued to meet every once in a while to check in with and support one another. Some group members have scheduled a couple of individual sessions with the group leaders to touch base and continue with goals set in the group. Do any of these options sound beneficial to you?

PARENT: I really like the idea of maintaining contact with other group members who have learned the same strategies and have had similar experiences as I have had. And maybe I could also set up an individual session if needed, once I've worked some more on my goals.

GROUP LEADER: I think this is a terrific idea. During the last group session, would you like to introduce the idea of maintaining contact with other group members after the group is over?

PARENT: It would be great if you brought it up, and then I can express my wish to keep in touch.

GROUP LEADER: Sure. I can do that. It sounds like a plan! Do you feel a little better about the group ending and having a plan for what happens next?

PARENT: Yes. This has been very helpful, and now that we came up with a plan, I'm feeling better about the group coming to an end.

GROUP LEADER: I'm glad you expressed your concerns and that we had a chance to talk about it before the last group. I bet a lot of group members are feeling the same way and this may be helpful to them, too. Great work! I'll see you next week!

**TIP**

Create a template for a contact list so that group members can fill in their contact information during the session. Then, you can make copies and give one to each group member to take home.

## APPENDICES

# Reproducible Forms

*Note.* Documents included in the Appendices are examples. Refer to your agency/program/company and school district for approved, legal forms, especially in the cases of suicidal assessment and consent/assent for group inclusion.

# Program Summary

(Name of Group/Program)

**What will the children participating in this group learn?**
- (Group Topic 1)
- (Group Topic 2)
- (Group Topic 3)
- (Group Topic 4)

**The children will participate in a total of _____ group meetings at school with a counselor over the course of _____ weeks.**

### Weekly Group Meeting Topics:

**Session 1:** Group Introduction and Rules

**Session 2:** (Session 2 Title)

**Session 3:** (Session 3 Title)

**Session 4:** (Session 4 Title)

**Session 5:** (Session 5 Title)

**Session 6:** (Session 6 Title)

**Session 7:** (Session 7 Title)

**Session 8:** (Session 8 Title)

**Session 9:** (Session 9 Title)

**Session 10:** Review Session

**Session 11: End of the Group Celebration!!!**

---

**Parents/caregivers can participate in a parent group too!!**

**Topics for Parent Groups include:**

**Session 1:** Introductions, Overview, and Group Rules

**Session 2:** (Session 2 Title)

**Session 3:** (Session 3 Title)

**Session 4:** (Session 4 Title)

---

# Consent/Permission Form

(School/Name of Group/Program)

(Address)

## Parent Permission Form for Individual and Group Counseling

Name of Child: _____

Address: _____

_____

Birth Date: _____

Name of Parent or Guardian: _____

I, _____, give permission for my child,
　　　　　　(Name of Parent or Guardian)

_____, to participate in the _____.
　　　　　　(Name of Child)　　　　　　　　　　　　　　　　　　　(Name of Group/Program)

This counseling program will be provided by _____.
　　　　　　　　　　　　　　　　　　　　　　　　　　(Name of Group Leader and Position)

I understand that this service is being made available in order to help my child learn techniques and skills to be successful in school.

I understand that any information divulged in counseling sessions is confidential and will not be shared with anyone except an officially designated professional supervisor, except in situations in which the safety and welfare of the students or others may be in jeopardy.

_____

(Signature)

_____

(Relationship)

_____

(Date)

# Student Assent Form

We are the group leaders at _____ and we are inviting you to be in a group that helps students learn techniques and skills to be successful in school.

## Group times:

The group will take place on (day of week) from (start time) to (end time).

## Do I have to be in this group?

You do not have to participate in this group. It is up to you. Most students find the group to be fun and rewarding. But no one will be upset with you if you decide not to participate.

## Will being in this group hurt or help me in any way? (edit based on group content)

Being in this group will bring you no harm. Within this group you will learn skills and techniques that will help you to be successful in school and develop positive peer relationships with group members. During each group we will watch videos, participate in activities, practice using learned skills and techniques, and enjoy a snack.

## Confidentiality:

## What will you do with information about me?

Everything that is shared in group will remain within the group environment. The only time that your group leaders would need to share information from group is if someone in the group shared information about hurting oneself or someone else.

## If you have questions about the group, contact:

(Group leader's contact information)

## Agreement:

By signing this form, I agree to be in the group described above.

Name: _____

Signature: _____ Date: _____

**You will receive a copy of this form.**

# Teacher Nomination Form

(Name of Group/Program)

Please rank order the students in your class according to the degree or extent to which each exhibits the behaviors* below. The student who exhibits the greatest degree of these behaviors is ranked first and so on, until 10 students (or as many students who apply) are rank ordered.

- When teased or threatened, he/she gets angry easily and strikes back.
- Claims other children are to blame in a fight.
- When accidentally hurt, he/she assumes that the peer meant to do it and reacts with anger/ fighting.
- Gets other kids to gang up on somebody that he/she doesn't like.
- Uses physical force (or threatens to use physical force) in order to dominate other kids.
- Threatens or bullies others in order to get his/her way.

Most ↑

1. _____
2. _____
3. _____
4. _____
5. _____
6. _____
7. _____
8. _____
9. _____
10. _____

Least ↓

*Note.* These names **will not** be shared with anyone other than the group leader.

*The behaviors to be listed on the nomination form will change based on the group's focus.

# Caregiver Contact Log

(Name of Group/Program)

Name of Child: _____    Phone Number: _____

Name of Caregiver(s): _____    Address: _____

Name of Child's Teacher: _____

| Date | Time | Purpose of contact (e.g., recruitment, reminder call, follow-up after group absence) | Outcome (e.g., no contact made, left message, reason caregiver denied consent, reason for not attending parent group) |
|---|---|---|---|
| | | | |
| | | | |
| | | | |
| | | | |
| | | | |
| | | | |
| | | | |
| | | | |
| | | | |
| | | | |
| | | | |
| | | | |
| | | | |
| | | | |
| | | | |
| | | | |
| | | | |
| | | | |
| | | | |
| | | | |
| | | | |

# Recruitment Script

IF TALKING BY PHONE, BEGIN: Hello, may I speak to (Name of Parent/Caregiver)?

Hi, my name is (Name of Group Leader) and I am a counselor from (Elementary School Name). How are you doing? I wanted to talk to you briefly about a free program we are offering at the school. The program is called the (Name of Group/Program) and is taught to children who are in the (Number) grade. (Name of Child) is currently in (Number) grade and has been selected to participate in the program.

The main goal of the (Name of Group/Program) is to teach children how to deal with peer pressure; problems that face children with other peers, teachers, and parents; and also how to set long-term and short-term goals. The program will run for (Number) sessions and meet once per week. The space is limited; we plan to have no more than six students participating in the program.

Additionally, we invite the parents and caregivers of the participating children to attend parent group meetings. The parent group will be held at a time convenient for you and dinner (or Food and Drinks) will be provided. The parent group brings together parents to discuss issues and to learn about the techniques taught in the child groups to help their children do better at home and at school. It has been shown through research that while children benefit from the child group component alone, the children get the maximum benefit when parents attend the parent group meetings as well.

I am contacting you to let you know about this opportunity and to see whether you are interested in having your child participate in the child group. Further, I would like to ask you about days and times that could work for you to attend the (Name of Group/Program) parent group.

If you are interested in having (Name of Child) participate in the group, I will need you to sign and return a consent form.

IF TALKING TO PARENT IN PERSON: What questions do you have before we look over the consent?

IF TALKING TO PARENT OVER PHONE: I will send home the consent form along with some additional information about the (Name of Group/Program) and a questionnaire about your preferences for the parent group times. What questions do you have about the child or parent groups?

BEFORE ending the conversation, determine the following:

1. Is the parent willing to consent to the child's participation in the group?

2. Are the parents interested in participating in the parent group?
   a. What are possible days and times they could participate?
   b. What barriers may get in the way of their participation?
   c. Are other caregivers likely to participate in the parent groups?
   d. Will child care be needed for participation in the parent groups?
   e. Will transportation be an issue for participation in the parent groups?

3. Do you have the correct address and phone number for contacting the parents?
   a. What are the best times of the day to call?

# Parent Group Survey

You are invited to attend the (Name of Group/Program) parent group.
All groups will be held at (Name of School/Location).
<u>A meal will be provided at each meeting</u>.

Please complete this form and return as soon as possible. Send this form back with your child to help him/her earn points that he/she can put toward earning prizes from the prize box! Thank you!! We truly appreciate your input!

YOU WILL BE NOTIFIED ABOUT THE DATES AND TIMES OF THE PARENT GROUPS AT THE COMPLETION OF THIS SURVEY.

<u>Please check</u>:

\_\_\_\_ Yes, I would like to attend.

\_\_\_\_ Sorry, I am <u>not able to attend</u> for the following reason:

_____

_____

Name of Parent: _____

Name of Child: _____

Address: _____

_____

_____

Phone Number: _____

Best Time to Call: _____

\_\_\_\_ I need more information, please call me.

| The BEST <u>days</u> for parent groups for me would be: | | The BEST <u>times</u> of day for parent groups for me would be: | |
|---|---|---|---|
| \_\_\_\_ Monday | ☐ | \_\_\_\_ Early morning | ☐ |
| \_\_\_\_ Tuesday | ☐ | \_\_\_\_ Late morning | ☐ |
| \_\_\_\_ Wednesday | ☐ | \_\_\_\_ Early afternoon | ☐ |
| \_\_\_\_ Thursday | ☐ | \_\_\_\_ Late afternoon | ☐ |
| \_\_\_\_ Friday | ☐ | \_\_\_\_ Early evening | ☐ |

# Letter to Parent/Caregiver

Dear Parent/Caregiver,

(Name of Group/Program) is a FREE program at (Name of School/Group Location) taught by (Name of Group Leader and Position). (Name of Group/Program) includes a child group and a parent group. Students will meet once a week for approximately 45–60 minutes during normal school hours. Group sessions will be held during resource blocks so that the students are not taken from their main academic coursework. You are also invited to attend a parent group to help support the new skills that your child is learning.

Your child is being offered this opportunity to support his/her strengths, such as positive classroom behavior, academic strengths, school spirit, and friendship skills. Additionally, this program will help your child when he/she transitions to middle school.

Topics covered will include:

- (Topic 1)
- (Topic 2)
- (Topic 3) . . .
- (Topic 4)
- (Topic 5)

It is my pleasure to offer you and your child the opportunity to be a part of the (Name of Group/Program). If you would like for your child to be a part of these activities, please fill out the attached consent form and return it to (Name of Group Leader) as soon as possible. Additional information regarding the parent groups will be provided at a later date. Please feel free to call (Name of Group Leader) at (000-000-0000) if you have further questions.

Thank you!

Sincerely,

---

# Parent Group Reminder Flier

### A Friendly Reminder . . .

**Session 2: (Session 2 Topic)**

**Please join us for our parent group meeting on:**

**Day:** _____

**Date:** _____

**Time:** _____

**Place:** _____

**Upcoming Meetings:**

**Session 3: (Session 3 Topic)**

**Session 4: (Session 4 Topic)**

-------------------------------------------------------------------------------

Please detach and return this form to let us know if you will be attending Session 2. Please check one of the choices below and send this form back to school with your child to help him/her earn 2 points that he/she can put toward earning prizes from the prize box. As long as your child returns the form (no matter whether you can attend the group or not), he/she will receive the points!

_____ Yes, I plan on attending Session 2.

# Parent Group Invite Letter

Dear Parents/Guardians of (Number)-Grade Students,

Being a parent can be tough. Even when children are well behaved, raising a child takes time, energy, and a lot of hard work. At times parenting can be frustrating and demanding, especially when other daily issues (e.g., jobs, other relationships) are also time-consuming. Nobody is perfect! We can all learn to better communicate, play, and build relationships with children. Children do not come with manuals, and they constantly keep us on our toes! Have you ever felt this way?

Parent groups are a good way to gain experience, bond with others, and learn skills that you may not have tried. My name is (Name of Group Leader) and I am the counselor from (Program) who works at your child's school. I will be running a parent group beginning in January and ending by the end of the school year. Parents with different parenting needs are being invited to attend. Some parents need a lot of help with their child's behavior because of issues they are experiencing every day, and other parents may want to change something that occurs only every once in a while with their child.

The group will cover specific topics, such as positive engagement, praising appropriate behaviors, ignoring inappropriate behaviors, behavior management, setting rules and expectations, and administering effective consequences. Although there will be specific topics covered in the program, parents will also have the chance to share real-life examples, practice skills, and review videos of positive and negative examples of what we are learning.

The group will be held one day per week for 1 hour. Food will be served and prizes will be given during sessions. If you are interested in participating in this group, please sign the form below and have your child return it to me at school. We will choose a day and time based on the majority! There are only 15 spaces in the group, so the first 15 parents who are able to commit to the group will be invited to be in the group. I look forward to hearing back from you!

-------------------------------------------------------------------------------------

Name of Child: _____

Name of Parent: _____

Signature: _____ Date: _____

Phone Number(s): _____

What day(s) are best for you? (please circle)

    Monday     Tuesday     Wednesday     Thursday     Friday

What time(s) are best for you? (please circle)

    Early morning     Late morning     Early afternoon     Late afternoon

## Parent Group Invite Flier

As a parent, you work hard!! Raising a child takes time, energy, and a lot of hard work . . .

Join the (Name of Group/Program) parent group to
connect with other parents and enhance your parenting skills, including:

- Skill 1
- Skill 2
- Skill 3 . . .

| (Group/Program Name) Parent Group Will Focus on Parenting Children Ages 4–7. | Group Leaders Are (Leader Names) |
|---|---|
| **Group Location: (Location of Group)** **Group Day/Time: (Day/Time of Group)** | |

Please return the bottom portion of this form to the main office or give it directly to (Name of Group Leader). Thanks!

--------------------------------------------------------------------------------

Name of Child/Student: _____

Date: _____

Name of Parent: _____

Phone Number: _____


What day(s) are best for you? (please circle)

    Monday      Tuesday      Wednesday      Thursday      Friday


What time(s) are best for you? (please circle)

    Early morning      Late morning      Early afternoon      Late afternoon

# Planning Ahead Checklist—Child Group

In general:

☐ Establish your schedule for meetings and distribute a copy to:

    ☐ School counselor

    ☐ School principal

    ☐ School custodian

    ☐ Other relevant individuals

☐ Plan for a weekly meeting with your co-leader

☐ Review the program

For each meeting:

| To do | 1 | 2 | 3 | 4 | 5 | 6 | 7 | 8 | 9 |
|---|---|---|---|---|---|---|---|---|---|
| Goal sheet reminder | | | | | | | | | |
| Call parents to check in (as needed) | | | | | | | | | |
| Copy handouts | | | | | | | | | |
| Gather supplies (e.g., pens, paper, chart) | | | | | | | | | |
| Create agenda | | | | | | | | | |
| Order/buy food and beverages | | | | | | | | | |
| Update incentives list | | | | | | | | | |
| Gather prize box prizes | | | | | | | | | |
| Set up room (e.g., chairs, folders) | | | | | | | | | |
| Get video equipment ready | | | | | | | | | |

# Child Group Weekly Feedback Form

(Name of Group/Program)

Circle your answer:

1. I think what the group leaders were teaching us was:

   A. Easy to figure out—I understood everything.

   B. Pretty easy—I had trouble understanding some things.

   C. Hard—I did *not* understand the lesson.

2. I think the group leaders did a good job leading our group.

   A. Totally agree—they did a great job leading group.

   B. Somewhat agree—they did an OK job leading group.

   C. Disagree—they did a poor job leading group.

3. I think what I learned today was:

   A. Very helpful—I will use it *all* the time.

   B. Helpful—I will use it sometimes.

   C. NOT helpful—I will *not* use it.

4. I think that the role plays/activities we used to practice were:

   A. Very helpful—they really helped me understand the lesson today.

   B. Helpful—they somewhat helped me understand the lesson today.

   C. NOT helpful—they did *not* help me understand the lesson today.

5. What did you like the BEST this week?

   _____

   _____

   _____

   _____

6. What did you like the LEAST this week?

   _____

   _____

   _____

   _____

# Session Summary Handout—Teacher Version

(Name of Group/Program)
(Session #: Topic/Title)

The following material was highlighted during the group meeting. You may wish to ask the students to share with you what they discussed or learned during the group. The main ideas are shared below so you can elicit the information from them and help to reinforce that you are interested and support the program.

*Goals for the Week:*

1. Reviewed goals from last week.

2. Set new goals for this week.

*Reviewed Homework from Past Week:*

1. Students shared homework examples.

2. Discussed specific examples from homework.

*Session Topic:*

1. Discussed (list main ideas in the session).

2. Practiced (list main techniques used in the session).

MEMBER HOMEWORK

This week, students participating in the group have been assigned a task: _____

Each student was provided with (describe homework worksheet).

Each student was asked to (give specific homework instructions).

Each student can earn 2 extra points for returning their homework.

*Suggestions for How You Can Support the Group Members*

- Ask them about the goals they developed for this week.
- Remind them of their goals throughout the week and praise them for success.
- Have them show you (list techniques learned in group).
- Have a discussion with the entire class about (list ideas learned in group). Please remember to be general in your discussion as to not single out the members of the group.
- Remind them to complete the group member homework.

# Session Summary Handout—Parent Version

(Name of Group/Program)
(Session #: Topic/Title)

We talked about the following material during the group meeting. You may want to ask your child to share with you what he/she learned during the group. The main ideas are shared below so you can talk with your child and show that you are interested and support the program.

*Goals for the Week:*

1. Reviewed goals from last week.

2. Set new goals for this week.

*Reviewed Homework from Past Week:*

1. Students shared homework examples.

2. Discussed specific examples from homework.

*Session Topic:*

1. Discussed (list main ideas in the session).

2. Practiced (list main techniques used in the session).

## YOUR CHILD'S HOMEWORK

This week, your child has been assigned a task: _____

_____

Your child was provided with (describe homework worksheet).

Your child has been asked to (give specific homework instructions).

Your child can earn 2 extra points for returning his/her homework.

*Suggestions for How You Can Support Your Child*

- Ask your child about the goals he/she developed for this week.
- Remind your child of his/her goals throughout the week; praise your child for success.
- Have your child show you (list techniques learned in group).
- Have a discussion about (list ideas learned in group).
- Check in and remind your child to complete his/her homework a couple times this week.

(List definitions and summarize key ideas)

# Planning Ahead Checklist—Parent Group

In general:

☐ Establish your schedule for meetings and distribute a copy to:

    ☐ School counselor

    ☐ School principal

    ☐ School custodian

    ☐ Other relevant individuals

☐ Plan for a weekly meeting with your co-leader

☐ Review the program

For each meeting:

| To do | 1 | 2 | 3 | 4 | 5 | 6 | 7 | 8 | 9 |
|---|---|---|---|---|---|---|---|---|---|
| Send home reminder fliers | | | | | | | | | |
| Make reminder phone calls | | | | | | | | | |
| Copy handouts | | | | | | | | | |
| Gather supplies (e.g., pens, paper, chart) | | | | | | | | | |
| Create agenda | | | | | | | | | |
| Order/buy food and beverages | | | | | | | | | |
| Confirm child care | | | | | | | | | |
| Confirm transportation | | | | | | | | | |
| Gather raffle prizes | | | | | | | | | |
| Set up room (e.g., chairs, folders) | | | | | | | | | |
| Get video equipment ready | | | | | | | | | |

# Donation Letter

(Date)

(Company Name)
(Company Address)


Dear _____,

(Name of Program/Company) is implementing the (Name of Group/Program) in the (School District). (Name of Group/Program) is a group intervention that targets children in the late elementary school and early middle school years who show signs of risk for serious behavior problems later in life, including substance abuse and affiliation with delinquent peers. This intervention has both a child and parent component. (Name of Group/Program) is based on an empirical model of risk factors for substance use and delinquency and addresses key factors including social competence, self-regulation, and positive parental involvement. A two-page summary of the intervention is included.

The purpose of this letter is to request a donation to provide incentives to parents/caregivers who attend the (Name of Group/Program) parent group meetings. There are many barriers to parent and caregiver attendance to interventions outside their home. A donation from your establishment would be used to provide incentives for parent participation. These incentives would be in the form of raffle prizes and refreshments to parents attending groups. Your support in this manner will be greatly appreciated. All donations would be recognized as donated from your establishment during the groups.

(Name of Group/Program) is currently being offered to 24 children and their parents from the following four elementary schools in (School District). The mental health clinicians in the schools are conducting the groups.

We would like to request your company's assistance in providing this intervention to the children and parents of participating (School District). Your donation would be greatly appreciated. These funds would be used to purchase gift cards to raffle during each parent group, light refreshments/snacks, and small incentives for group participation.

If you have any questions or would like additional information, please contact (Name of Group Leader) at (000-000-0000). Send e-mail inquiries to (E-mail Address of Group Leader).


Sincerely,

# "Thank You for Donating" Letter

(Date)

(Company Name)
(Company Address)

Dear _____,

(Name of Program/Company) and the Elementary Schools involved in implementing the (Name of Group/Program) in the (School District) would like to thank you for your kind donation.

Your donation has allowed us to provide incentives in the form of raffle prizes and refreshments to parents and caregivers who attend the parent group sessions, which has shown to work in the past to increase attendance and participation at parent group meetings. Your donation has also allowed us to provide incentives to the children in the form of prizes for good behavior and homework completion. Your support in this manner is greatly appreciated. All donations are recognized as being donated from your establishment during the groups.

We are greatly appreciative of your company's assistance in helping to provide this intervention to the children and parents of participating (School District). You have truly helped us to provide quality services to children who are at risk for serious behavior problems later in life, including substance abuse and affiliation with delinquent peers.

If you have any questions or would like additional information, please contact (Name of Group Leader) at (000-000-0000). Send e-mail inquiries to (E-mail Address of Group Leader).


Sincerely,

# Child Care Permission Form

(Name of Group/Program)

There will be child care available during the (Name of Group/Program) parent group if parents are in need of someone to watch their children so that they are able to attend the parent group. The child care will be held in (Name of School/Group Location) during the time of the parent group. The child care worker is from (Company Name of Child Care Worker). Games, movies, and snacks will be made available to the children while in the child care setting.

All children are required to follow all rules and regulations set forth by (Name of School/Group Location). There may be a certain degree of risk, including the potential of injury to persons and property. Parents/guardians agree to understand and acknowledge such risks and hereby voluntarily assume these risks. Parents/guardians further agree to release, indemnify, and forever hold harmless, Clinician A, Clinician B, Clinician C, Child Care Worker A, (Name of School/Group Location), (Name of Program/Company) if anyone is injured or any property of the participant is damaged while under the supervision of any employees of the above-named institutions.

I, _____, have read the above information and I am giving my permission for my child/children to be looked after by Child Care Worker A from (Child Care Worker's Company), while I am attending the (Name of Group/Program) parent group.

_____

Parent/Guardian Signature

_____

Date

## "Thank You" Note to Parent

# Thank You!

Thank you for attending the (Name of Group/Program) parent group last week! We are looking forward to working with you and your child this year. We hope you will be able to attend the next meeting on (Date) from (Start Time to End Time). Lunch will be provided! Please call me if you have any questions: (000-000-0000) (ext. 000).

—Clinician A and Clinician B

## "We Missed You" Note to Parent

We Missed You!

We hope you will be able to attend our next parent meeting on (Date) from (Start Time to End Time)! Lunch will be provided! Please call me if you have any questions: (000-000-0000) (ext. 000).

—Clinician A and Clinician B

# Parent Encouragement Form

(Name of Group/Program)

Name of Parent: _____

(Session #)

Did you complete your homework? How did it go? _____

_____

_____

_____

My goal for this week: _____

_____

_____

_____

Message from my group leader: _____

_____

_____

_____

(Session #)

Did you complete your homework? How did it go? _____

_____

_____

_____

My goal for this week: _____

_____

_____

_____

Message from my group leader: _____

_____

_____

_____

# Parent Group Feedback Form

(Name of Group/Program)

Circle your answers:

1. I think what we learned in this session was:

   A. Not helpful—I will not use it.

   B. Somewhat helpful—I will use it sometimes.

   C. Very helpful—I will use it a lot.

2. The group leader's teaching and leadership skills were:

   A. Below average—The leader did a poor job leading the group.

   B. Average—The leader did an OK job leading the group.

   C. Above average—The leader did a great job leading the group.

3. The group discussions and interactions were:

   A. Not helpful—I will not use it.

   B. Somewhat helpful—I will use it sometimes.

   C. Very helpful—I will use it a lot.

4. The use of role plays and video examples were:

   A. Not helpful—I did not think they were useful.

   B. Somewhat helpful—They were somewhat useful.

   C. Very helpful—I will use this information a lot.

5. What did you like the BEST about the session this week?

   _____

   _____

   _____

   _____

6. What did you like the LEAST about the session this week?

   _____

   _____

   _____

   _____

"Cool Down" Thermometer

# "Cool Down" Corner

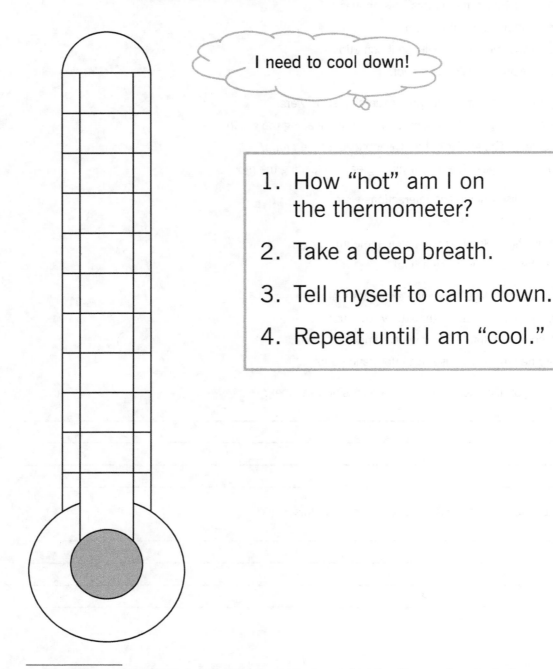

I need to cool down!

1. How "hot" am I on the thermometer?

2. Take a deep breath.

3. Tell myself to calm down.

4. Repeat until I am "cool."

# Goal Sheet

(Group/Program Name)

Name: _____ Week of: ____/____/____

This week my goal is: _____

_____

_____

_____

I, _____, have chosen the above goal and am responsible for doing my best to meet this goal, having my teacher sign this sheet, and returning it to group each week.

Monday          Y   N          _____

_____

Tuesday         Y   N          _____

_____

Wednesday       Y   N          _____

_____

Thursday        Y   N          _____

_____

Friday          Y   N          _____

_____

Teacher: Please sign your name on the line provided and indicate whether or not the goal was met by circling Y (Yes) or N (No). If the child did not meet the goal, please provide a brief explanation as to why. Praise and encouragement are recommended for student commitment to goals.

Teacher Signature: _____

Student Signature: _____

# Good Behavior Sticker Chart

| Name ↓ Session # → | 1 | 2 | 3 | 4 | 5 | 6 | 7 | 8 | 9 | 10 |
|---|---|---|---|---|---|---|---|---|---|---|
| | | | | | | | | | | |
| | | | | | | | | | | |
| | | | | | | | | | | |
| | | | | | | | | | | |
| | | | | | | | | | | |

(Group Name/Program) Sticker Chart

# Parent Group Agenda

(Group/Program Name)

1. Check-ins, success stories, and frustrations.

2. Review homework and key points from last session.

3. Introduction to (topic).

4. Video examples.

5. Role plays and practice activities.

6. Wrap-up.

7. Homework.

8. Raffle and closing.

# Great Work!

# Suicide Assessment Form

Name of Group Member: _____ Date: _____

1. Instance in group session: _____
   _____

2. Ideation

   When did the student begin to consider suicide? _____

   How often does the student think about suicide? _____ times per hour/day/week

3. Current plan

   ____ yes ____ considering means/vague ____ no

   *Specify:* Time frame _____ Place _____

   Means _____

4. Access to method

   ____ yes ____ no ____ unclear

5. Intent

   ____ denies ____ endorses ____ unclear/passive ____ evasive

6. Immediate intervention procedures (*check all that are applicable*):

   ____ School principal was notified. Date: _____ Time:_____

   ____ Parent/guardian was notified. Date: _____ Time:_____

   ____ Student linked with other staff for additional support: _____

   ____ Student referred to outside agency: _____

   ____ Student escorted to/met at ER. Date: _____ Time:_____

   Hospital: _____ Admitted? ____ yes ____ no

   ____ Safety plan established via written Contract for Safety.

   ____ Student able to explain positive aspects of living/express hope/future orientation.

   ____ Student has person(s) or agency(ies) to contact if does not feel safe.

   ____ Student understands steps to take if does not feel safe.

   ____ Student willing to sign document.

7. Follow-up

   ____ Group leader will call student/guardian.

   ____ Group leader will meet with student/guardian.

   ____ Group leader will contact agency.

_____        _____
Group Leader Signature                                                          Date

# Safety Contract

This is an agreement between my group leader, _____, and

myself, _____, to help keep me safe from harm.

1. I agree that if I have thoughts about physically hurting myself or anyone else while I am at school, I will tell my group leader, counselor, and/or teacher.
2. If I am at home and I have these thoughts, I agree to tell one of my adult supports,* OR call the National Suicide Prevention Lifeline at 1-800-273-8255, OR call 911.
3. Signing my name on this paper means that I agree not to hurt myself or anyone else.

I understand that my group leader wants to make sure that I am safe and that others around me are safe. This means that my group leader may need to talk to my parent/guardian to make sure I am safe when I am not at school. Also, my group leader may need to call 911 or may need to escort me to the hospital.

_____    _____
Group Member                                          Witness/Group Leader

## MY SUPPORTS

SUPPORTS are people who are there for you when you need them. You can talk to them and share your feelings with them. Most importantly, you can go to them for help. Your group leader may be one example of an adult support. You might have family members, neighbors, or teachers who are also supports for you. It is good to know who can support you at school AND who can support you at home.

Who are two adults who you can talk to when you are at home (not in school)?

1. Name: _____    Phone Number: _____

2. Name: _____    Phone Number: _____

3. Name: _____    Phone Number: _____

Who are two adults you can talk to at school?

1. Name: _____    Phone Number: _____

2. Name: _____    Phone Number: _____

| AGENCY | NUMBER | HOURS OF OPERATION |
|---|---|---|
| National Suicide Prevention Lifeline (*https://suicidepreventionlifeline.org*) | 1-800-273-TALK (1-800-273-8255) | 24 hours/7 days per week |
| National Hopeline Network (*www.hopeline.com*) | 1-800-SUICIDE (1-800-784-2433) | 24 hours/7 days per week |

***Please call 911 if you are in immediate danger. Tell the operator you are in suicidal danger.**

# Final Group Feedback Form

(Group/Program Name)

Date: _____

*Please answer the following questions by indicating one response.*

How important was it for you to attend this group?

☐ not at all important    ☐ somewhat important    ☐ fairly important    ☐ very important

How helpful was the group for you?

☐ not at all helpful    ☐ somewhat helpful    ☐ fairly helpful    ☐ very helpful

How difficult was it for you to be part of this group?

☐ very difficult    ☐ mostly difficult    ☐ somewhat difficult    ☐ not difficult

Was the amount of time and effort you put into this group worth it?

☐ not worth it    ☐ somewhat worth it    ☐ mostly worth it    ☐ very worth it

How confident are you that you can use the new skills you learned in the group?

☐ no confidence    ☐ somewhat confident    ☐ fairly confident    ☐ very confident

Overall, how do you feel about being part of this group?

☐ very negative    ☐ somewhat negative    ☐ fairly positive    ☐ very positive

How helpful did you find the information provided by the group leader?

☐ not at all helpful    ☐ somewhat helpful    ☐ fairly helpful    ☐ very helpful

What tips can you provide for making the groups work even better in the future? _____

_____

_____

What did you like *best* about the group? _____

_____

_____

What did you like *least* about the group? _____

_____

_____

## Certificate of Completion

(School/Program)

## Certificate of Completion

is hereby granted to

# (Group Member's Name)

to certify that she has completed

## (Group Name/Program)

Awarded: "Exceptional Praiser!"

Granted: (Date)

_____
(Group Leader)

_____
(Group Leader)

# References

Achenbach, T. (1992). *Manual for the Child Behavior Checklist/2–3*. Burlington: University of Vermont Department of Psychiatry.

Advocates for Youth. (2012). *Science and success: Sex education and other programs that work to prevent teen pregnancy, HIV and sexually transmitted infections* (3rd ed.). Washington, DC: Author.

Albano, A. M., & Kendall, P. C. (2002). Cognitive behavioral therapy for children and adolescents with anxiety disorders: Clinical research advances. *International Review of Psychiatry, 14*(2), 129–134.

American Psychological Association Presidential Task Force on Evidence-Based Practice. (2006). Evidence-based practices in psychology. *American Psychologist, 61*(4), 271–285.

Bandura, A. (1977). Self-efficacy: Toward a unifying theory of behavioral change. *Psychological Review, 84*(2), 191–215.

Barrett, P. M., Lowry-Webster, H., & Turner, C. (2000). *FRIENDS program for children: Group leaders manual*. Brisbane, Australia: Australian Academic Press.

Beck, A. T., Ward, C. H., Mendelson, M., Mock, J., & Erbaugh, J. (1961). An inventory for measuring depression. *Archives of General Psychiatry, 4*, 561–571.

Birmaher, B., Brent, D. A., Chiappetta, L., Bridge, J., Monga, S., & Baugher, M. (1999). Psychometric properties of the Screen for Child Anxiety Related Emotional Disorders (SCARED): A replication study. *Journal of the American Academy of Child and Adolescent Psychiatry, 38*(10), 1230–1236.

Botvin, G. J. (2000). *Life Skills Training curriculum manual*. Princeton, NJ: Princeton Health Press.

Botvin, G. J., & Eng, A. (1980). A comprehensive school-based smoking prevention program. *Journal of School Health, 50*(4), 209–213.

Botvin, G. J., & Griffin, K. W. (2002). Life skills training as a primary prevention approach for adolescent drug abuse and other problem behaviors. *International Journal of Emergency Mental Health, 4*(1), 41–48.

Brown, C. (2004). *The Curriculum-Based Support Group (CBSG) program: Curriculum manual*. Dallas, TX: Rainbow Days.

Burlingame, G. M., Fuhriman, A., & Johnson, J. E. (2001). Cohesion in group psychotherapy. *Psychotherapy: Theory, Research and Practice, 38*(4), 373–379.

Clarke, G. N., Lewinsohn, P. M., & Hops, H. (1990). *Adolescent coping with depression course: Leader's manual for adolescent groups*. Portland, OR: Kaiser Permanente.

Clarke, G. N., Rohde, P., Lewinsohn, P. M., Hops, H., & Seeley, J. R. (1999). Cognitive-behavioral treatment of adolescent depression: Efficacy of acute group treatment and booster sessions. *Journal of the American Academy of Child and Adolescent Psychiatry, 38*(3), 272–279.

Costello, E. J., Mustillo, S., Erkanli, A., Keeler, G., & Angold, A. (2003). Prevalence and development of psychiatric disorders in childhood and adolescence. *Archives of General Psychiatry, 60*(80), 837–844.

Darney, D., Reinke, W. M., Herman, K. C., Stormont, M., & Ialongo, N. (2013). Children with co-occurring academic and behavior problems in first grade: Distal outcomes in twelfth grade. *Journal of School Psychology, 51*(1), 117–158.

DeRosa, R., Habib, M., Pelcovitz, D., Rathus, J., Ford, J., & Sonnenklar, J. (2006). *Structured psychotherapy for adolescents responding to chronic stress (SPARCS): A trauma-focused guide for groups.* Manhasset, NY: North Shore University Hospital.

DeRosa, R., & Pelcovitz, D. (2008). Igniting SPARCS of change: Structured psychotherapy for adolescents responding to chronic stress. In D. Brom, R. Pat-Horenczyk, & J. Ford (Eds.), *Treating traumatized children: Risk, resilience and recovery* (pp. 1–20). New York: Routledge.

Dishion, T. J., & Patterson, G. R. (1992). Age effects in parent training outcome. *Behavior Therapy, 23*(4), 719–729.

Dodge, K. A., Lansford, J. E., Burks, V. S., Bates, J. E., Pettit, G. S., Fontaine, R., et al. (2003). Peer rejection and social information-processing factors in the development of aggressive behavior problems in children. *Child Development, 74*(2), 374–393.

Farmer, E., Burns, B., Phillips, S., Angold, A., & Costello, E. J. (2003). Pathways into and through mental health services for children and adolescents. *Psychiatric Services, 54*(1), 60–66.

Faulstich, M. E., Carey, M. P., Ruggiero, L., Enyart, P., & Gresham, F. (1986). Assessment of depression in childhood and adolescence: An evaluation of the Center for Epidemiological Studies Depression Scale for Children (CES-DC). *American Journal of Psychiatry, 143*(8), 1024–1027.

Goodman, R. (1997). The Strengths and Difficulties Questionnaire: A research note. *Journal of Child Psychology and Psychiatry, 38*(5), 581–586.

Greenberg, M. T., Domitrovich, C., & Bumbarger, B. (1999). *Preventing mental disorders in school-age children: A review of the effectiveness of prevention programs.* University Park: College of Health and Human Development, Pennsylvania State University.

Greenberg, M. T., & Kusché, C. A. (2006). Building social and emotional competence: The PATHS curriculum. In S. R. Jimerson & M. Furlong (Eds.), *Handbook of school violence and school safety: From research to practice* (pp. 395–412). Mahway, NJ: Erlbaum.

Greenberg, M. T., & Kusché, C. A. (2011). *Promoting Alternative Thinking Strategies (PATHS): Curriculum manual.* South Deerfield, MA: Channing Bete.

Greenberg, M. T., Kusché, C. A., Cook, E. T., & Quamma, J. P. (1995). Promoting emotional competence in school-aged children: The effects of the PATHS curriculum. *Developmental Psychopathology, 7*(1), 117–136.

Gresham, F. M., & Elliott, S. N. (1990). *Social Skills Rating System.* Circle Pines, MN: American Guidance Service.

Hedl, J. J., Jr. (2009). *Reducing interrelated risks for substance abuse, delinquency and violence: Effects of the Rainbow Days' Curriculum-Based Support Group Program.* National Registry of Evidence-Based Programs and Practices.

Herschell, A., D., McNeil, C. B., & McNeil, D. W. (2004). Clinical child psychology's progress in disseminating empirically supported treatments. *Clinical Psychology: Science and Practice, 11*(3), 267–288.

Jaycox, L. (2003). *Cognitive Behavioral Interventions for Trauma in Schools: Curriculum manual.* Dallas, TX: Sopris West.

Jaycox, L., Kataoka, S. H., Stein, B. D., Langley, A. K., & Wong, M. (2012). Cognitive Behavioral Interventions for Trauma in Schools. *Journal of Applied School Psychology, 28*(3), 239–255.

Jemmott, L. S., Jemmott, J. B., III, & McCaffree, K. (1994). *Be Proud! Be Responsible! Strategies to empower youth to reduce their risk for HIV infection: Curriculum manual.* New York: Select Media.

Jemmott, L. S., Jemmott, J. B., III, & McCaffree, K. (1998). *Making Proud Choices: Curriculum guide.* New York: Select Media.

Jemmott, L. S., Jemmott, J. B., III, & McCaffree, K. (2003). *A safer-sex approach to HIV/STDs and teen pregnancy prevention: An overview of the curriculum.* New York: Select Media

Kamphaus, R. W., & Reynolds, C. R. (2008). *Behavioral and Emotional Screening System.* Bloomington, MN: Pearson.

Kendall, P. C. (2006). *Cognitive-behavioral therapy for anxious children: Therapist manual* (3rd ed.). Ardmore, PA: Workbook.

Kendall, P. C., & Hedtke, K. (2006). *Cognitive-behavioral therapy for anxious children: Therapist manual.* Ardmore, PA: Workbook.

Kendall, P. C., Robin, J. A., Hedtke, K. A., & Suveg, C. (2005). Considering CBT with anxious youth?: Think exposures. *Cognitive and Behavioral Practice, 12*(1), 136–148.

Keyton, J. (1993). Group termination: Completing the study of group development. *Small Group Research, 24*(1), 84–100.

Kratochwill, T. (2007). Preparing psychologists for evidence-based school practice: Lessons learned and challenges ahead. *American Psychologist, 62*(8), 829–843.

Kratochwill, T. R., & Shernoff, E. S. (2003). Evidence-based practice: Promoting evidence-based interventions in school psychology. *School Psychology Review, 33*, 34–48.

Lochman, J. (1995). Screening of child behavior

problems for prevention programs at school entry. *Journal of Consulting and Clinical Psychology, 63*(4), 549–559.

Lochman, J. E., & Wells, K. C. (2002). The Coping Power program at the middle-school transition: Universal and indicated prevention effects. *Psychology of Addictive Behaviors, 16*(4), 40–54.

Lochman, J. E., Wells, K. C., & Lenhart, L. (2008). *Coping Power: Child group facilitator's guide.* New York: Oxford University Press.

McIntosh, K., Reinke, W. M., & Herman, K. C. (2010). School-wide analysis of data for social behavior problems: Assessing outcomes, selecting targets for intervention, and identifying need for support. In G. Peacock, R. Ervin, E. Daly, & K. Merrell (Eds.), *Practical handbook of school psychology: Effective practices for the 21st century* (pp. 135–156). New York: Guilford Press.

McKay, M. M., Hibbert, R., Hoagwood, K., Rodriguez, J., Murray L., Legurski, J., et al. (2004). Increasing evidence-based engagement interventions into "real world" child mental health setting. *Brief Treatment and Crisis Intervention, 4*(2), 177–186.

McKay, M. M., McKernan, M., Atkins, T., Hawkins, C., & Lynn, C. J. (2003). Inner-city African American parental involvement in children's schooling: Racial socialization and social support from the parent community. *American Journal of Community Psychology, 32*(1), 107–114.

Merrell, K. W. (2011). *Social and Emotional Assets and Resilience Scales (SEARS).* Lutz, FL: Psychological Assessment Resources.

Merrell, K. W., Carrizales, D., Feuerborn, L., Gueldner, B. A., & Tran, O. K. (2007). *Strong Kids— 3–5: A social and emotional learning curriculum.* Baltimore: Brookes.

Merrell, K. W., Juskells, M. P., Oanh, K. T., & Buchanan, R. (2008). Social and emotional learning in the classroom: Evaluation of Strong Kids and Strong Teens on students' social–emotional knowledge and symptoms. *Journal of Applied School Psychology, 24*(2), 209–224.

Merrell, K. W., Parisi, D., & Whitcomb, S. A. (2007). *Strong Start—Grades K–2: A social and emotional learning curriculum.* Baltimore: Brookes.

Merrell, K. W., Whitcomb, S. A., & Parisi, D. A. (2009). *Strong Start—Pre-K: A social and emotional learning curriculum.* Baltimore: Brookes.

Morrissey-Kane, E., & Prinz, R. J. (1999). Engagement in child and adolescent treatment: The role of parental cognitions. *Clinical Child and Family Review, 2*(3), 183–198.

National Academy of Sciences and Institute of Medicine. (2009). *Preventing mental, emotional, and behavioral disorders among young people: Progress and possibilities.* Washington, DC: National Academies Press.

National Research Council & Institute of Medicine. (2009). *Preventing mental, emotional, and behavioral disorders among young people: Progress and possibilities.* Washington, DC: National Academies Press.

Neil, A. L., & Christensen, H. (2009). Efficacy and effectiveness of school-based prevention and early intervention programs for anxiety. *Clinical Psychology Review, 29*(3), 208–215.

Nock, M. K., & Kazdin, A. E. (2005). Randomized controlled trial of a brief intervention for increasing participation in parent management training. *Journal of Consulting and Clinical Psychology, 73*(5), 872–879.

Pelham, W., Gnagy, M., Greenslade, K. E., & Milich, R. (1992). The Parent/Teacher Disruptive Behavior Disorder Scale. Retrieved from *http://ccf.buffalo.edu/pdf/DBD_rating_scale.pdf.*

Rappee, R. M., & Lyneham, H. (2006). *Cool Kids Child & Adolescent Anxiety Program therapist manual.* Sydney, Australia: Macquarie University Centre for Emotional Health.

Reynolds, C. R., & Kamphaus, R. W. (2004). *Behavior Assessment System for Children (BASC-2).* Bloomington, MN: Pearson.

Runyon, M. K., & Deblinger, E. (2013). *Combined Parent–Child Cognitive Behavioral Therapy: An approach to empower families at-risk for child physical abuse: Therapist guide.* New York: Oxford University Press.

Runyon, M. K., Deblinger, E., & Steer, R. A. (2010). Group cognitive behavioral treatment for parents and children at-risk for physical abuse: An initial study. *Child and Family Behavior Therapy, 32*(3), 196–218.

Salloum, A. (1997). *Grief and Trauma Intervention (GTI) for children: A manual for practitioners.* New Orleans, LA: Children's Bureau of New Orleans.

Salloum, A., & Overstreet, S. (2008). Evaluation of individual and group grief and trauma interventions for children post disaster. *Journal of Clinical Child and Adolescent Psychology, 37*(3), 495–507.

Sanders, M. R. (1992). *The Triple P—Positive Parenting Program: Curriculum guide.* Queensland, Australia: Triple P International.

Sanders, M. R. (1999). Triple P—Positive Parenting Program: Towards an empirically validated multi-level parenting and family support strategy for the prevention of behavior and emotional problems in children. *Clinical and Family Psychology Review, 2*(2), 71–90.

Shortt, A. L., & Fox, T. L. (2001). Evaluating the FRIENDS Program: A cognitive-behavioral group treatment for anxious children and their parents. *Journal of Clinical Child and Adolescent Psychology, 30*(4), 525–535.

Shure, M. B. (1993). I can problem solve (ICPS): Interpersonal cognitive problem solving for young children. *Early Child Development and Care, 96*(1), 49–64.

Shure, M. B. (2001a). *I can problem solve: Curriculum manual* (2nd ed.). Champaign, IL: Research Press.

Shure, M. B. (2001b). I can problem solve (ICPS): An interpersonal cognitive problem solving program for children. *Residential Treatment for Children and Youth, 18*(3), 3–14.

Spence, S. H. (1994). Spence Children's Anxiety Scale. Retrieved from *www.scaswebsite.com/docs/scas.*

Spitzer, R. L., Kroenke, K., Williams, J. B. W., & Lowe, B. (2006). A brief measure for assessing generalized anxiety disorder: The GAD-7. *Archives of Internal Medicine, 166*(10), 1092–1097.

Stormont, M., Reinke, W. M., & Herman, K. C. (2011). Teachers' importance ratings for evidence-based behavioral interventions. *Behavioral Disorders, 37*(1), 19–29.

Stormont, M., Reinke, W. M., Herman, K. C., & Lemke, E. (2012). *Academic and behavior supports for at-risk students: Tier 2 interventions.* New York: Guilford Press.

Stormshak, E. A., Dishion, T. J., Light, J., & Yasui, M. (2005). Implementing family-centered interventions within the public school: Linking service delivery to change in student problem behavior. *Journal of Abnormal Child Psychology, 33*(6), 723–733.

Sue, D., Bingham, R. P., Porché-Burke, L., & Vasquez, M. (1999). The diversification of psychology: A multicultural revolution. *American Psychologist, 54*(12), 1061–1069.

U.S. Department of Health and Human Services. (2014). Mental health: A report of the surgeon general. Retrieved from *www.samhsa.gov/ebp-web-guide.*

Volpe, R. J., & Fabiano, G. A. (2013). *Daily behavior report cards: An evidence-based system of assessment and intervention.* New York: Guilford Press.

Walker, H. M., & Severson, H. (1992). *Systematic Screening for Behavior Disorders* (2nd ed.). Longmont, CO: Sopris West.

Watson, T. S., & Steege, M. W. (2003). *Conducting school-based functional behavioral assessments: A practitioner's guide.* New York: Guilford Press.

Webster-Stratton, C. (1999). *How to promote children's social and emotional competence.* Thousand Oaks, CA: SAGE.

Webster-Stratton, C. (2005). *The Incredible Years: A trouble-shooting guide for parents of children aged 2–8 years* (Rev. ed.). Seattle, WA: The Incredible Years.

Webster-Stratton, C. (2013a). *The Incredible Years Parenting Programs: Parent group facilitator's guide.* Seattle, WA: The Incredible Years.

Webster-Stratton, C. (2013b). *The Incredible Years Small Group Dinosaur Curriculum: Child group facilitator's guide.* Seattle, WA: The Incredible Years.

Webster-Stratton, C., & Reid, M. J. (2003). The Incredible Years parents, teachers and children training series: A multifaceted treatment approach for young children with conduct problems. In J. R. Weisz & A. E. Kazdin (Eds.), *Evidence-based psychotherapies for children and adolescents* (pp. 224–240). New York: Guilford Press.

Webster-Stratton, C., Reid, M. J., & Hammond, M. (2004). Treating children with early-onset conduct problems: Intervention outcomes for parent, child, and teacher training. *Journal of Clinical Child and Adolescent Psychology, 33*(1), 105–124.

Wells, K., Lochman, J. E., & Lenhart, L. (2008). *Coping Power: Parent group facilitator's guide.* New York: Oxford University Press.

World Health Organization. (2004). Prevention of mental disorders: Effective interventions and policy options (Summary Report). Retrieved from *www.who.int/mental_health/evidence/en/prevention_of_mental_disorders_sr.pdf.*

Yalom, I. D. (1995). *The theory and practice of group psychotherapy* (4th ed.). New York: Perseus.

Yalom, I. D., & Rand, K. (1966). Compatibility and cohesiveness in therapy groups. *Archives of General Psychiatry/JAMA Psychiatry, 15*(3), 267–275.

# Index

Note: *f* following a page number indicates a figure; *t* indicates a table.

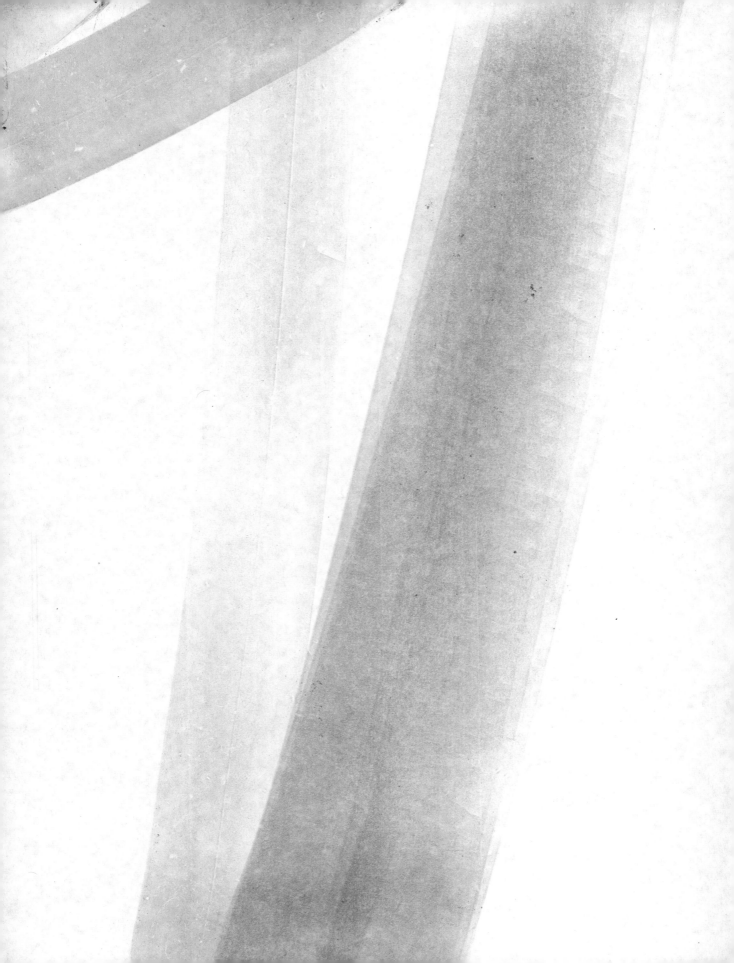